British

British Library Occasional Papers 10

Chinese Studies

Papers presented at a colloquium
at the School of Oriental and African Studies,
University of London
24–26 August 1987

Sponsored jointly by the British Library,
the School of Oriental and African Studies,
University of London and
the China Library Group

Edited by Frances Wood

The British Library 1988

© 1988 The Contributors

Published by
The British Library
Great Russell Street
London WC1B 3DG
and 27 South Main Street, Wolfeboro,
New Hampshire 03894–2069

British Library Cataloguing in Publication Data

Chinese Studies: papers presented at a colloquium at the
School of Oriental and African Studies, University of
London, 24–26 August 1987, sponsored jointly by the
British Library, the School of Oriental and African Studies,
University of London and the China Library Group.—
(British Library occasional papers; 10).
1. Chinese studies. Information sources
I. Wood, Frances II. British Library
III. Series
951'.007

ISBN 0–7123–0516–9

Designed by Alan Bartram
Typeset in Lasercomp Bembo
by August Filmsetting, Haydock, St Helens
Printed in England on permanent paper ∞
by St Edmundsbury Press,
Bury St Edmunds, Suffolk

Contents

Editor's preface		
List of participants		
List of abbreviations		

Overview of resources for Chinese studies

The role of collection development	B C Bloomfield	2
Singular lassitude: some historical and comparative perspectives on Chinese studies in the United Kingdom	T H Barrett	9
The development of the Chinese collections in SOAS Library	Charles d'Orban	54
Chinese materials in the India Office Library and Records	Anthony Farrington	61
Chinese collections in the British Library's Science Reference and Information Service	Raymond Kyang	71
Archives and manuscript collections relating to China in SOAS Library	Rosemary Seton	76
Chinese maps and globes in the British Library and the Phillipps Collection	Helen Wallis	88
Curiosities of the British Library Chinese Collection	Frances Wood	97

Paper and the book in China

Painters of the Tang period in Dunhuang and Turfan	Zhang Gong	108
The evolution of the Tang household records and census system reflected in Dunhuang manuscripts	Song Jiayu	114
An introduction to the Dunhuang manuscript, *Shi yao zi yang*	Yanwen Liu and David Arrandale	119

Dice, dominoes and card games in Chinese literature: a preliminary survey	Andrew Lo	127
Books and things: Ming literary culture and material culture	Craig Clunas	136
The Morrison Papers	Lo Huimin	145
Research materials in the National Palace Museum	Nancy Wang	152
The *Chinese catalogue of rare books* and its criteria of inclusion	Ji Shuying	161
The Dunhuang and Central Asian manuscripts and the history of books	Jean-Pierre Drège	171
The origin of papermaking in the light of scientific research on recent archaeological discoveries	Pan Jixing	176
Conservation of Chinese materials in the British Library	Peter Lawson	181

Automation and co-operation

Automation and Chinese studies	John Cayley	186
Chinese bibliographic data processing	Zhou Shengheng	198
RLIN–CJK: a review of the first four years	John W Haeger	205
The OCLC Library Network of Chinese, Japanese and Korean Characters	Andrew Wang	210
The China Library Group	Charles d'Orban	218
The European Association of Sinological Librarians	David Helliwell	221

Editor's preface
Frances Wood

The colloquium, held on 24–6 August 1987, was jointly sponsored by the British Library and the School of Oriental and African Studies (University of London) and the China Library Group. We were honoured by guests from as far away as Australia, many from China, some from the USA and particularly strong support from European colleagues, many of whom stayed on to meet as the European Association for Sinological Librarians after the colloquium was over.

The sessions were devoted to (a), an overview of resources for Chinese studies with special reference to the British Library and the School of Oriental and African Studies; (b), paper and the book in China; and (c), automation and co-operation, themes which were continued in the subsequent EASL sessions.

The papers are set out in the order in which they were presented, followed, where appropriate, by a short summary of the ensuing discussion. The absence of such a summary should not be taken as an indication that the paper was met with stony silence; the only brake on otherwise enthusiastic discussions was lack of time. The papers have all been edited to adapt them to British Library house style and I have imposed (according to British Library cataloguing rules) the pinyin romanisation on all except in cases of antiquarian context. All the sessions of the colloquium were recorded on tapes which are available at the British Library National Sound Archive.

We are all very grateful to everyone who attended the colloquium and helped to make it a warm and lively event, but I must express special thanks to colleagues in the Chinese section and Mrs Xiaowei Bond who was co-opted to assist with administration, to the staff of SOAS, particularly the catering staff for the efficient hospitality and, in the production of these proceedings, Mrs Banya and her staff for typing and retyping and Anne Young for eagle-eyed editing work.

List of participants

Dr Sarah Allan	Department of the Far East, School of Oriental and African Studies
Mr David Arrandale	Brotherton Library, University of Leeds
Mr Charles Aylmer	Library, Cambridge University
Prof T H Barrett	School of Oriental and African Studies
Ms Jill Barrett	Department of Law, School of Oriental and African Studies
Ms Marina Battaglini	Biblioteca Nazionale, Rome
Ms Lao Bing	Library, Polytechnic of Central London
Mr B C Bloomfield	Collection Development, British Library
M Rene Boisguerin	Chinese Section, Bibliotheque Asiatique des Missions etrangères, Paris
Ms Xiaowei Bond	Oriental Collections, British Library
Mrs Yuying Brown	Oriental Collections, British Library
Miss Barbara Burton	Library, School of Oriental and African Studies
Mr John Cayley	Oriental Collections, British Library
Lama Radha Chime	Oriental Collections, British Library
Ms Ruth Chu	Westminster Public Libraries
Mr John Clews	Document Supply Centre, British Library
Dr Craig Clunas	Victoria and Albert Museum
Mr Tom Collings	[Paper conservationist]
Ms A d'Eye	Camden Libraries
Ms Sara Dent	Research Department, Foreign and Commonwealth Office
Mr Charles d'Orban	Library, School of Oriental and African Studies
Dr J P Drège	Equipe de recherche sur les documents de Touen-Houang, CNRS, Paris
Dr Helga Dressler	Berlin
Ms Jo Drew	Lancashire China Centre
Dr A Dufey	Bayerische Staatsbibliothek
Mr Michael Egloff	Far Eastern Library, Universität Zurich
Ms Elizabeth Eide	Faculty of Arts Library, Universitetet i Oslo

Ms Susanne Ettl	Bayerische Staatsbibliothek
Ms Harriet Evans	Polytechnic of Central London
Mr Anthony Farrington	India Office Library and Records, British Library
Mr Chin Foo-Kune	Document Supply Centre, British Library
Ms Liu Yanwen	China National Administrative Bureau of Cultural Relics and Historical Literature
Ms Leslie Forbes	Oriental Section, University of Durham Library
Mr Lars Fredriksson	Ostasiatiska Biblioteket, Stockholm
Dr Albertine Gaur	Oriental Collections, British Library
Mr Roger Greatrex	Forsknigspolitiska Institutet, Lunds Universitet
Dr John Haeger	Research Libraries Group, Stanford CA
Ms Pauline Haldane	Asian Studies Section, National Library of Australia
Mr David Helliwell	Bodleian Library, University of Oxford
Ms Rosalind Hibbens	Humanities and Social Sciences Automated Systems, British Library
Dr Luo Huimin	China Centre, Australian National University
Ms Jane Hwang	Bayerische Staatsbibliothek
Mr Anthony Hyder	Oriental Institute Library, University of Oxford
Chang-ming Janin	Bibliothèque du Centre de Recherche sur la Chine Contemporaine, Paris
Mr A Crispin Jewitt	Planning and Administration, British Library
Ms Rose Kerr	Victoria and Albert Museum
Mr Raymond Kyang	Science Reference and Information Service, British Library
Ms Kirsten Lauridsen Ronbol	Orientalsk Afdeling, Det Kongelige Bibliotek, Kobenhavn
Mr Peter Lawson	Preservation Service, British Library
Dr William Liu	Library, University of Edinburgh
Dr Andrew Lo	Department of the Far East, School of Oriental and African Studies
Weng-on Loke	Bibliothek, Universität Hamburg
Mr Anthony Long	Bibliographic Services, British Library

Dr Claudia Lux	Staatsbibliothek Preussischer Kulturbesitz
Mrs Beth McKillop	Oriental Collections, British Library
Ms Susan Morton	Research Department, Foreign and Commonwealth Office
Mlle Jacqueline Nivard	Bibliothèque du Centre de Recherche sur la Chine Contemporaine, Paris
Dr Yong-sook Pak	Percival David Foundation, London
Mlle Odile Pierquin-Tian	Bibliothèque du Centre de Recherche sur la Chine Contemporaine, Paris
Prof D E Pollard	Department of the Far East, School of Oriental and African Studies
Ms Jane Portal	Oriental Antiquities, British Museum
Ms Jessica Rawson	Oriental Antiquities, British Museum
Ms Kira Rohde-Liebenau	Bibliothek, Universität Bochum
Mlle Salavert	Bibliothèque Asiatique des Missions Etrangères, Paris
Ms Johanna Scheerlinck	China–Europe Institute, Katholicke Universitet, Leuven
Ms Rosemary E Seton	Library, School of Oriental and African Studies
Madame Ji Shuying	Special Collections, National Library of China
Mr J M Smethurst	Director General, Humanities and Social Sciences, British Library
Mr Jiayu Song	Institute of History, CASS
Dr Renate Stephan-Bahle	Bayerische Staatsbibliotek
Ms Pamela Stewart	Library, University of Newcastle
Dr Johann-Michael Streffer	Staatsbibliothek Preussicher Kulturbesitz
Dr Paul Thompson	Department of the Far East, School of Oriental and African Studies
Ms Catherine Till	Department of the Far East, School of Oriental and African Studies
Mr H Todd	Oriental Collections, British Library
Ms Regula Trauffer	Far Eastern Library, Universität Zurich
Mr Robin Twite	Books and Libraries Division, British Council

Dr Marsha Wagner	East Asian Library, University of Columbia
Ms Y Y Wah	Chinese Community Librarian, Manchester Public Library
Dr Helen Wallis	Map Library, British Library
Dr Hartmut Walravens	Staatsbibliothek Preussischer Kulturbesitz
Mr Andrew H Wang	Asian/Pacific Services, OCLC
Mrs Nancy Wang	Library, Palace Museum, Taibei
Ms Verity Wilson	Victoria and Albert Museum
Dr Frances Wood	Oriental Collections, British Library
Ms Joyce (Yung-tzu) Wu	Sinologische Institut, Leiden
Mr Zhang Gong	Institute of History, CASS
Mr Zhou Shengheng	Automation Development Department, National Library of China

List of abbreviations

ACOOM	Advisory Committee On Orientalist Materials
ALA	American Library Association
ASCII	American Standard Code for Information Interchange
BL	British Library
CASS	Chinese Academy of Social Sciences
CCCII	Chinese Character Code for Information Interchange
CCI	Contemporary China Institute
CLG	China Library Group
CUCRB	*Chinese Union Catalogue of Rare Books*
EACS	European Association of Chinese Studies
EASL	European Association of Sinological Librarians
EBCDIC	Extended Binary Coded Decimal Interchange Code
IFLA	International Federation of Library Associations
IOLR	India Office Library and Records
ISBDS	International Standard Book Descriptions
ISTIC	Institute for Scientific and Technical Information, China
LC	Library of Congress
LIBER	Ligue des Bibliothèques Européennes de Recherche
MARC	Machine Readable Cataloguing
NLC	National Library of China
OC	Oriental Collections
OCLC	Online Computer Library Centre
REACC	RLIN East Asian Character Code
RLIN	Research Library Information Network
RLIN-CJK	Research Library Information Network Chinese, Japanese and Korean system
SCOLMA	Standing Conference On Library Materials on Africa
SCONUL	Standing Conference On National and University Libraries
SOAS	School of Oriental and African Studies
SRIS	Science Reference and Information Service
UAP	Universal Availability of Publications
UBC	Universal Bibliographic Control

Overview of resources for Chinese studies

B C Bloomfield

The role of collection development

'Collection development' – the two words used in conjunction came into professional library literature in the 1960s, but there has been no really serious attempt to define their meaning. It is clear that the words imply more than the old phrase 'acquisitions policy' formerly employed to indicate what a particular library saw as its collecting policy for literature stored, preserved and made accessible to serve its readers. But the concept of service to readers was (is?) by no means universally accepted by all libraries; the idea of the library as a simple repository for the preservation of literature is not yet dead. However, 'collection development' clearly implies a more active role in managing a library's collections and indicates that that role will change and develop in response to changing conditions, and the most changing and challenging condition for librarians now is what readers and users expect or demand from libraries. In other words, 'collection development' represents an evolving concept of library collection management devised to answer changing reader demands on library collections: readers do not now simply demand access to those books catalogued, preserved and available within one institution; they demand bibliographic and surrogate access to material outside the library, outside the country, and often outside their specific knowledge. To manage these processes and continue to serve readers in such an extended framework, what to provide and how to finance it – these questions are the province of 'collection development'.

Collecting policies

How can this concept of 'collection development', itself developing and imprecisely expressed, relate to Chinese studies, which are themselves imprecise and changing? This relationship can be considered in the context of one institution, nationally and internationally. First I propose to consider it in relation to the British Library itself.

Other papers will present the strengths of the collections held by the British Library as they relate to Chinese studies, but it is legitimate to ask how those collections came to the Library and whether they are regarded as strengths or random acquisitions. What now are the collecting policies of the Library and do they seek to build on previous strengths or take new directions?

The British Library's main aims and purposes are set out in *Advancing with knowledge*, the strategic plan for 1985–90 (British Library, 1985) and, as they apply to the collections, on p. 19 we read:

Collection policies... are determined by experience of users' present needs and by assessment of the perceived requirements of future users, as well as with regard to the existing strengths of the collections. These judgements are made in the framework of longstanding public expectations that (i) all British and most overseas publications of research interest regardless of subject, language, date or place of publication, will be found in the British Library; (ii) the Library will hold extensive manuscript collections as well as printed resources in most areas; (iii) the needs of business and industry will be met with particular speed and ease of access; (iv) national and international treasures in book form will be extensively held and displayed... The priorities for acquisition of research material considered on a language and country basis are (i) material received under the UK legal deposit mechanism, (ii) material in English published overseas, (iii) material in any language about British civilisation; (iv) material in other widely accessible languages; (v) material, regardless of language, published in countries of major world importance, (vi) material of other origins which is of significant value and relates to the existing scope of the collections.

Further paragraphs deal with subject collecting priorities, now more clearly set out in the British Library's version of the Research Library Group's Conspectus schedules (British Library, 1986), shortly to be mounted on the RLIN Conspectus database in the USA and to form the basis of a planned UK Conspectus now in prospect. The collection development priorities of the Document Supply Centre at Boston Spa are also set out as:

(i) an extensive range of serial publications in all languages and from all countries; (ii) an extensive set of research level English language books, conference proceedings, doctoral dissertations, official publications and reports; (iii) an extensive collection of music scores; (iv) a selective collection of foreign language books and theses

and to these are added those of the Science Reference and Information Service (SRIS). Other special library materials and special formats are dealt with in detail, but these statements present a formidable array of criteria for building the collections of the British Library, backed up within divisions and departments by more detailed statements of policy and intentions for the existing collections (into which there is not space to go at present). However, the joint statement of the Oriental Collections and the India Office Library and Records is of obvious relevance here, since these departments contain the major historical strengths of the British Library's materials on China.

Even within these general statements of collection development policies there is ample food for speculation, explication and thought. British interest in China and Chinese studies among British Library readers comes mainly from the scholarly and academic communities, but scholarly users have been reduced severely in numbers by the cuts in university funding in the UK over the past ten years: there are probably no more than 300 university teachers now in post with an interest in China, and perhaps not more than 1000 students at all levels. On the other hand, economic and industrial interest in China has rapidly increased as the market for sales to China has opened to the outside world; similarly, political interest in China has increased as the Chinese themselves have become more outward looking and as the position on Hong Kong has been clarified. Both political and diplomatic interest in China may be expected to increase and to lead to further demands for literature and information.

But Chinese cannot by any stretch of the imagination be called a 'widely accessible language' and indeed it is doubtful if it can be considered one of the international languages of scholarship in any sense other than numerical. Yet in view of China's increasing political, industrial and economic importance, library materials in Chinese will qualify for collection as 'published in countries of major world importance'. The Library's collections of secondary material in English and major European languages will continue to be a major strength, as will anything dealing with the past contacts between the two countries, particularly on such subjects as the East India Company, the former opium trade, Hong Kong and other colonial and semi-colonial contacts.

In view of the British Library's increasing difficulty in funding and the likelihood of decreasing government support, there are obvious difficulties in reconciling these elements of small academic and scholarly interest, increasing commercial interest with political importance, source material in a 'difficult' language, and declining financial support for purchases. These difficulties are compounded by the potential size of the literature in Chinese that may be of interest, significance, or just plain grist to the academic research mill. The literature in Chinese is not subject to a high degree of bibliographic control and availability is difficult too in many cases, so that much printed and recent material is simply not easily available to overseas research workers. It seems obvious that, in spite of clear and limited collection development statements, readers' needs in Chinese cannot be satisfied without some relation to, and agreement with, libraries in China itself, as competent sources simply do not exist in the non-Chinese world.

International developments

Within the United Kingdom one clear way of lessening these difficulties must lie in cooperation and coordination between those libraries interested in China studies. They are few, and such coordination as exists has evolved through the work and publications of the China Library Group. In general, though, it has been a mapping of the territory rather than an attempt at formal coordination. Cooperation also needs extra finance to achieve success and this has never looked likely to materialise. Recent academic retrenchment has wreaked havoc with any planned distribution of studies combined with library resources, and this makes future cooperation in collection development an even more necessary imperative. (Here we may hope for better things in the future through the Parker report.)

And now that the United Kingdom is within the European Community, cooperation and coordination on a wider scale should become another objective of library collection development policy. Schools of Chinese studies in other European countries have specialities and distinctions it would be unwise and uneconomic to replicate here in the UK. But the largest schools and centres of Chinese studies outside China itself are in North America and Japan, and cooperation in collection development and bibliographic access with those libraries must be essential for future strategies. The British Library already has, for experimental purposes, a dedicated telecommunications link with the RLIN computerised database in Stanford, California, and experiments are proceeding with its use in searching and derived cataloguing; use in collection development must depend on continued guaranteed access and this depends on finance and future agreements being concluded. There is no reason not to hope for greater and cooperative developments in the future.

This is particularly true in the joint use of the Conspectus technique for describing the past or existing strengths of library collections and the recording of current collecting intensities. Once the technique is developed and in use, analysis of the recorded data will permit much greater integration of collecting policies, the assignment of primary collecting responsibilities within any grouping of libraries, national, regional or subject, and cooperation in conservation and other activities. Interrogation of the database by librarians and by scholars will facilitate the economical direction of research and also the distant consultation of computerised library catalogues through utilities and other networks. Without an accurate map of our existing library collections and a considered policy of acquisitions for the future, there is no possibility of fruitful cooperation to support Chinese studies throughout the world outside China itself.

Returning to the British Library itself, apart from the need to support indigenous Chinese studies and to serve the needs of industry and diplomacy, the Library recognises that it has a role to fulfil in international relationships with other libraries, especially other national libraries and information networks. This role is adumbrated in the Library's strategic plan (*Advancing with knowledge*, p. 29) where it is recognised that the strength of the historic collections entails obligations to preserve and make those collections available to scholars in countries overseas, for scholarship is international and knows no intellectual boundaries. Thus, Chinese scholars have visited the India Office Library and Records to consult and use the records of the East India Company relating to trade with China and have acquired microfilm of those records to continue their research; similarly, the Library has, on rare occasions, acquired from the National Library in Beijing microfilm of early rare printed books not available outside China itself. These contacts and exchanges should be developed and extended so that interdependence between our libraries can result in the most economical and effective use of the money made available by governments for libraries.

The position of libraries in China, and particularly of the National Library of China, is crucial here. It is axiomatic that Chinese studies depend on China, its people, its resources and its literature, libraries and information resources. If China itself succeeds with its plans for the development of libraries within the country, surveys its library resources, and makes arrangements for making those resources available to scholars, then libraries in countries outside China may, in cooperation, plan for their own readers an orderly access to literature in Chinese on a secure basis. Until that happy day, whatever libraries outside China may do and plan is in the nature of 'Hamlet without the Prince of Denmark'. For the Chinese authorities to tackle this problem – equally essential for the needs of scholars within China as for those without – would be an immense step forward in Chinese studies worldwide, and the keystone for collection development policies to support those studies. For example, Chinese participation in the work of the International Federation of Library Associations (IFLA) is only just beginning, but Chinese adoption of two IFLA core programmes of Universal Bibliographic Control (UBC) and Universal Availability of Publications (UAP) would be an immense step forward. But this may be where 'collection development' begins to trespass on political affairs, not normally considered to be part of library policies!

The British Library's other main role in international relations and information networks is to be found in the work of the Document Supply Centre (formerly the Lending Division). The original simple concept of a core collection of scientific and technical serials to serve, by return of post, any requests from users anywhere within the UK has been modified and expanded so that the core collection now serves the humanities and social sciences as well as science and technology, includes monographs (with the aid of many back-up libraries and other British Library collections) as well as journals, and now serves an enormous range of libraries throughout the entire world. More than three million requests for inter-lending are satisfied through the Document Supply Centre every year, and it serves Chinese studies throughout the world just as much as any other subject. It is intended that this fundamental role in service to scholarship and industry will continue and be open to all libraries world-wide. 'Collection development' policies within the British Library are coordinated to ensure that this role can continue and be developed in the most economical fashion. But since funding is short, the international development of such services will need to be on a secure cost recovery basis and on the basis of agreed standards for the recognition of the protected rights of intellectual property – a most intractable, contentious (not to say litigious) problem.

This brief introductory paper may seem to have wandered rather far from strictly library problems in discussing the contribution of 'collection development' to Chinese studies, but my intention has been to outline the specific role it can play in supporting Chinese studies, and the specific role it will assist the British Library to play in supporting such studies in the UK, Europe and world-wide. However, without the active cooperation of China and its libraries in these plans of library cooperation and development, progress will inevitably be slow and show few results, since the bulk of literature in Chinese is only available from China and its libraries, where cooperation in library planning, development and collection building is naturally retarded. But if we do not draw Chinese libraries and their collections into an international network of literature supply and document delivery, scholarship dealing with China and Chinese studies will consequently remain restricted in range and deficient in access to necessary source material – a sort of pimple on the bottom of international academic activity. Neither scholars nor librarians can or should contemplate this with equanimity; plans for 'collection development' are the most practical way out of this impasse. United we progress; divided we stagnate.

Bibliography

B C Bloomfield, 'Notes on library provision for Oriental and Asian studies in Great Britain', *Journal of librarianship*, 8 no. 2 (1976), pp. 111–21.

British Library, *Advancing with knowledge: the British Library strategic plan, 1985–1990* (British Library Board, 1985)

Stephen Hanger, 'Collection development in the British Library: the role of the RLG Conspectus', *Journal of librarianship*, 19, no. 2 (1987), pp. 89–107.

Brian G F Holt and Stephen Hangar, *Conspectus in the British Library* (British Library, 1986).

University Grants Committee, *Speaking for the future: a review of the requirements of diplomacy and commerce for Asian and African languages and area studies* (UGC, London, February 1986, Chairman: Sir Peter Parker, 'The Parker Report').

Discussion

In the subsequent discussion, points concerning exchange of materials and personnel and the future of funding for Chinese library resources were raised. Mr Bloomfield felt that given the problems in achieving cooperation from Chinese libraries, it was essential to maintain contacts with the Foreign and Commonwealth Office and to make sure that the Cultural Agreement was kept up to date and used as much as possible. This could facilitate getting our librarians to China and Chinese librarians over to the UK, important exchanges if funding permitted. The Cultural Agreement should also be used to promote exchanges of books and materials as sinological librarians had great difficulties in getting microfilms or surrogate copies of earlier material printed in China: such material appeared to be difficult to locate within China and difficult to copy. This sort of problem concerning the flow of material, together with the question of access to libraries and archives, should be brought up through normal diplomatic channels.

In the exchange of personnel, the British Council acted as an important conduit and source of funding. The British Library also has an agreement with ISTIC (and the Library Association with its equivalent in China) providing for the exchange of delegations, and such formal apparatus was important because it was easier for the Chinese authorities.

On the question of the future funding of university libraries and the consequent worry that sinological collections might not be maintained in future, a problem which was beyond the scope of the librarian to solve, Mr Bloomfield pointed to Holland where draconian relocation of library resources had been carried out. The University Grants Committee might well feel a similar need to forcibly relocate staff and resources, for the academics within the universities had not themselves tackled the problem. In Sweden, the new Ostasiatiska Biblioteket represented a successful centralisation of library resources on Asia. Pauline Haldane of the National Library of Australia told the colloquium that a 'National Library summit' had been planned for March 1988, when it was hoped to get guarantees from state and university libraries that they would maintain certain collections.

T H Barrett

Singular Lassitude: some historical and comparative perspectives on Chinese studies in the United Kingdom*

To the outsider librarianship sometimes seems a peculiarly hopeless profession. Of making books there is assuredly no end; acquisitions and cataloguing departments must simply make what shift they can to cope with the rising tide of publications. No matter how sophisticated our information technology becomes, we still seem far from having solved the problems created by the invention of the book – hardly an encouraging level of progress, one would have thought, after more than two millennia. For the sinological librarian, and especially the sinological librarian in Britain today, there is every reason for the levels of desperation to be markedly higher: selecting and acquiring books from the other end of the earth, when but one of the major sources of supply publishes new titles at the rate of several tens of thousands annually – to say nothing of several thousand periodicals[1] – and cataloguing the purchases when they are all written in a script which in itself subverts half the assumptions of conventional librarianship is no easy task, especially given the generally inadequate staffing levels in most of our libraries.

Under such circumstances the range of activities which a librarian may indulge in contracts towards a straightforward concern with crisis management, leaving little time for such niceties as conservation or the publication of catalogues. Thus a conference which allows us to take stock of resources for Chinese studies in our libraries is an unexpected luxury, and one for which all users of Chinese collections should be grateful to the British Library, the School of Oriental and African Studies and the China Library Group, for their concerted efforts in bringing such a gathering into being.

Yet there is, I fear, an inevitable temptation in such a conference to over-accentuate the positive. Given the opportunity to relax and enjoy the unaccustomed pleasure of reflection, it is far more agreeable to stress the uniqueness of the rarities among our holdings, the sophistication of the research into bibliographical topics that may be achieved on the basis of our current resources, or the utopian prospects afforded by the latest advances in automation,

---

* A partial version of Professor Barrett's paper was read at the Colloquium by Charles d'Orban.

rather than to contemplate topics already far too familiar, such as the severe limitations upon our collections, and the day to day struggle of maintaining them at anything like an acceptable level. But it is not simply in order to redress a potential imbalance that the following survey of the broader context of time and space, of history and of the global academic community, in which our own work is pursued, stresses by contrast the negative side of the story. Rather, nothing short of a frank admission of the failure of Chinese studies to establish themselves in Britain will do justice to the historical record as it stands to date.

Chinese books and the real China

The very fact that not a single publication has been devoted up till now to the history of Chinese studies in this country *as such* speaks for itself. Where aspects of that history have been dealt with – as, for example, in a detailed study, now almost fifty years old, of the Chinese language competence of the East India Company,[2] or in an excellent short account of the Chair of Chinese in London, prefaced to an inaugural lecture[3] – it has been made quite plain that the past achievements of the British nation in this field of endeavour have been rather less than distinguished.

It is, of course, all too easy to deride the failures of men of past ages from our present vantage point, forgetting that in future our own work will doubtless appear very foolish indeed. The prudent historian, to be sure, is mindful of the handicaps under which his forebears laboured, and accords them a due measure of respect. None the less, the history of the study of China invites comparison, if not between times past and present, then at least between the relative degree of understanding achieved by the various nations of the West. The study of past sinology as part of the general intellectual history of the Western world is only now getting under way,[4] but again enough has been done to show that names other than that of Great Britain are sure to loom far larger in any eventual treatment of the story taken down to our own times. We already possess a most fluent and readable summary of the development of Chinese studies in France by Paul Demiéville, which itself owes much to the outstanding chronicler of China, Henri Cordier (1849–1925)[5] – and Cordier's name is but one of the many which adorn the history of sinology in Demiéville's adopted country.[6] The history of Chinese studies in the United States of America is by contrast far shorter, yet an entire monograph has already been devoted to a revaluation of American historiography on China so far.[7]

My own remarks (I should warn you) amount to no more than a lightning sketch of a topic that would really require a far fuller treatment; it is based purely upon a rapid trawl through the existing secondary literature, supplemented by one or two incidental observations. Some aspects of the story, such as the history of the collecting and appreciation of Chinese art in this country, I have left aside entirely. I have, however, tried to lay some emphasis particularly upon the accumulation of library resources in Britain, not simply with a view to my immediate audience, but also because I believe that the acquisition of such resources is a precondition for the successful development of Chinese studies. Certainly the acquisition by British subjects of the Chinese language is another necessary precondition, and the title of this essay, which is a characterization of British attitudes towards Chinese studies made by Sir John Davis (1795–1890), Governor of Hong Kong was made with language studies in mind.[8] But learning to speak Chinese is not enough; the exploitation of Chinese books in order to arrive at a more accurate understanding of China provides a far more reliable index of progress in a broader sense.

At the risk of preaching to the converted, such an approach requires a word or two of explanation. For the importance of Chinese books, and especially premodern Chinese books, as a means towards studying China is not necessarily apparent to all, not even to those who are fluent in Chinese. Indeed, the newly proficient Chinese speaker, set down in the midst of a vibrant and rapidly developing society, might be pardoned more readily than most for thinking that all written records of Chinese civilisation were worthless when confronted with the very novel reality of China today. A civilisation so different from our own strikes the observer on the spot with an overwhelming immediacy, so that it becomes quite incandescently obvious that no book could capture the least fraction of it, and that only a library composed of press cuttings (perhaps fortified with statistical surveys, as available) could provide even a pale reflection of a phenomenon so protean and so vast. Certainly, the new arrival feels, anything in classical Chinese relates only to a world long since vanished.

One can sympathise immediately with such a view: the ancient *Chan* masters, after all, were already aware of the inadequacy of written records in capturing the truth. Yet they themselves did not dispense with the 'finger pointing to the moon', even when they knew that it was the moon they wanted. Nor should reading about China in the library necessarily prevent us from crying for the moon of The Real China. And books, vast quantities of books, increasing in numbers by several thousand million copies annually,[9] are undeniably part of that reality. Given that China was the first country to discover both paper and printing, how could it be otherwise? Neither can we simply forget about the books of the past. I have tried to argue elsewhere that the apparent dispensability of the Chinese past springs as much from notions of change that have prevailed in China since long ago as from the reality of recent change.[10] And the more acute observers of contemporary China can certainly point to some rather startling examples to shake one's belief in the totality of its recent transformation: to the existence in the 1980s of clan schools teaching the traditional, classical Confucian curriculum; to well-placed Chinese witnesses of the momentous events of the 1970s discussing them in terms of analogies contained in an eleventh-century historical masterpiece, the *Zi zhi tong jian* of Sima Guang.[11] In a country where references to works centuries old occur even in popular comedy routines, can we afford to ignore the literary heritage of the past?[12] Why bother to learn the language if we do not know what they are talking about?

Early European sinology, the Iberian phase

The Chinese book in Western libraries still seems to too many a wildly exotic interloper, just as much a mere curiosity as the first recorded arrival, well over four and a half centuries ago. That volume, we are told, was sent as a gift by the King of Portugal to Pope Leo X (1513–21) – in conjunction with an elephant.[13] Fortunately for sinological librarianship, this inconvenient practice of dual donations did not become an established procedure, though what became of these presents I do not know. But in fact the ready availability of Chinese books to the Iberian seafarers who finally established continuing direct relations between China and Europe in the sixteenth century meant that the first deliberate steps we know of to discover more about China (as opposed to the dissemination of travellers' accounts like those of Marco Polo) were taken by a scholar who had no knowledge of Chinese whatsoever. João de Barros (1496–1570) was already making use of Chinese books by about the middle of the century to produce studies of China, thanks to the assistance of a Chinese slave, purchased along with his sources.

Regrettably much of what Barros wrote is now lost, and we do not even know the name of this slave, the hapless forerunner of a host of Chinese research assistants, most of whom have won no greater recognition for their efforts.[14] His pioneering work, however, helped to establish the Iberian peninsula as the first home of sinology in Europe. Its libraries remain important to this day – it is in Spain that we find the earliest known translation of a Chinese-language work (albeit one compiled in Korea) into a European language, executed by Juan Cobo in 1592 at the latest.[15] Their oldest holdings already exhibit that peculiarity of Western collections which would have been seen by any Chinese scholar in those times as an unseemly vice, but which is now seen as their greatest virtue: a readiness to preserve ephemeral works such as popular fiction alongside more acceptable literature.[16]

As is well known, the first account of China to see a wide readership in Europe was Gonzalez de Mendoza's *Historia de las cosas mas notables, ritos y costumbres del Gran Reyno de la China* (Rome, 1585), which was based in large part on a report by Fr Martín de Rada, who visited Fujian in 1575.[17] We know that Rada brought a considerable number of books from China to the Philippines, where he studied them with the help of Chinese-speaking converts. By the time that the results of his researches were published, there were Chinese books not only in the libraries of the Iberian peninsula (the Queen of Portugal had a couple of Chinese books by 1577) but also in the Vatican, where Montaigne saw a Chinese book in 1581, and where the now somewhat expanded holdings had been firmly disassociated from the menagerie and placed in the classical section of the library.[18] By the start of the seventeenth century Catholic Europe as a whole had become involved in the attempt to bring Christianity to China. The work of missionary translators such as Matteo Ricci (1552–1610) and the Chinese-language missionary press in the Philippines testify, at times, to a level of competence in Chinese which remains impressive, even today.[19]

The first Sino-British contacts

Meanwhile our Tudor ancestors had to make do with translations into English of works like Mendoza's: the translator who had all China divided up into thirteen 'shyres' shows how dangerously misleading such second-hand accounts could be.[20] Even direct contact with overseas Chinese proved at first singularly unenlightening. Sir Francis Drake did encounter one eager Chinese informant in the Malacca Archipelago in 1579, during his circumnavigation of the globe, but was treated to a complete cock-and-bull story about his new-found friend's descent from the founder of the Ming dynasty.[21]

On the basis of such abortive contacts Queen Elizabeth I did try dispatching messages to the Emperor of China, some couched (in a fashion which may only be described as half-intelligent), in Latin. There is no sign, though, that they ever reached their destination.[22] Absurdly enough, the practice of addressing the Emperor of China hopefully in Latin persisted into the nineteenth century, when one observer was finally prompted to remark: 'At all events the practice of sending letters with Latin translations, addressed to the Emperor and left to their own fate, seems highly improper and impolitic'[23] – surely something of an understatement.

Yet Elizabeth's immediate successor appears to have redoubled these efforts at communicating using no more than plain English, or so to judge from an example of James I's correspondence now languishing in a very different destination from that which was intended for it, the James Ford Bell Library of the University of Minnesota: 'The Report of the greatnesse of your power and dominion, in those Easterne parts of the World, hath stirred up great desire in our Subjects to undertake a voyage, into your Countrey to sollicite your friendshippe, towards the settling of a Trade and Commerce with your people...'[24] 'Friendshippe' has proved a sadly mutable goal in British relations with China; not so the settling of trade and commerce.

This letter seems to have been sent as a follow-up to one dispatched in 1612, which we know did get as far as Bantam in the East Indies before it had to be redirected to Japan: 'Touching his Majestey's (of England) letters to the Emperor of China here we can get none to translate them much less to convey them, and have therefore sent them to Mr Cocks in Firando if haply he through his friend Captain Dettis can get them done and sent. This Dettis is a Chinaman...'[25] Other sources reveal that the improbably named but undoubtedly Chinese Andrea Dettis (or Dittis) relieved the unhappy Mr Cocks in Japan of considerable sums of money to be used in bribing the Ming authorities to grant concessions to the British, all to no avail whatsoever.[26] No wonder King James had to try again.

Fortunately, by the time that the first British merchant vessel did establish contact with the Chinese authorities in Canton in 1637, a more helpful intermediary happened to be on the scene. We know of Captain John Weddell's experiences mainly through the account of a companion, a Cornish adventurer named Peter Mundy (1608–67). Mundy introduces us to this friend and intercessor as 'Antonio A Capher Eathiopian Abissin or Curled Head'; subsequently he refers to him more briefly as 'Antonio the Caffer'.[27] This man, who as far as we know was the first interpreter to try to impart a knowledge of Chinese to Englishmen, was one of a number of black slaves from Macao who managed to escape into Chinese territory.[28] Presumably Antonio and Mundy conversed in Portuguese;

earlier Anglo–Chinese translations appear to have taken place through the intervening medium of Malay.[29] Mundy gives a rendering of the Chinese numerals in his manuscript, and also records his own attempts to teach some English phrases to a native speaker: 'How Doe you Doe. Ve-ry well. But they pronounce it vely wen'.[30] It will be remarked that he succeeds here in creating, instantaneously and before our very eyes, a stereotype of the comic Chinaman (to say nothing of the African Antonio) which still appears far too frequently in our mass media even today.

As the British became more established in Far Eastern waters they saw little need to learn Chinese themselves, and continued much as they had started. Noting how the Ming loyalist Koxinga had displaced their rivals the Dutch from Taiwan, they formed the belief that his successor might reconquer the mainland, and accordingly sent a letter in English from Bantam in the name of King Charles II to the 'King of Tywan' which includes a reference to the intermediaries upon whom they relied: '. . . we have sent on this our ship Capt. Sooke, with eight other Chinamen, who have for long time traded and been acquainted with us and our Nation'.[31] It was not until after the Manchu conquest that the Directors of the East India Company concluded: 'Taiwan is good for nothing now, and we will not have you settle any factor there again'.[32] In the mean time, it seems, some written materials in Chinese were conveyed thence back to Britain, for both the Bodleian and the British Library contain almanacs published under the Taiwan loyalist regime.[33]

The Seventeenth Century

But these were by no means the earliest Chinese printed materials to reach this country. There is good evidence that at least a portion of a Chinese book had come into English hands at the very start of the seventeenth century, in the form of a fragment in the Bodleian which was studied by J J L Duyvendak. This bears upon it a note in English to the effect that its owner obtained it from Paulus Merula, a Dutch scholar whose dates are 1558–1607.[34] In the latter year Sir Thomas Bodley was certainly building up an Oxford Chinese collection, for he writes to his Librarian: 'Of the China bookes, because I cannot giue their titles, I haue written on euery volume the name of the giuer',[35] meaning, however, the donor of the funds used, so that a note in Bodley's hand on one Chinese volume (upside-down on the end flyleaf) giving the earlier date of 1604 may not represent the date of the purchase but of the benefaction drawn upon.

By the time of Bodley's death in 1613, the library already possessed fragments from seventeen Chinese works, mainly from medical texts that must originally have formed a single collection. More filtered in during the remainder of the century, and though much remains to be published concerning British accessions of Chinese books in the seventeenth century, it is clear that the Bodleian Chinese collection at least was (as it is today) much indebted to Dutch scholarship, from Merula's gift onward. Only one Dutch benefactor, Festus Hommius, is listed in connection with Chinese books, but I understand that fragments of at least one work in the medical collection, namely some portions which, after passing through the hands of the Duke of Buckingham, formed the earliest Chinese accessions in Cambridge, had earlier belonged to the library of the Leiden Arabist Thomas Erpenius, who died in 1624.[36] At the very end of the century, in 1696, another large group of Chinese books which had been kept at Leiden was bought by Narcissus Marsh, Bishop of Armagh, and added to the Bodleian holdings.[37]

They arrived too late to be listed in the first published catalogue in Britain to mention Chinese books, which appeared in 1697, but which in the case of this part of the Bodleian collection relied upon work carried out a decade earlier by a visiting Chinese. This man, Shen Fuzong (called, quite unaccountably, Shin Foburgh in one contemporary English source) had been brought to Europe by Fr Philip Couplet in 1683, and had subsequently travelled rather widely before dying on his way back to China in 1692. In England he evidently met James II, for when the monarch later visited his erstwhile employer, Dr Thomas Hyde (1636–1703), Librarian at the Bodleian, who had paid him six pounds for his work, the two conversed briefly concerning him. 'He was a little blinking fellow, was he not?' James is reported to have said.[38] Maybe the little blinking fellow had the last laugh in the end: the catalogue of 1697 gravely lists a popular novel as a copy of the *Mencius*, perhaps because of a mischievous streak in Shen's character, or else because Hyde, who had tried to avail himself of Shen's presence to turn himself into a China expert, was rashly overconfident of his own mastery of Chinese, or even because the two men (who communicated in Latin) simply failed to understand each other.[39]

Hyde was not the only would-be sinologist in late seventeenth-century Britain: the scientist Robert Hooke (1635–1703) seems to have acquired a Chinese dictionary and other materials, and to have applied a considerable intelligence to examining them.[40] Of others, however, perhaps the less said the better.[41] Almost without exception the British public continued throughout the century to depend on translations of works from other European languages for their knowledge of China. We find, for example, two particularly popular works on 'contemporary China' published together in 1655 as translated anonymously 'by a person of quality' – a claim which, though evidently designed to reassure the potential reader, fails to suggest technical qualifications for the job any superior to those of the Tudor translator mentioned above.[42]

If other Protestant countries were at a similar disadvantage (apart, perhaps, from the Dutch),[43] then at least it is possible to point to deliberate steps taken elsewhere to establish an independent capacity for Chinese studies, steps which won the full support of a Protestant ruler at a time when the King of England found an encounter with a Chinese visitor merely amusing. Friedrich Wilhelm (r.1640–88), Elector of Brandenburg, prompted by the scholar Andreas Müller (1630?–94), laid the foundations of a Chinese collection in his library through extensive purchases from a Dutch admiral. Though Müller's scholarship may have been 'laughable by today's standards',[44] he did publish catalogues of his ruler's collection in 1679 and 1683, ahead of Thomas Hyde, and the collection did grow for a while at a very gratifying rate: by 1683 there were 25 titles in 300 Chinese volumes, and by 1702 no less than 400 volumes were present.[45]

The Eighteenth Century in Britain

Indeed, while the eighteenth century in Europe as a whole was marked by a considerable willingness to take China seriously – one can even point to a thesis on China completed at a Finnish university in 1749, albeit largely on the basis of a very brief visit to Canton[46] – the average British writer seems to have gone out of his way to debunk the notion that China was anything special.[47] One might even suggest that the complete change in tone of descriptions of China witnessed at the start of the nineteenth century, usually attributed to the silencing of the subtle Jesuit interpreters of Chinese civilisation who had played such a large part before,[48] was perhaps rather due to the increased stridency of a typically Anglo-Saxon voice in Chinese affairs which had long since assumed its own characteristics. These characteristics, for their part, were largely formed in a profound ignorance of things Chinese, which is all the more remarkable in view of the ever increasing importance of British trade with China throughout the period.

True, these trading contacts did occasionally result in stimulating the interests of one or two individuals to the point where some efforts towards a deeper understanding were made, but those efforts were apparently so rare that they attracted considerable contemporary attention, and so we know enough about them to form by contrast a rather depressing picture of how much interest the average Englishman in East Asia took in the culture surrounding him. In 1699 we do hear briefly of a certain Lloyd who is said to have known Chinese,[49] but the earliest indications we have that any employee of the East India Company actually managed to come to grips with the written language relate to the famous episode of the translation of the *Hao qiu zhuan*. This seventeenth-century Chinese novel of romance and adventure became, thanks to the good offices of Bishop Thomas Percy (1729–1811), the first work of Chinese prose fiction to be brought before the British public. The appearance of the *Hau Kiou Choann or The Pleasing History* in London in 1761 excited considerable attention, and modern scholarship has accordingly done much to throw light on the background to this event.[50]

In fact the translation had been executed more than 40 years earlier in 1719 by a man named James Wilkinson, evidently as an exercise in learning Chinese from a tutor who was a Portuguese (or at least a Lusophone), with the result that when Percy was contacted by the Wilkinson family with a view to publishing the manuscript posthumously, he was confronted with a rendition of the Chinese mostly into an English translation which simply required a little literary polish, but also partly (where the tutor had completed the exercise) into Portuguese; Percy accordingly had to teach himself Portuguese in order to complete his task. Though the results of this somewhat involved process of translating and editing do betray inevitable lapses in conveying the original, the *Pleasing History* was not in origin a paraphrase, and the appearance of a French and a Dutch version of Percy's publication mark it as the one British (or at any rate Anglo–Portuguese) sinological success of the century.

But even though it was probably the first work of Chinese literature ever translated into a European language, by the time that it found its way into Percy's hands, Joseph de Prémare had already, in 1731, rendered a Yuan drama into French, and more than one edition of Prémare's work in English was already in circulation.[51] All other translation work from the Chinese during the eighteenth century was, for that matter, completely dominated by Jesuit publications in French, which continued to appear (thanks to a considerable backlog of materials already completed in manuscript) long after the suppression of the order in 1773. This predominance was indeed simply a continuation of that established by their translations into Latin of the preceding century.[52] And as it happens, the only other known British involvement in Chinese studies, at Canton in the early eighteenth century, relates to the transcription, in 1738–9, of a partial manuscript of the New Testament in Chinese, apparently of Jesuit (or at least French Catholic) origin.[53]

All the same, the publication of the *Pleasing History* seems to have pointed the way in Britain towards a marginally greater spirit of sinological independence. The Royal Society, hitherto no exception to the general rule that Britain at this point learned about China mainly through France,[54] took the novel step of approaching the East India Company's Canton Factory for 'one or two good Dictionaries of the Chinese Tongue and Characters with a litteral explanation attached thereto; and also some other capital books of the Chinese, both with and without translations, as they can be had': such works were duly forwarded in 1765.[55] But though some further supplies of Chinese books reached Britain from the same source in the next decade, and one small Chinese collection formed elsewhere in Europe which had come to London earlier in the century even found its way to Scotland at about this time,[56] no independent British competence in Chinese studies resulted. True, Sir William Jones (1746–94), founder of the Royal Asiatic Society of Bengal, dabbled in Chinese in between more serious Persian and Indian studies, but Arthur Waley dismisses the outcome of his efforts in a single page.[57]

The Eighteenth Century in Russia and France

Such a state of affairs in Britain contrasts sharply with the experience of Russia during the eighteenth century. The eastward expansion in influence of both nations brought them into contact with the Chinese for the first time at a comparable stage during the seventeenth century, and the Russians were certainly no better prepared then than the British to establish any form of diplomatic relations. A letter addressed to the Chinese authorities in 1619 was still awaiting translation in 1676, and no translators of official correspondence had yet been trained even in 1726.[58] But already in 1725 a German sinologist had been invited to St Petersburg to compile a dictionary, and by 1738 a native speaker of Chinese had been employed in Moscow.[59] The Russian ecclesiastical mission in Peking was perhaps not all that far in advance of the Canton Factory as a centre of intellectual activity, but when one of its first sinological trainees of any distinction returned to St Petersburg in 1740, he did take one hundred Chinese books back with him, and in 1753 he was even able to order successfully more purchases from Peking – something of a breakthrough for sinological librarianship in Europe which most centres of learning were unable to emulate until our own century.[60] The St Petersburg collection had been started in 1730 with works acquired through the Jesuits; by 1741 a catalogue had been published and by 1794 202 titles were held.[61]

Even so, eighteenth-century Russian awareness of China was heavily influenced by Paris sinology, which was at quite a different level of sophistication.[62] The Chinese collection in the Bibliothèque du Roi in fact only emerged as pre-eminent in Europe during the eighteenth century itself – prior to 1647 it only had four Chinese books, and it was not until 1697 that it acquired 49 more[63] – but it is in Paris that we must seek the beginnings of sinological librarianship as a distinct profession. A young Chinese named Arcadius Hoang, who had arrived in France in 1702, was given charge of the collection, and held this responsibility until his death in 1716. Although he had acquired, as had Shen Fuzong, a conventional Jesuit training, he appears to have cut a far more dashing figure: he took to wearing a hat and sword after the fashion of the day, and even married a French wife.[64] Though he does not seem to have been replaced as librarian, the collection continued to grow, thanks to the substantial contributions of Chinese-language materials made by French Jesuits based in China. Foremost among these collections of materials was that acquired from Jean-Francois Foucquet (1663–1740) in 1722. This was the result of a request for Chinese books sent by the Director of the library to Canton, which this Jesuit scholar had taken in hand. It is a pity that the catalogue of his acquisitions which he prepared remained unpublished until 1902, since it exhibits a systematic classification scheme applied with a certain amount of rigour; books on Confucianism, however, naturally predominate over all others.[65]

Unfortunately when the first catalogue of the Bibliothèque's Chinese holdings did appear, it was made neither by a librarian of Chinese origin, nor yet by a missionary scholar, but by one of the Paris savants in the field of Oriental languages who had been stimulated by the activities of the Jesuits to try their own hand at Chinese studies. The 'Catalogus Librorum Bibliothecae Regiae Sinicorum' of E Fourmont, attached to his *Linguae Sinarum Mandarinicae Hieroglyphicae Grammatica Duplex* of 1742,[66] is assuredly not one of the masterpieces of eighteenth-century French Catholic sinology, and with the rise of professional, secular sinology in Paris in the early nineteenth century its inadequacies came to be cruelly, though justly, ridiculed.[67] Listing all the popular novels and dramas in amongst the dictionaries seemed, in retrospect, inexplicably quirkish, whilst describing one of them, that famous depiction of a doomed love affair the *Xi xiang ji*, as an 'Historia comica' did not seem entirely apt.[68] It should be remembered, however, that to Fourmont's Jesuit mentors works of popular literature served mainly as a means to learning the spoken language and that literary judgements as to their contents were subordinated to this educational aim: the *Xi xiang ji* must have seemed merry stuff after the hours of study of the Confucian Classics which necessarily dominated the curriculum.

Also, whilst admitting that translations such as 'Familiae hù orationes' to indicate the famous *Shuo wen* dictionary must have been decidedly unhelpful,[69] it must be said that Fourmont's work does show some elements of good sense. The ten subject divisions (Grammar, Geography, History, Classics, etc.), though less closely allied to the classification scheme used in China itself than the divisions adopted by Foucquet in his then unpublished work, demonstrate an attempt, however flawed, at imposing a scheme of order upon the catalogue. By contrast, nearly all British catalogues of Chinese books up until very recent times have simply listed their contents in alphabetical order of the titles in transcription, if not completely at random.[70]

Despite its defects, moreover, the use of Chinese characters (from a font prepared for the printing of the *Grammatica Duplex*) does allow a fair picture of the nature of the collection. Of the 389 entries, 122 are categorised as theology – in other words, Christian works mainly compiled by Europeans. The presence of other translations of European works in the mathematics section, and of non-Chinese books (such as Japanese and Vietnamese works) towards the end also reduces the number of entries for works of purely Chinese origin, but clearly the library held well over two hundred such separate titles: a mere drop in the ocean when compared to the (already somewhat restricted) number of 10,254 titles given in the imperial *Si ku quan shu zong mu* of 1782, but a start none the less.

Yet it is precisely an awareness of their own limited knowledge which marks perhaps the highest achievement of the better French Jesuit scholars of the eighteenth century. This strikes home with a certain force even today: 'China is the America of men of letters. European scholars are like the Portuguese who boast of having conquered the Indies because they discovered them and built a few little forts on their coasts'.[71] The contrast with the mixture of ignorance and arrogance which has normally characterised British attitudes towards China could not be more manifest. Certainly publication of the *Pleasing History* was a particularly happy episode in the development of British sinology. But one cannot leave the eighteenth century without remarking on another famous episode, one which can only be accounted a complete disaster.

East India Company sinology

This was the celebrated Flint incident, in which an East India Company employee of a somewhat later period than James Wilkinson attempted to turn his studies of the Chinese language to a more practical end, with consequences unfortunate for himself and fatal for his tutor. Until, in the middle of the century, James Flint established himself as a recognised interpreter for the Company, its traders had been forced to rely on the services of local Chinese known (not entirely appropriately) as 'linguists', who utilised a limited form of pidgin adequate for immediate commercial purposes.[72] Flint soon showed the advantage to be gained by cutting out these middlemen and dealing with the Chinese directly in their own language, though whatever his spoken fluency it seems that a good written style in classical Chinese (essential in official communications) lay beyond his grasp. The John Rylands Library in Manchester in fact possesses a petition to the Emperor dated 1759 in tolerable classical Chinese said (according to a note upon it) to have been composed by a French trader who was the only European in Canton who commanded such a skill.[73] In this very year Flint, who had already been involved in moves to open up to trade ports less restrictive than Canton, sailed north to try to deliver a petition of his own devising. By thus attempting to bypass the normal channels of communication through Canton, Flint so provoked the Emperor's wrath that he himself was imprisoned, and the unfortunate Chinese who had helped him to cast the petition in the appropriate style, a certain Liu Yabian, was detained and executed.[74]

During the earlier part of Flint's career (which had seen one Chinese amanuensis arrested by the authorities for assisting him as early as 1753) the East India Company had been sufficiently encouraged by his success to invest somewhat in language training, so that after his departure from the scene another man, Thomas Bevan, was able to take his place until 1773, when illness forced him to retire. But given the natural reluctance of any more Chinese to martyr themselves in the cause of British sinology, the number of language students trained remained barely adequate for the Company's needs, and the last two decades of the century found the British entirely dependent on members of the Danish and French Houses in Canton for their dealings with Chinese officials.[75]

At this point the inadequacies of this struggling tradition of Chinese language studies fostered purely by commercial considerations became cruelly exposed when Britain at length decided upon an official diplomatic mission to China under Lord Macartney. There was simply no one in the country who could act as an interpreter. Very fortunately, however, an Italian would-be student of Chinese named Antonio Montucci (1762–1829), who was eventually to make a career for himself as a sinologist in France,[76] was working at the time as a language tutor in England, and he suggested to Sir George Staunton (1737–1801), Secretary to Macartney's mission, that interpreters might be obtained from the Chinese College in Naples. Prior to this Sir George had only been able to find a retired China missionary in Paris, who had forgotten most of his Chinese since leaving twenty years earlier, and who felt no inclination to renew his acquaintance with the country whatsoever.[77] The Chinese College in Naples had been established by an Italian missionary, Matteo Ripa, in 1732 to train young Chinese for the priesthood; in time it provided the basis for Chinese studies at Naples University. Well into the nineteenth century it must have been the only place in Europe where Chinese (especially educated Chinese) could be expected to be found. An English translation of Father Ripa's *Memoirs* published in the second half of that century appends a German account of a visit to the College which conveys something of the wide-eyed curiosity with which such rare aliens were viewed: 'The colour of their faces is yellow, but not disagreeably so ... When they laugh, and this they do incessantly, owing to their childish good humour, it is with a grin which shows all their teeth.'[78]

One of the pair of interpreters secured by Staunton from Naples did not entirely conform to this agreeable, if ingenuous, stereotype; the other proved during the course of the voyage and mission from 1792 to 1794 a firm favourite, and his surname of Li was Anglicized with good-humoured jocularity, so that he became known to all as 'Mr Plumb'.[79] Even more of a success was Sir George Staunton's son, also named George (1781–1859), the eleven-year-old page to Macartney. Both he and the Comptroller, John Barrow, attempted to learn Chinese on the outward voyage, but at their first practical test Barrow turned out to be unintelligible to the mission's hosts, whilst (as his father proudly observed) young George, 'whose organes were more flexible, proved already a tolerably good interpreter'.[80] Further efforts to extend the embassy's linguistic resources proved more problematic: a young Spanish-speaking Chinese was briefly recruited, but in the presence of Chinese officials he became so overawed as to render the remarks of his employers into impossibly abject Chinese.[81]

As is well known, the Macartney mission foundered on problems far more fundamental than a lack of suitable interpreters, but there are signs that in the wake of this signal failure in the development of Anglo-Chinese relations, a little more thought was devoted to the question of securing adequate means of communication. The East India Company persuaded a Chinese in the relative safety of Macao to start teaching the language to its employees once more;[82] in 1800 a certain Tchong A-sam was set on board a ship for England, apparently against his will, with a view to providing a native speaker in London, but after his vessel fell into the hands of the French he found himself conveyed to Paris instead.[83] As a result, the nineteenth century dawned in Britain on a land which, for all its commercial contacts with China, still could not boast a single teacher of Chinese. Even the younger Staunton had gone – returned to the East in 1798 to work for the East India Company.

The early nineteenth-century sinologists

But the country could at least boast one potential student, a man of the highest intellectual calibre, motivated neither by commercial nor religious interests, but by a profound spirit of intellectual enquiry. The remarkable Thomas Manning (1774–1840), a graduate of Caius College, Cambridge, and an accomplished mathematician, the friend of Richard Porson and Charles Lamb, 'began to brood upon the mysterious empire of China' in about 1798.[84] Noting the scientific accomplishments of the Jesuits which commended them to China's emperors, he trained as a physician, but had it not been for the Treaty of Amiens in 1802, which allowed him to go to France, he would have been completely baulked in his Chinese studies. In Paris he was able, for two years, to study with Joseph Hager (1757–1819),[85] and it is said that Napoleon himself allowed him free passage to leave the country when Anglo-French hostilities resumed. He sailed to Canton in 1806, but after failing to gain entry to China or to Annam finally decided at least to venture into Chinese-controlled territory by heading, accompanied by a single servant, into Tibet. The opposition of the Chinese authorities forced him to withdraw, but not before a meeting with the Dalai Lama. He accompanied the Amherst mission to Peking in 1817, but after returning from the Far East to Britain published no book on China and won a reputation for marked eccentricity.[86]

But the journal he kept of his Tibetan adventure did survive, and was later published. From this one might rather be tempted to conclude that, far from being a hopeless eccentric, he was one of the most farsighted men of his age, and that his failure to publish the results of his researches into things Chinese stemmed perhaps from an awareness that 'all the world was drunk and he alone was sober', to use the Chinese expression. At any rate the following diary entry, penned deep inside Tibet but giving his reflections on the mentality of the East India Company, who had refused to allow his trip any official status, shows that his own thinking had moved ahead from a consideration of the linguistic difficulties which had impeded the Macartney embassy, to question the very idea of sending out ambassadors ignorant of the speech of their Chinese hosts: 'I cannot help exclaiming in my mind (as I often do), what fools the Company are to give me no commission, no authority, no instructions. What use are their embassies when their ambassador cannot speak to a soul, and can only make ordinary phrases pass through a stupid interpreter? No *finesse*, no *tournure*, no compliments. Fools, fools, fools, to neglect an opportunity they may never have again!' Sure enough, the first Chinese magistrate he met started to hint at the possibility of Anglo–Chinese trade through Bhutan, but to no avail.[87]

Though the notion that diplomats might do well to speak Chinese in China was still only a visionary eccentricity at this stage, some progress had been made towards this goal even by the time that Manning set out for Canton, in that 1805 marked the first appointment of a Professor of Chinese to give instruction to British students.[88] But this appointment was not in London, nor for that matter in Canton, where the East India Company was employing a Father Rodriguez to do its language teaching,[89] but at Fort William College in Bengal. Here the Baptist missionary Joshua Marshman (1768–1837) and his family were given instruction by Joannes Lassar, an Armenian Christian from Macao. Lassar's arrival in this pioneering academic post was the result of pure serendipity. His family background in Macao was comparatively wealthy, and his parents had hired two Chinese tutors for him, simply to indulge a childhood whim. Though this had led to a mastery of both spoken and written Chinese, he had arrived in Calcutta in 1804 as part of a family trading venture, and there is no reason to suppose that he entertained any hopes that his hobby would ever serve him well in a professional capacity, least of all in India.

Marshman and his Baptist associates were, however, anxious to learn Chinese at the first opportunity, in order to prepare a Chinese translation of the Bible, in their eyes an essential preliminary to further missionary efforts among the Chinese. Together he and Lassar embarked upon this work, publishing the results as they became available, at first using woodblocks and later moveable metal type. St Matthew's Gospel was the first portion of the Bible to appear from the Mission Press, Serampore, in 1810; the complete Bible was finally published in 1822, for the first time ever in Chinese. But in the following year the publication of some revised portions had already become necessary, since Canton had also been, from 1810 onwards, the scene of Bible translation work. This, due to the added benefit of far greater numbers of available native-speaker Chinese informants (Marshman appears to have had only one),[90] tended to eclipse the Serampore pioneers' version in quality, even if the complete translation resulting from the parallel project was not published until 1823 in Malacca, somewhat later than its Bengal-based rival.[91]

This second, Canton–Malacca Bible was the work of Robert Morrison (1782–1834) and W Milne (1785–1822), both of the London Missionary Society. Morrison had first started learning Chinese in London in 1805, and twenty years later became the first British teacher of Chinese to hold classes there.[92] For although he was to some extent self-taught (making use of the dictionaries obtained by the Royal Society), he was also able to avail himself of the assistance of a Chinese named Yang Sam Tak, who had landed up in Clapham after a (voluntary) trip from Canton – in return for removing Yang from lodgings mainly occupied by students from Sierra Leone and putting him up at 14 Pitt Street, Fitzroy Square.[93] The years following Morrison's arrival in Canton in 1807 can be said to mark the first true flowering of British sinology. Missionary influences, though strong, were not the only ones at work: Morrison himself was obliged (given the lack of opportunity for evangelization) to work for the East India Company from 1809 onwards, and the year that saw the publication of his first translation from the Bible into Chinese (the Book of Acts, 1810) also saw the publication by his fellow employee Sir George Staunton (the younger Staunton; the father had died in 1801) of a translation of the Qing penal code, the first entire work rendered into English from Chinese since Bishop Percy completed James Wilkinson's efforts of almost a century before.[94]

Even this had been preceded by a rather poorly handled partial attempt at the *Analects*, published in Serampore by Marshman in 1809.[95] But the lead won by Marshman and Lassar for the 'Bengal school' of British sinology remained precarious throughout its existence. Although Marshman talked of Chinese forts on the Tibetan border menacing East India Company territory in which no one was linguistically equipped to deal with the enemy, it seems that Lassar's professorship was provided for throughout by private funds, rather than the regular Fort William College payroll, and soon after a change of Governor-General in 1813 we find Marshman's official support cut off in favour of patronage directed to Morrison.[96] Soon, too, Morrison was producing the basic learning aids (a grammar, a dictionary) which allowed Milne's Anglo–Chinese College, founded in Malacca in 1818, to provide for prospective missionaries an education in Chinese more firmly grounded than anything the East India Company itself had ever been able to secure.[97]

These early Protestant missionary scholars still had their limitations, of course, which were duly pointed out by their contemporaries in Paris,[98] and any Briton looking for an education in Chinese for non-missionary purposes might prefer to go elsewhere – as Thomas T Meadows (1815–68) preferred (or was obliged) to learn Chinese from Karl Freidrich Neumann (1793–1870) in Munich, prior to starting his career as a government interpreter.[99] For the Anglo–Chinese College, at least in its early days, tended to be marked by a distinctly partisan approach to scholarship.[100] David Collie, who on Milne's death achieved the position of Professor of Chinese there in 1823, after only about a year's worth of language instruction from Morrison,[101] produced before his early death in 1828 a translation of the 'Four Books' of Confucianism which had some influence on Thoreau and

Emerson, but which exhibits in its footnotes a quite virulent contempt for Chinese thought.[102]

Rather unsurprisingly, then, whereas there are signs that the French were at first willing to concede a certain parity between themselves and the British in the study of the spoken language, and to applaud the way in which Morrison's costs in producing his dictionary were underwritten by the East India Company to the tune of £2000, the Franco–British co-operation which led to the publication of a grammar written in the preceding century by Prémare seems to have been an isolated occurrence.[103] At any rate, Morrison's injudicious remark in a China guide of 1817 that 'No person in Europe has succeeded in acquiring the language to any extent' provoked the tart comment that no one seriously involved in Chinese studies in Europe would have made the errors discernible in Morrison's work.[104]

Chinese studies in nineteenth-century London

But the studies of men like Morrison, Staunton and Manning, whether impelled by religious, commercial or purely intellectual motives, did result in the building up of sinological libraries which, in the course of time, found their way back to Britain. There little had happened since the 1770s to increase the stock of Chinese books: Macartney's mission was evidently responsible for the importation of some fragments of an important Chinese illustrated manuscript,[105] but given the linguistic difficulties it encountered, it is hardly strange that the idea of systematically collecting source materials in Chinese does not seem to have occurred to anyone.

The East India Company, perhaps as part of its subsequent heightened concern for language studies, did form the habit, from about the start of the nineteenth century, of occasionally sending parcels of Chinese books back to London, where they lay, for the time being, unopened.[106] In Canton, however, from 1806 onwards it built up far more of a working library, which at the time of its dispersal in 1832 consisted of some 1600 titles in English, French and Chinese.[107] The private libraries of its employees also appear to have been considerable: when Sir George Staunton in 1824 drew up a list of his Chinese books for donation to the Royal Asiatic Society, which he had helped to found, it contained 186 separate works.[108] This marked the first accession of a substantial collection of Chinese materials to a public institution ever in this country, one year ahead of the donation by 'Mr Fowler Hull of Sigaur' which laid the basis for the British Museum's nineteenth-century Chinese holdings.[109] Manning's Chinese books, too, some two hundred in all, went to the Royal Asiatic Society in the end: this indeed was only proper, since Manning himself had held the post of Honorary Chinese Librarian in the Society, thus providing sinological librarians in this country with a forerunner every bit as individual as Arcadius Hoang.[110]

Morrison's library, now in the School of Oriental and African Studies, took a different course, and one far more beneficial to the development of Chinese studies in this country than even the establishment of the Royal Asiatic Society. For his executor was none other than Sir George Staunton, who was now given a second opportunity to make a substantial donation of Chinese books to an institution of his choice. A Robert Morrison Education Society did exist in Macao to perpetuate his name in good works, but this had apparently already been the beneficiary of part of the Canton Factory library upon its dispersal,[111] and in any case Sir George, who had since 1817 been comfortably retired from an active participation in Chinese studies in East Asia to become a Hampshire country gentleman,[112] was clearly more concerned with promoting ventures closer to home. Armed with Morrison's excellent collection as an inducement, he persuaded University College, London, much against the wishes of some of the elements within it, to appoint a Professor of Chinese for a period of five years in return for the books. In 1837 an agreement was concluded and a Professor elected, at a salary of £60 *per annum*.[113]

Accustomed as we are in an age subject to bouts of giddying inflation to assume that figures such as these must have represented a considerable sum so long ago, it is worth reporting the observations of the pioneer translator Robert Thom, writing in the preface of his bilingual version of *Esop's Fables* in Canton in 1840 '... while some objected to the establishing of a Chinese Chair altogether — others (and they were the majority) agreed to set aside for the re-imbursement of a learned gentleman — who had spent many years of his life in the acquiring of this most difficult of all languages — a sum — about equal to half that — which an English gentleman awards to a good Cook, or a smart Valet-de-chambre!'[114]

So, although it was thanks to a legacy of Chinese books that Staunton was able to put Chinese studies in Britain on a professional footing and so achieve a goal which had been the subject of fruitless discussion since at least John Barrow's time some four decades earlier,[115] we should note the very guarded enthusiasm of those who found it too little, too late. The translator of Aesop does not mention it, but he was almost certainly aware that in 1837 a further chair of Chinese had simultaneously been established in Russia at Kazan, by decree of the Tsar, and that the state had funded not only the post itself, but library provision too.[116] In fact Kazan was equipped with a valuable collection of materials derived through the Russian mission in Peking from the eighteenth-century Jesuits.[117] At least Thom expresses no regrets about the choice of learned gentleman, though the Reverend Samuel Kidd (1799–1843) was clearly not a man of Morrison's own intellectual stature. He had been for many years a teacher at the Anglo–Chinese College in Malacca, where he had succeeded to Collie's professorship and had published a well-known Protestant tract in Chinese translation, but in 1832 had been obliged by ill health to retire to Britain.[118]

Though doubtless an able teacher of the language (he was James Legge's first teacher of Chinese),[119] his sinological attitudes seem more reminiscent of the eighteenth or even seventeenth centuries than of the age of the great Stanislas Julien (1797–1873), who already held a chair in Paris at the time of Kidd's election. Kidd's published ruminations on the relationship of Chinese to the 'common primordial language of mankind' fall within a long tradition of speculation linking China and Egypt, whilst his catalogue of books of the Royal Asiatic Society library contains entries even more bizarrely inappropriate than anything in the work of

Fourmont or Hyde: listing the novel *San guo yan yi* under 'statistical works' is a typical example.[120]

No wonder, then, that after his death in 1843 the chair was allowed to lapse, and that Staunton had to start work all over again at King's College, London, where, however, he was obliged to finance this second chair through an endowment raised by public subscription. Although the chair at King's was filled more or less without interruption throughout the remainder of the century, there were embarrassing interregna. During the first of these, in 1851, one would-be sinologist was complaining that 'While Paris, Petersburg, Munich and even Naples contain Chinese professorships ... we are without the means of studying a language in which more than in most others assistance is required' – though by the time these remarks were published in 1854 the situation had been remedied.[121] Since the chair at University College was also revived rather more sporadically until the death of Samuel Beal (1825–89),[122] nineteenth-century London could from time to time boast two professors as a result of Staunton's efforts. But it should be pointed out that Paris, too, possessed two chairs of Chinese, one at the Collège de France, founded in 1814 for classical Chinese, and another for modern Chinese at l'École des Langues orientales, founded in 1843. Not all occupants of these chairs were as distinguished as Julien (though for six years he contrived to occupy them both), but they did exhibit a level of scholarship consistently higher than that of their London contemporaries, with the possible exception of Beal, who like Julien was a pioneer in Chinese Buddhist studies.[123]

German scholarship likewise could point to two Professorships of Chinese earlier than those in London. One was held by Neumann at Munich, as mentioned above, where he concurrently taught Armenian and had charge of the very large Chinese library collection he had himself built up.[124] The other, nominally in Berlin, had been awarded to Julius Klaproth (1783–1835), who was permitted to reside in Paris.[125] Klaproth did, however, produce a copiously annotated catalogue of the holdings of the Royal Library in Berlin which covers less than 50 titles (including large parts of the same medical collection, first acquired by the Dutch, which had also contributed to Sir Thomas Bodley's acquisitions) but which set standards of thoroughness sufficient to render Kidd's efforts all the more embarrassing.[126]

Nor, despite the limits on the Berlin collection, could the libraries acquired in Britain by the Royal Asiatic Society, the British Museum and University College be said to represent an exceptional influx of Chinese books by comparison with the rest of Europe. The Kazan and Munich acquisitions we have already mentioned; the flamboyant Russian sinologist N Ia Bichurin (1777–1853) is also reported to have brought back fifteen camel-loads of books after his stay in Peking,[127] while the voluminous translations of August Pfizmaier (1808–87), who started to teach in Vienna from 1848 onwards, testify to a considerable collection in that capital too.[128] The shortcomings of early nineteenth-century British studies are further underlined by the fact that the first Professor at King's, a former interpreter named Fearon, was certainly not the College's first choice for the job. The Dutch scholar Johann Joseph Hoffman, for many years an assistant to the famous Japanologist P F Von Siebold, was offered the post, but at the last moment was given a position by his own government to forestall his leaving the country.[129]

The late nineteenth century

None the less, the start made in London University did provide a valuable precedent for developments later in the nineteenth century. The late Victorian and Edwardian eras saw the establishment of further chairs at other universities and the expansion of Britain's Chinese collections in a number of public and private libraries. Government service rather than missionary endeavour now became the principal incentive in bringing about expansion, but it is also possible to see continuities between these two phases of growth. We have already noted that James Legge (1814–97) was at first a student of Samuel Kidd, but his missionary career soon took him to the Anglo-Chinese College, of which he became the Principal in 1839. Dissatisfaction with the work of David Collie and his like led him to embark on his great project of translating or retranslating all the Confucian Classics. This task was to occupy him for the greater part of his career, but it did produce a basically sound corpus of work remarkable in its own time and still useful today.[130]

His eventual installation at Oxford as Professor of Chinese in 1876, though it marked in some ways a new era in British sinology – with (once again) the possible exception of Beal, he was the first professional British scholar in Chinese studies to win an international reputation – also showed a marked continuity with the past. For it was still not the university which saw any need of a Professor of Chinese; rather, Legge's friends clubbed together to provide for the Chair – and, indeed, managed to raise a sum resulting in an improved but still modest yield of £95 *per annum* – on the proviso that James Legge was its first occupant.[131] By way of comparison it may be noted that even Belgium had installed a sinologist in a university chair some years before this.[132]

What he did for books at first, other than use his own, is unclear: the holdings accumulated 200 years earlier in the Bodleian were hardly adequate for modern research. They had been expanded somewhat by 1876, as a catalogue published in that year by Joseph Edkins (1823–1905) shows. But this list still runs to less than 300 titles, including about 40 works by Protestant missionaries, and some other items in Japanese and Mongol, as well as a few paintings and maps. Edkins, incidentally, seems to have been a worthy successor to Kidd: the famous pornographic novel *The Prayer-mat of Flesh* is rendered here with Lewis Carollesque whimsy as *The Meat and Spinach Garden*.[133] In 1881 and 1882 these resources were expanded by the purchase of the library of Alexander Wylie (1815–87), a missionary scholar whose career in China, principally in the service of the British and Foreign Bible Society, had been cut short by failing eyesight.[134]

Next, we find a third university acquiring a Chair of Chinese, but this time (as with that at University College) the Chair itself was a by-product of a donation of books, which arrived in 1886 at Cambridge. This benefaction, running to over 650 titles in Chinese, came from Sir Thomas Wade (1818–95), who had served as an interpreter and diplomat in China until 1882. In the letter offering his collection Sir Thomas did point out (having no Sir George Staunton to do it for him) that 'while presenting it as a free gift, I press for but one condition, namely that, for the rest of my life, I be allowed free access to it, and that, so long as my powers of mind and body permit, I be constituted its special curator or guardian'.[135] In 1888 he was duly appointed to a new Chair of Chinese, and, just to make sure that he might continue to enjoy his books undisturbed, further remarked in his inaugural lecture 'I assume that my pupils, should I have any, will be intending missionaries or interpreters... My advice to applicants in either category is that they should make their own way to China with all speed...[136]

Sir Thomas is best known today for his work with the romanisation of Chinese, which resulted in the Wade–Giles system, still much used today. But his successor at Cambridge, Herbert A Giles (1845–1935), though he too had started as an interpreter in the consular service, seems to have had a poor opinion of the man whom he succeeded in 1897 and with whom he is now thus customarily linked. Noting Wade's disparaging characterisation of Legge's translations as 'wooden', Giles comments: 'In my opinion, Legge's work is the greatest contribution ever made to the study of Chinese, and will be remembered and studied ages after Sir Thomas Wade's own paltry contribution has gone, if indeed it has not already gone, to the dustheap'.[137]

At the start of the present century a fifth professorship was founded at Manchester for Edward Harper Parker (1849–1926), yet another ex-consular service official who had been teaching since 1896 in Liverpool.[138] Parker, a prolific but resolutely mediocre scholar, was apparently succeeded by a Reader in Chinese who taught there until World War Two,[139] after which, despite post-war expansion, we hear no more of Chinese in Manchester University. Apparently his collection of books survives in that city yet, along with the earlier Bellot collection, and, in the John Rylands Library, an excellent nineteenth-century collection of Chinese books which was initially kept at Haigh Hall, Wigan.[140] The long-forgotten prominence of Wigan in the story of British sinology was entirely due to the efforts of Alexander William Crawford Lindsay, 25th Earl of Crawford (1812–80). He is described by the *Dictionary of National Biography* as 'sincerely religious', though a sufferer from ill health; the library of the School of Oriental and African Studies contains one or two publications by him on Aryans, on ancient Israel and on other such topics no longer fashionable.

Yet although his Chinese collection formed but a part of the library of this wealthy bibliophile (and a part whereof he himself was able to read not a single syllable), the professionalism he displayed in building up his collection far eclipsed that of any other librarian in Britain responsible for Chinese books at the time. For whilst the nucleus of his Chinese holdings was acquired at one stroke in 1863, by the purchase of a private sinological library from Belgium, he also made use of a Peking agent to expand it further.[141] This we learn from the preface to a catalogue prepared at the behest of his heir, James Ludovic Lindsay, the 26th Earl, under the direction of J P Edmond. Unfortunately, listings such as the description of an edition of the ancient *Travels of King Mu* as 'Respectful terms for addressing the Emperor and superiors generally' do not inspire too much confidence in the body of the catalogue,[142] but a first-hand inspection of the Lindsay Chinese books might well repay the effort.

In sheer size, of course, the Lindsay, Wade and Wylie collections were already easily eclipsed by the holdings of the British Museum. These had been increased in part as the result of the use of force – Queen Victoria bestowed on the institution in 1843 materials captured by her troops at Canton in 1842[143]– and in part through the acquisition of Chinese collections which had happened to become available in Britain. Thus, when James Legge's collaborator Wang Tao (1828–97) passed through London in 1869, he disposed of 203 works from his own library for £65 10/–.[144] This is hardly the munificent donation of 11,000 *juan* which Wang later claimed,[145] but when the price paid is compared to the figures for academic salaries given above, and when it is compared with the annual library acquisitions budget of £20 maintained by the Royal Asiatic Society at this time,[146] the British Museum appears relatively liberal in its use of funds.

I know of no evidence, however, that the British Museum pursued anything other than a sporadic opportunistic acquisitions policy with regard to Chinese, let alone made any use of a regular agent in Peking.[147] By contrast other libraries elsewhere in Europe were already sending out agents to East Asia to make purchases on their behalf. For example, K F Neumann had visited Canton prior even to Morrison's death, in order to acquire more books for Munich and the Royal Library in Berlin.[148] As far as I am aware, no such purchasing trip was mounted from Britain until over a century later.

Instead, the librarian in charge of the Chinese collection at the British Museum from 1863 to 1905, Robert Kennaway Douglas (1838–1913), occupied himself with the production of a series of catalogues dismissed even by Giles as 'a monument of immature scholarship'.[149] Meanwhile the lack of any system of classification within the library itself rather took the first Chinese mission to Britain by surprise – even if the inclusion of Taiping placards cheek by jowl with imperial edicts, though blasphemy to them, did ensure that after the fall of the Qing, London became the first port of call for Republican historians of the anti-Manchu struggle.[150] Douglas was yet another ex-consular official, though the combination of his post with a professorship at King's College suggests a somewhat more active disposition than many of his contemporaries similarly retired from service in the Far East.[151] In 1904, just before his retirement from this further career, he was joined at King's (the University College chair had now been abolished) by a second professor, Sir W C Hillier (1849–1927).[152] Thus, at the high noon of British imperialism, the country could afford no fewer than five professors of Chinese, a number it has never attained since. Yet all too soon the foundations of this apparent prosperity were to be shaken by the first of the many inquiries into the effectiveness of British Oriental Studies which have so far punctuated this century.

The early twentieth century in Britain

The *Reay Report*, to use the title generally given to the volume produced for the Treasury in 1909 by a committee under Lord Reay's chairmanship, was in fact more circumscribed in its terms of reference than any of its successors, since it considered only the organization of Oriental Studies in London. Although it led in time to the creation of the School of Oriental Studies (now the School of Oriental and African Studies), it had been prompted in large part by persistent problems with the teaching of Chinese in particular in London – only Hillier, it seems, achieved any success as a teacher – and so was in a sense a somewhat parochial response to a broader problem, 'A Chapter of National Inefficiency', as *The Times* leader on the *Report* put it.[153] The inefficiency uppermost in the minds of most of the initiators of the *Reay Report* was the complete failure of the retired diplomats and missionaries of Britain to keep pace with their counterparts in Germany and France in the teaching of spoken Chinese, which had already started to work to the disadvantage of British economic interests.[154]

But, in the light of hindsight, some of the most poignant evidence heard by the committee came from Herbert Giles, describing his own career in Cambridge. He had had, he said, during his time as Professor 'only one student at Cambridge who really wished to learn the language for its own sake'.[155] In other words, aspiring diplomats and missionaries might be obliged to learn Chinese to further their objectives, but as in Manning's day, only the occasional rare eccentric felt that China might be the object of serious academic study. Even more depressing is the following exchange between Giles and the committee:

> Have you got a native assistant?—No, I have not.
> And do you think it would be desirable to have one; should you like to have one?—I should like to have one very much indeed; I am afraid Cambridge University would not rise to that.[156]

It might, admittedly, have been a little hard to find a Chinese assistant at a time when study abroad (except in Japan) was still something of a rarity in a Chinese career – there was only one Chinese in Oxfordshire at the beginning of this century, for example.[157] But reading some of the distinguished (and extremely long-serving) Professor's woollier contributions to sinology – 'Traces of Aviation in Ancient China', for example, or his pieces identifying Xi wang mu with Hera, or paintings of the founders of China's Three Teachings as representations of the Trinity ('Art Thou the Christ?')[158] one forms an impression of a man who, in the absence of his sons, had absolutely no one to talk to, no one to talk him out of his own private mystical musings.

Something of the situation of Chinese studies in Britain in the years immediately following the publication of the *Reay Report* (the recommendations of which took almost a decade to implement) may be seen in the story of Sir Edmund Backhouse (1873–1944) and his quest for the Professorship of Chinese at Oxford, a story which, thanks to Lord Dacre, is one of the few episodes in the history of Chinese studies in this country which is common knowledge beyond sinological circles themselves. And it is not a very edifying story either: Sir Edmund must clearly be ranked amongst the most duplicitous fantasists and forgers in the history of the West, even if his contemporaries seem to have had only the vaguest inklings of the true scale of his deceptions.

Yet, eccentric as Backhouse was, Lord Dacre is all too right in observing that he was 'unquestionably a scholar – a far more sensitive scholar than the retired consular officials and missionaries who would be his competitors'.[159] Perhaps it had even been to his advantage never to have studied Chinese under any British academic – for as far as we are aware he was entirely self-taught. It may be objected that despite his candidacy for the Oxford chair, he was ultimately disappointed in his hopes. But he was elected to the chair of Chinese in London, which, had he taken up the post, would have yielded £300 a year for him, as against £150 a year at Oxford.[160] In any case, the manner of his campaign at Oxford shows that little had changed in the way such issues were decided in Britain since the early nineteenth century: his famous donation of books to the Bodleian recalls not only Wade's donation to Cambridge, but also Staunton's gift of Morrison's library to University College.

At least the Bodleian tried, after a fashion, to make use of Backhouse as a buying agent in Peking and paid up for expenses incurred.[161] When Backhouse had earlier sold a number of Chinese books through Luzac's in London in 1908, the University Library in Cambridge had resorted to that other time-honoured method of supporting Chinese studies – private subscription – in order to raise the money to purchase its share of the collection.[162]. Both libraries, however, were basically still pursuing a policy of building their collections through occasional enlightened opportunism. The consequences were inevitable: though the Bodleian gained the greater advantage from its association with the former scapegrace Oxford undergraduate and undoubted bibliophile Sir Edmund, its Chinese collection in the 1930s still exhibited some most startling gaps – no copy of Li Bai's poems, for example.[163]

Rising standards in Europe and America

Thus, for all Sir Edmund's munificence, Britain's Chinese collections on the eve of the First World War presented a sorry contrast to those of France. The Bibliothèque Nationale in 1913 possessed not only the most complete collection of Chinese books outside the Far East, but also a worthwhile published catalogue of its holdings – in Pelliot's judgement the first serious catalogue in Europe.[164] And not only that: at a time when Giles and Backhouse represented the best that British sinology had to offer, a generation of French scholars were making use of these library resources in Paris to give France such a commanding lead in the academic study of China that in some areas their achievements have not been bettered even today. The scholarship of E Chavannes (1865–1918) and his students P Pelliot (1878–1945) and H Maspero (1883–1945) is too widely admired to require comment. But the close relationship between their astonishing advances into areas untouched not only by earlier Western but even by East Asian research and the materials available to them in their libraries can be readily demonstrated.

A good example is the field of Taoist studies, where French-language scholarship, even in the 1980s, maintains a dominance which in most other fields has passed to the United States since the Second World War. In 1912 Chavannes and Pelliot were celebrating the arrival of the first copy of the Taoist canon (albeit an incomplete one) in Europe; in 1913 they were already citing it in their joint research; in 1919 Chavannes won the posthumous honour of having the first translation of a text made directly from the Taoist canon published in Paris; by

1935 Maspero's writings showed that he was now reading extremely broadly in Taoist literature; in 1950 one volume of Maspero's posthumous works was devoted to the Taoist religion, the first book in a Western language to be based on extensive research in the Taoist canon itself. Though since the 1950s publications in English on the history of Chinese science have made use of the Taoist canon, it is only within the last decade that the French monopoly of books on the Taoist religion as such, based on canonical sources, has been broken.[165]

Of course, not all these contributions in French have been made by scholars native to France. At the start of this century only France possessed any lengthy tradition of professional scholarship in Chinese studies, but other nations of continental Europe soon established schools of sinology which vied with that of Paris in their commitment to the highest academic standards. Otto Franke (1862–1949) in Germany and J J L Duyvendak (1889–1954) in The Netherlands did pass some of the earlier days of their careers in consular services, but by the end of the First World War were both full-time scholars; Bernhard Karlgren (1889–1978) in Sweden appears to have enjoyed this status throughout.

By contrast, Britain was still appointing superannuated old China hands, when its universities bothered to make any appointments at all. Despite the *Reay Report*, London was still without a professor from 1914 to 1925; Giles was not replaced at Cambridge until five years after his retirement in 1928; it took Oxford six years to decide not to appoint Sir Edmund Backhouse; and Parker in Manchester was never replaced at all. Of the men who succeeded to these chairs, only A C Moule (1873–1957) at Cambridge, a missionary scholar from a famous family of missionaries and scholars, won any recognition from his peers in Europe. Despite the fact that he was already 60 at the time that he took up his professorship, he proceeded to publish a number of valuable studies – including two volumes on Marco Polo in collaboration with Pelliot – and devoted a great deal of attention to the Chinese holdings in the University Library; he is even credited with starting systematic buying to build up the collection, though perhaps this overstates his contribution.[166]

It would at any rate be a mistake to see British sinologists of this period as entirely ignorant of the extent to which standards of scholarship were rising elsewhere in the West. William Edward Soothill (1861–1935), the missionary educator who was eventually chosen in preference to Backhouse at Oxford, accompanied Lord Willingdon to China in 1925 as part of the Government Advisory Committee charged with deciding what use to make of Boxer Indemnity funds. He is said to have realised that substantial endowments for British sinological studies were needed to catch up with both the Continent and America, but as a former university administrator in China he also knew how much more Chinese education required support.[167] In fact, when the deliberations of this 1925 committee did lead, in 1931, to the establishment of the Universities' China Committee in London, its main objectives lay where Soothill's conscience had told him they should, and only a portion of the £200,000 from the China Indemnity Fund (to give it its official title) was, and is, devoted to the support of Chinese studies in this country.

By contrast, the foundation in 1928 of the Harvard–Yenching Institute alone involved the sum of $2,000,000,[168] and (as Soothill seems to have been aware) a rapid expansion of Chinese studies in other American universities was concurrently taking place against a background of funding undreamed of in this country. It was to take another world war and a third official enquiry before the opportunities missed in Britain during the 1920s became apparent.

The origins of Chinese studies in the United States may, like our own, be traced back into the nineteenth century, but almost from the start very marked differences from the pattern of development in this country become evident. I do not know what circumstances led to the creation of a chair of Chinese at Yale in 1876, though its first occupant, the missionary scholar Samuel Wells Williams (1812–88), is said to have helped to start the Chinese collection in that university. The employment of his son and eventual successor, Frederick Wells Williams (1857–1928) in taking care of the books, though the father was quite without students, suggests something of the cosy retirement of a Legge or a Wade.[169] But the next three chairs created were each the result of donations of money or other assets by wealthy individuals connected in some way with China, and each post was filled not with an American citizen returned from China, but with a scholar selected from abroad.

Thus, in 1877 Francis F Knight of Boston, who had been a resident in China for many years, raised a fund of $8750 which provided for a Mr Ke Gunhua of Ningbo to take up a chair in 1879; the books which Ke brought with him were donated to the university to start its collection. In 1895 $50,000 from the estate of Senator Edward Tompkins went to establish the Agassiz Professorship at Berkeley; the first occupant of this chair, the Englishman John Fryer (1839–1928), likewise donated his Chinese books (mainly, though, translations done by himself into Chinese whilst employed by the Qing government in the Tong wen guan) to his university. Tomkins was an early regent of the university; his prophecy (as early as 1872) that; 'The child is now born that will see the commerce of the Pacific greater than that of the Atlantic', may have been slightly premature, yet it looks commendably prescient today.

In 1901 General Horace W Carpentier, a Columbia graduate who had made a fortune in gold mining and who was impressed with the patience and faithfulness under provocation of his Chinese servant, Dean Lung, gave an initial $100,000 to establish an entire department of Chinese at his alma mater, headed by a Dean Lung Professor; Carpentier later added another $113,000 and the servant $12,000 of his own.[170] The first Professor was the German sinologist Friedrich Hirth (1845–1927), but in this case the endowment was so lavish that the department was able to start systematic acquisitions of Chinese books for the East Asian Library straight away, far in advance not only of its rivals but even of the Library of Congress. By 1913, however, that institution, already the beneficiary of several donations, started to commission its own purchases on a regular basis, while a few years later a gift from Carpentier to Berkeley of another $100,000 enabled its library to do the same.[171]

Though at Harvard 'a few volumes were added yearly' to Ke's collection (implying perhaps some deliberate policy of continuing acquisitions), it was not until after 1927, with the appointment of Dr A Ch'iu as Librarian in charge of the collection, that this trickle became a spate of tens of thousands of volumes annually. Although 'volume' in this case means the Chinese *ce*, the published annual statistics, even in the early days of the library, are awesome.[172] By the Second World War Chicago and Pennsylvania had joined the select group of American universities with full programmes in Chinese studies (though Chinese was also taught elsewhere, from Hawaii to Dartmouth) and some American professional sinologists (H G Creel, for example, or Derk Bodde) had already found posts in these institutions.[173] But it was Europe, especially France and Holland, which set the standards, and it was to men like Pelliot that the promoters of American sinology turned for advice, on librarianship in particular.[174] Academics with a missionary background, such as Kenneth Scott Latourette (1884–1968), who taught at Yale, might also be found in American universities at this time, but hardly dominated the scene to the same extent as in Britain.

Britain between the wars

If one could speak of professionals at all in British sinology between the wars, it would have to be in connection with the British Museum. Lionel Giles (1875–1958), son of Herbert, entered the Museum in 1900, not long before Sir Aurel Stein secured (to use a neutral term) a good portion of the manuscripts then recently discovered at Dunhuang and shipped them back to London in 1907. Exactly 50 years later, long after 'young Giles' had retired from his work with the Chinese collection, his catalogue of these materials was published. Not exactly quick work, but the first volume of the catalogue of the other main portion of the Dunhuang manuscripts, brought back to Paris by Pelliot, only appeared in 1970 after passing through several hands, and it has been followed by but one further volume (Volume Three!) since then.

The British Museum was also home for a time to Arthur Waley (1889–1968), certainly the best-known British Orientalist of this century, thanks to the exceptional literary value of his many translations from Chinese, Japanese and other languages.[175] Waley entered the service of the Museum in 1913 and left in 1930; his own catalogue of the paintings in the Stein collection was published with commendable celerity in 1931 – though to be fair to Lionel Giles, the paintings are numbered in hundreds, the manuscripts in thousands. But Waley's career as a cataloguer was, as it were, by the way. Like Thomas Manning, and like Herbert Giles' lone unknown student (a victim of the First World War?), but unlike nearly all other British sinologists prior to the Second World War – one hesitates over the case of Sir Edmund Backhouse – Waley was motivated in his Chinese researches by sheer intellectual curiosity. Entirely self-taught in the language, he started to publish translations at a very early stage in his studies, and once he had the financial means to devote himself exclusively to reading and writing, congenial to himself alone, eschewed all but the least taxing professional commitments with decided finality – when tempted with a chair at Cambridge, for instance, he is said to have replied 'I would rather be dead.'[176] For despite the excellence of his translations and the competence of his mature scholarship, he perhaps found the academic study of China, as exemplified by his continental contemporaries (let alone his British colleagues), a little boring.[177] His informal contributions to the general level of scholarship on China in this country were manifold and immense, but his highly individual talent avoided any institutional entanglements.

Thus Chinese studies in British universities presented a very bleak prospect indeed, in spite of Waley's publications, until amost the eve of the war. Although it was Britain's involvement in a global conflict suddenly requiring a quite unforeseen number of military personnel trained in East Asian languages that brought a dramatic end to the lassitude of centuries, in the three universities of London, Oxford and Cambridge some developments, in most cases indirectly connected with the gathering war clouds in Europe, were already under way in the late 1930s. In every case, too, library provisions in Chinese formed an important part of these developments.

In Oxford, for instance, despite the absence of a Professor after Soothill's death, the Chinese scholar Xiang Da was employed to draw up, in 1936, a report on the Chinese collection, and £600 was then devoted to covering the major gaps. Then, in 1939, an Honours School in Chinese was established, though the training in the language is described as 'written, not spoken'.[178] The moving spirit behind these modest advances appears to have been E R Hughes (1883–1956), a former missionary who had been teaching Chinese religion and philosophy at Oxford since 1933.

In 1938 the arrival of a new Professor in Cambridge also led to changes in the Library. Gustav Haloun (1898–1951), a product of the Leipzig school of German sinology founded by August Conrady (1864–1925), had already accumulated several valuable years of service in Göttingen, where he had paid particular attention to building up the library resources for Chinese, before the trend of events forced him to move on to Britain. In 1939 he initiated a comprehensive book purchase scheme for Cambridge University Library, though its implementation was delayed by the outbreak of war.[179]

Post-war expansion in Britain

Meanwhile, in 1936, SOAS had welcomed as a refugee from Germany Ernst Julius Walter Simon (1893–1981), who was both a Professor of Chinese and a qualified academic librarian, though yet again it was initially 'certain anonymous donors' rather than the university authorities who raised the money necessary to guarantee his presence at the School.[180] Simon attained the position of Reader within two years of his arrival, but over ten were to pass before he was given a Chair of Chinese. This was a new creation, since the professorship first created a century earlier had been filled from 1939 by E D Edwards (1888–1957), a former missionary schoolmistress who had been teaching at the School since 1921.

The unprecedented expansion represented by the introduction of this second chair (Simon's Department of the Far East as a whole was to expand from three posts to twenty-six) was of course a consequence of the Second World War, but even as late as the academic year 1943–4 we find some fairly damning comments still being passed on the existing state of affairs in Britain: 'I was once sent by the University of Hong Kong to discover a Professor of Chinese for that University. The people out there were under the delusion that such a man should be an Englishman. I went everywhere and found no one who was willing to come and who fitted the bill in any way... If I wanted any advice about Chinese, I found I had to go to Paris.'[181]

Yet by 1949 the sinologists of Paris were ready to declare their admiration for the level of state funding accorded Chinese studies in this country and to seek lessons applicable to France itself in the extensive reorganisation and development which this funding made possible.[182] Obviously Britain's wartime experience in having rapidly to train large numbers of linguists in languages hitherto deemed unworthy of too much attention formed the larger background to the Report of the Commission under the Earl of Scarborough, which was published after over two years' work in 1946. But, as was well appreciated in Paris, the original initiative in setting up the commission came from none other than Sir Anthony Eden, for better or worse the only Orientalist Foreign Secretary (let alone Prime Minister) we have ever had.[183]

By no means all the plans drawn up at this stage were never realised – Cambridge's target of a Professor and three other posts in Japanese, for instance, was only achieved in 1985, and that in the case of the professorship by private subscription in Japan rather than British state funding. But library provision was something the Scarborough Commission took seriously (Paragraph 115.19 of the *Report*), and soon Haloun and Simon were off to the Far East equipped with substantial non-recurrent grants for book purchases (£6000 in the former case). Such library expansion also necessitated the appointment of new personnel: in 1946–7 Miss (later Dr) M I Scott had already become the Curator in Oriental Literature at the University Library, Cambridge, beginning an association that was to last well over thirty years; in 1950–1 she was appointed to an assistant librarianship in charge of the Chinese holdings.[184]

In Oxford the situation was somewhat more complex. Towards the end of the war the University had appointed the leading Chinese historian Chen Yinke (1890–1969) to succeed Soothill, but he found his eyesight inadequate to the task, and returned to China to resume his academic career there, where there were plenty of trained researchers ready and willing to read his Chinese for him.[185] In 1947, still lacking a suitable British candidate, Homer Hasenpflug Dubs (1892–1969) was invited from the United States to fill the chair. Dubs, a missionary scholar of wide experience and varied attainments (he was, for example, an enthusiastic bassoonist) maintained the existing emphasis on Classical Chinese at the expense of the spoken language, but could not maintain the relationship which Hughes had evidently enjoyed with the Bodleian: accordingly, £2000 went to that library, while £8000 went to Dubs to start a library of his own, the nucleus of the present Chinese collection in the Oriental Institute.[186]

It is, however, important to bear in mind that Great Britain was not the only country to witness a period of expansion following the war. Though the eventual territory of West Germany possessed but four centres of Chinese studies in 1939, by 1952 Chinese was taught at no less than ten universities.[187] By contrast in Britain it was not until 1959 that a fourth university started to teach Chinese – this in the person of a Spalding Lecturer in Chinese at Durham who was simultaneously Curator of the Gulbenkian Museum and in charge of the Far Eastern Section of the University Library.[188] In North America, moreover, the direction taken by post-war expansion was to have in the longer term a profound and revolutionary influence on the way Chinese studies came to be regarded in the West, as the involvement of the United States in East Asian studies came to outweigh by far the contribution formerly made by the countries of Europe.

'The marriage of sinology and social science came only as a shotgun wedding during and after World War II', according to John K Fairbank.[189] But, however unduly delayed and reluctant this union was, it certainly took place much earlier in the United States than elsewhere. As a consequence the Paris-based type of sinology which Americans had striven to emulate in the past began to look very trivial by comparison with the theoretically more daring approaches of the social scientist. Fairbank himself described the affiliation of Paris sinology in these terms: 'The accumulation of factual bricks to build an edifice of learning (or at least pile up a heap of knowledge) created the tradition of micro-sinology, which was nourished by the tradition of *k'ao cheng hsueh* (establishing textual facts for facts' sake).'[190] Arthur F Wright (1913–76) further complained about the consequences of this tradition; 'Chinese studies remain a retarded and underdeveloped field of Western scholarship.'[191]

In fact both Fairbank and Wright studied (as historians, not sinologists, of course) in Oxford during the 1930s – something which might perhaps have provoked a particular disdain for European scholarship on China. Yet such sentiments were widely shared during the heyday of Area Studies in the United States: in response to a symposium on Chinese Studies organised by the *Journal of Asian Studies*, the main organ of the new Area Studies approach, the 'lone cheer for sinology' came not from an American, but from a British historian trained in sinology by Haloun; otherwise a substantial agreement prevailed that sinology represented an approach now entirely outmoded.[192]

In some circles, too, it was further suggested that since China had now rejected her own past so decisively all historical research on China should be downgraded in importance in favour of a far greater emphasis on contemporary studies.[193] Certainly such a view did not win universal acceptance, but it would have been much more difficult even to contemplate such a shift had not American library collections already in 1945 taken the first step in deciding to build up holdings of contemporary materials.[194] This decision was in turn facilitated by the presence of Americans already in North China and elsewhere who could act as buying agents.[195]

From Scarborough to Hayter

It would be unfair to see the Scarborough Commission as leading simply to a perpetuation of a rather conservative form of continental sinology in this country.

Many of the post-war generation of recruits to Chinese studies had Japanese as their first East Asian language, so they were able to make use (as none of their predecessors save Waley had done) of Japanese studies of China. They were thus able to benefit from the unique blend of competence in traditional sources and awareness of more modern possibilities in interpretation which has characterised the best Japanese scholarship of this century. As long as Britain's armed forces, through the medium of National Service, continued to play a leading role in Chinese language training, the advances made in the teaching of modern spoken Chinese during the war were not lost either, even though some universities still felt reluctant to accord the spoken language more than a minor part in the syllabus. None the less, the only major innovation in Chinese studies in the years following the Commission's report was in a sense also an anachronism, harking back to the time when things Chinese in British universities were the concern only of men with other careers behind them.

I refer, of course, to the work of Joseph Needham, the first volume of whose *Science and Civilisation in China* was published in 1954; fourteen further titles in the series have appeared to date. This widely admired project has not by any means been pursued in the academic isolation which characterised the work of Giles and his like, but it has impinged on the course of professional, established Chinese studies in this country hardly at all so far – though the appointment of a China specialist to the new post in the History of Asian Technology created at SOAS this year does at last offer the prospect of bringing this aspect of Chinese civilisation into the regular curriculum there. Otherwise it is worth noting that the existence of the Needham Research Institute as an established continuation of the project has come about as the result of donations received mainly from outside the United Kingdom, and that these donations have been attracted to the Institute in large part because of its unique library.

But the creation of the Needham Research Institute has taken well over a quarter of a century, and during the last quarter of a century the mainstream of Chinese studies has itself moved on, even though it has followed at times a rather uncertain course. In 1961 a sub-committee of the University Grants Committee under Sir William Hayter addressed itself to a review of post-Scarborough development, and concluded that radical changes bringing Chinese studies in this country closer to the American model were necessary. 'Enthused by the American example,' to quote Sir Peter Parker, 'it concentrated on the establishment of regional centres of area studies.'[196] A fifth department of Chinese was created at Leeds University in 1963, specialising in modern Chinese studies, while SOAS added economic and political studies, geography and sociology to its teaching. Some further developments followed: in 1965 Edinburgh University established the teaching of Chinese on its own initiative, while in 1967 the Ford Foundation made a grant of $325,000 to SOAS in order to set up the Contemporary China Institute; the new institute opened formally on 12 June 1968.[197] The same American foundation simultaneously gave $50,000 to the Library of the University of Leeds to help create the bibliographic resources necessary for the new centre there.[198]

But the Hayter Sub-committee's approach was subject to criticism from the start. In 1961 it was already observed that the: 'Hayter Sub-committee's preoccupation with short-term and fundamentally unacademic expedients threatens, if their outlook is widely adopted by British universities, to perpetuate the tradition that the field of modern Chinese studies at least is one for the amateur and the journalist rather than for the serious scholar.'[199] One American visitor was still told in 1965 by a British university member that: 'We simply send our students who are interested in modern China to the United States'. The visitor's own feeling was that European studies of modern China as a whole were inadequately funded, especially since: 'Although we started earlier and have had twenty years to build up a reservoir of manpower from which to recruit, financing modern and contemporary China studies becomes more and more difficult. But Europeans must start from scratch'.[200]

A 1971 Ford Foundation report, too, while noting plenty of problems in the development of Chinese studies in the United States, observed that: 'In Great Britain, the traditional interest has survived, but has not flourished,' and after reviewing the rather mixed benefits of the Hayter expansion concluded: 'The failure to develop and mobilise social scientists to work on China indicates China's modest place in British intellectual and national concern.'[201]

Though there have been one or two innovations since this date (for example, the establishment of the Contemporary China Centre at Queen Elizabeth House, Oxford, in 1980), the years 1967–71, during which I received my own training in Chinese, probably marked the apogee of development in Chinese studies in this country. It was at this time, for example, that the *Cambridge History of China*, on which planning started in 1966, began to take shape. But here again the qualified success of post-war development in Britain is suggested by the scale of American involvement, financial and academic, in this continuing project. And within a decade severe retrenchment had set in, and posts created during the Scarborough and Hayter eras had started to disappear. None of the six existing departments of Chinese has been lost (though an attempt to establish Chinese studies in Glasgow proved a failure), but in the meantime like provision in the United States has risen to some 100 departments, and in West Germany to a score or so.[202] The number of professional China specialists in academic life in this country is hard to estimate: about 40 to 50 are concerned with teaching Chinese; perhaps about another 50 (if that) have Chinese studies posts related to their disciplines.[203] By contrast China specialists in the USSR 'may approach one thousand' in number, while in the United States the figure has been estimated at about 3000.[204]

British studies of China in retrospect

The process of decline in Britain has now been halted, thanks to the completion in 1986 of the report 'Speaking for the Future' by Sir Peter Parker, which has resulted in the provision of funds to cover a certain number of posts and studentships – and library resources besides. The net result of this provision, however, can hardly be described as amounting to expansion: the future may not now be as bleak as it once looked, but it would be an exaggeration to call it rosy.

For having come so far with the story of Chinese studies in Britain, it is perhaps worth a backward glance or two before confronting the problems that lie ahead. One immediate conclusion that may be drawn from the preceding pages is that in its attempts at understanding China, this country has always depended on the kindness of strangers – Chinese like Cocks's fine friend Andrea Dittis; little, blinking Shen Fuzong; the martyr Liu Yabian; the genial Plumb; the conscripted Tchong A-sam; a host of nineteenth-century co-workers or 'moonshees', ranging from the inadequate Yang Sam Tak to the outstanding Wang Tao; more modern men of letters like Lao She and Hsiao Ch'ien and scholars like Joseph Needham's collaborator Lu Gwei-djen; Joannes Lassar, the Armenian Professor of Chinese; the African ex-slave Antonio; Europeans like the unknown co-translator of the *Pleasing History*, the Italian tutor Montucci and the missionary Father Rodriguez, or more recently academics like Simon and Haloun; Americans like Homer Hasenpflug Dubs – the list could be extended indefinitely.

With one or two exceptions,[205] British sinology was at its most self-sufficient in the century between the appointment of Kidd and the retirement of Moule. But that era, despite a few outstanding individual talents, can be termed great and glorious only by comparison with the preceding centuries, when the needs of commerce had engendered such a short-term, utilitarian view of the desirability of Chinese studies as to produce results almost uniformly pathetic.

In the last half-century, the complete inability of this country to achieve adequate standards in Chinese studies without outside assistance (and even outside funding) has been particularly marked. Simon and Haloun must be given credit for the increase in professionalism following the Scarborough expansion;[206] the rise of modern Chinese studies in the post-Hayter era has depended conspicuously on American help.[207] At the three oldest centres of Chinese studies there has never been a time since Haloun's arrival when all three chairs of Chinese have been held by scholars of British origin; the more recent chair at Leeds has never been filled by a British scholar at all and is currently vacant. Of course, the internationalism of the academic profession is one of its major strengths, and the number of Chinese, Europeans and Americans who have filled and continue to fill posts in our Chinese departments have contributed richly to our university life; many British graduates in Chinese, for their part, teach in Australia, Canada, New Zealand, the United States and even in other parts of the world where the medium of instruction is not English.

But if we look at British exploitation of our own library resources it becomes clear that behind the normal patterns of academic interchange lies a less welcome picture of British failure. Our library holdings are for the most part nothing out of the ordinary: standard works of reference show that more substantial collections of Chinese books exist elsewhere in Europe and particularly in the United States – comparison with East Asia itself is, of course, a little unfair.[208] In terms of quality we may point to three main areas of strength: popular literature not collected by traditional Chinese bibliographers; politically subversive materials (Taiping, Triad, etc.) suppressed by earlier Chinese governments; and the Dunhuang manuscripts.[209] Yet the names of British scholars who have made use of these materials (and certainly there are some who have taken the opportunity to study the rarities to hand here) have been completely overshadowed by those visitors to this country – Liu Tsun-yan, Xiao Yishan, J C Cheng, Hu Shih and Wang Shumin, just for example – who have done far more to put them on the map.

The fate of the Dunhuang documents taken to Paris affords a telling comparison with that of our own collection. True, Paris has shown itself somewhat tardy by comparison with London in its publication of catalogues (though both centres have now been far outstripped by Tokyo), but a monograph series has for some time been in existence there to publish research on their manuscripts, while in recent years a steady stream of collective publications from a team of scholars working on these materials has further added to French-language scholarship on Dunhuang. British scholarship has always been far less collaborative – especially with so few scholars to collaborate – and even the productivity of our most outstanding individual sinologists has been of no bibliographic benefit to this country: James Legge's books are in the New York Public Library; Arthur Waley's papers are in Rutgers.

The consequences of failure

The continuing failure of Chinese studies in Britain to make good use of the opportunities which history has afforded us has both reasons and consequences, which must now be squarely addressed. For our libraries the most immediate message of the foregoing survey concerns consequences. We must expect, for the short-term future at least, not to be able to fill vacancies in Chinese studies in Britain with British recruits to the profession. Yet attempts to recruit abroad, especially in the United States but increasingly in continental Europe also, will be doomed to failure if British libraries are seen to fall behind the standards now being set elsewhere. Research funding is insufficient in this country to guarantee frequent trips to make use of library facilities abroad, and if our own collections are seen to be inadequate for research purposes, we will be written off by the outside world. And not by the outside world alone – it will surely become impossible to keep even the trained staff working here at present.

Nor will it be possible in future to skimp on library provision by cutting back, concentrating either on pre-modern or modern China (though some division of labour between libraries may be desirable), since the trend of the best scholarship, in the United States in particular, is now strongly against such compartmentalization. There both old-fashioned sinology and the Area Studies approach have been consigned to the past.[210] If anything, the emphasis has switched back to a renewed appreciation of the value of studying pre-modern China, and a reaffirmation of the relevance of an historical approach to China in the twentieth century.[211] At the same time the greater accessibility of contemporary Chinese materials as the result of post-Cultural Revolution developments, to say nothing of research on the spot, has laid open opportunities which other nations are certainly not neglecting. An increasing volume of secondary literature is appearing, not only in English, from the USA, Australia and elsewhere, but also in French, German and Russian, whilst a command of Japanese literature on China is today even more necessary than a generation ago. Without adequate funding we could be left very far behind.

Why not, then, drop all pretensions to academic excellence for its own sake, and concentrate on 'practical Chinese', sufficient for our purposes as a nation? After all, other English-speaking countries publish enough on China to keep us reasonably well informed without having to trust to the services of self-declared 'persons of quality'. The answer is that the promotion of practical Chinese has, in effect, been the policy which we have tacitly been pursuing all along, and which we are pursuing today – and that is precisely the reason why our studies have always been so ineffectual. Thus, Sir Peter Parker, in line with his predecessors, was asked simply 'to enquire into the provision of Oriental and African languages and associated area studies which is required to meet the demands of commerce and diplomacy'.[212] But consider the following verdict on the failure of H A Giles to match the sinological standards set elsewhere, culled from an entirely sympathetic contemporary Chinese assessment of his work:

The word, 'TRADE', is written large in the history of the British contact with China. The demand was for an efficient understanding of the oral and written language. If commercial treaties can be signed and official documents can be deciphered, there is no need for further study.[213]

A century earlier, things were much the same, as W C Taylor observed in reviewing the prospects for Oriental literature as a whole: 'In no other Nation is it so difficult to introduce a new object of study, or extend the cultivation of an old one, without demonstrating its immediate pecuniary advantages.[214] Sixty years earlier still, a visiting French Orientalist made a number of observations on learning and letters in Britain which, as Arthur Waley remarked in his summary of them in 1952 'to some extent still hold good'; the most basic was that: 'Outside the two university towns learning, unless directly useful to commerce, has no prestige at all'.[215]

It may seem reasonable to ask for academic studies to prove themselves cost effective, but in the case of Chinese during the first century in which it was taught here it is quite clear what happened. Having mastered a useful skill, only those who by reason of age or infirmity were incapable of putting it any longer to some good purpose returned to this country to pass on their knowledge. Far from promoting excellence in teaching, this led at best to a random selection of less than dynamic has-beens attempting to teach one of the most difficult languages in common use.

We are now in danger of the same situation, or worse, recurring: during the years that I have been teaching, I have seen plenty of bright students with the intellectual curiosity which Giles found so rare, but without exception they have despaired of any academic prospects and turned elsewhere: diplomacy, commerce or posts overseas. A whole generation of students has been lost to us for good, since they lack the qualifications needed in our age to return to university life. Now that I have had posts to fill at last, I have been thankful to find scholars older than myself who have eked out a living for years outside university employment waiting to make use of an academic training long since completed. Such men and women are rare, and becoming rarer: few younger persons are willing to face the risks of an academic career when a knowledge of Chinese can provide immediate rewards.

The promotion of no more than practical Chinese seems to me, in short, utterly impracticable, and a waste of time and money. Surely what we need in any case is not simply more language experts – though basic language teaching, so difficult in a university context but almost impossible elsewhere, must remain a priority. For mere experts are not good enough. Can we afford to scoff at those, far more successful in Chinese and other Asian studies than we are, who assert that 'language training should be seen as a fundamental part of the humanities, of value in its own right', that their 'intellectual life will be impoverished without the inclusion of the creative achievements of the great Asian civilisations'?[216] The dissemination of a broader knowledge of China in our society at the moment is quite scandalously inadequate. In history teaching, for example, two established journals which at their outset promised readers coverage of Far Eastern or even specifically Chinese history were found at the start of this decade to be devoting 0.2% and 0.3% of their coverage respectively to what has been, after all, the historical experience of a quarter of mankind.[217] No wonder Sir Peter Parker quotes the Director of the School of Oriental Studies, Durham, as saying: 'I cannot but say that Britain is seen to underrate the 'practical' value of 'ancient' subjects in terms of cultural politics, especially by comparison with the French.'[218]

Rather than simply assuming that the remoter, deeper cultural background to modern China can be simply ignored, it might be more profitable to look at our own history and try to discover how such a bizarre notion could come into being. If our own country were truly as devoid of an interest in the past and of an interesting past as we assume China to be, we would be many millions of pounds worse off in terms of revenue from tourism – and in the struggle to attract tourists China has not yet begun to fight. The material products of the Chinese past, for that matter, command ever-increasing prices in our auction rooms. Is a knowledge of the background that produced these objects not practical knowledge? That unappealing genius Sir Edmund Backhouse certainly realised that it was, and tried to turn it to his advantage in his forgeries.

In his day, of course, the less intellectually subtle could make money out of China as Backhouse did in his more straightforward moments by simply looting Chinese treasures. Those days are gone, but still Waley's observations on the attitudes of Sir Aurel Stein illuminate an interesting facet of more general attitudes to Asia which may perhaps have some bearing on our current problems. Stein, he notes, belonged firmly in a tradition of archaeologists used to operating in societies 'where conversion to Islam had long ago completely divorced the inhabitants from their remote past'.[219] Indeed, in some of the areas most familiar to Europeans, it is our past to which these inhabitants are the most recent heirs. Of what value is a study of the ruins of Ephesus to an understanding of modern Turkey? But the relationship of modern China to the remains of its ancient civilisation is in fact far more intimate than even the relationship of modern Greece to the Parthenon. And in a civilisation where stone and metal were little used in architecture, and where it was literary remains which provided monuments more lasting than brass, it is the written legacy of the past that we must look to first in order to gain a deeper perspective on China.

Well-stocked, well-funded, well-staffed libraries covering both pre-modern and modern Chinese studies are, I would submit, every bit as practical an aid in our dealings with China as tapes and videos for language learning. They may seem expensive, but they do function simultaneously to guarantee the presence of academics – and in a world of jumbo jets, an exodus of scholars can happen rather swiftly. Remote and ineffectual academics may appear, but past history suggests that it is precisely as the practical benefits of knowing Chinese become greater and greater that it becomes less and less likely that anyone else will consider it worth their while to teach Chinese language and culture, so, paradoxically, enough of an exodus of scholars could spell commercial disaster in the longer term. The opportunities afforded by this conference I described earlier as a luxury in terms of the daily grind of sinological librarianship; in terms of the future of Chinese studies in this country a co-ordinated review of our resources is, surely, a very urgent necessity.

Notes

1. Though others may be able to provide more detailed and up-to-date figures, those I have seen for the early 1980s are disheartening enough: see Liu Guojun and Zheng Rusi, *The Story of Chinese Books* (Beijing, 1985) pp. 118–22.
2. Susan R Stifler, 'The language students of the East India Company's Canton factory', *Journal of the North China Branch of the Royal Asiatic Society* 69, 1938, pp. 46–82.
3. D C Twitchett, *Land Tenure and the Social Order in T'ang and Sung China* (London, 1962) pp. 3–13.
4. The impact of a first-hand awareness of China on European thinking during the seventeenth century has been demonstrated by a number of studies by Edwin J Van Kley and by David E Mungello. The most recent monograph by the latter, *Curious land: Jesuit accommodation and the origins of sinology* (Stuttgart, 1985) demonstrates the way in which speculation concerning the Chinese language related to pre-existing theories stretching back to mediaeval thought. But although much has been written about the relationship between the influence of writings about China and the eighteenth-century Enlightenment, for the later period less has been done to demonstrate the intellectual context in which Chinese studies themselves were carried out.
5. Henri Cordier is, of course, best known for his monumental *Bibliotheca Sinica*, 2nd, revised ed. (Paris, 1904–08) in four volumes; supplementary volume, 1924), but apart from this indispensible bibliography he also completed a number of studies of the development of French sinology, which are listed in n. 1, pp. 59–60 of the last such piece to appear, 'Les études chinoises sous la Révolution et l'Empire', *T'oung Pao* 19(1920) pp. 59–103.
6 'Aperçu historique des études sinologiques en France', *Acta Asiatica* 2 (1966), pp. 56–110. For German sinology, see below, note 148.
7. Paul A Cohen, *Discovering History in China: American Historical Writing on the Recent Chinese Past* (New York, 1984). The appearance of this volume has itself sparked considerable debate in the United States. On p. 212, n. 78, Cohen notes that he includes one British historian with strong American links in his survey.
8. See Stifler, 'Language students', p. 46.
9. Luo and Zheng, *The Story of Chinese Books*, pp. 118–19.
10. 'How to forget Chinese history', *Bulletin of the British Association for Chinese Studies* (1986) pp. 10–21.
11. Lynn Pan, *The New Chinese Revolution* (London, 1987) pp. 164, 232.
12. See Hei long jiang ren min chu ban she, ed., *Quan tong xiang sheng xuan* (Harbin, 1979), pp. 167–79, for one such example.

13. D F Lach, *Asia in the Making of Europe*, vol. 2, book 2 (Chicago, 1977) p. 227.
14. On Barros, *see* C R Boxer, 'Some Aspects of Western Historical Writing on the Far East, 1500–1800', pp. 308–9, in W G Beasley and E G Pulleyblank, eds, *Historians of China and Japan* (London, 1961), pp. 307–21.
15. *See* p. 44 of Paul Pelliot, 'Notes sur quelques livres ou documents conservés en Espagne', *T'oung Pao* 26 (1929) pp. 43–50. More recent studies on this work have been published in Japanese: *see* the summary by Wm. Theodore de Bary on p. 1 of de Bary and JaHyun Kim Haboush, eds, *The Rise of Neo-Confucianism in Korea* (New York: Columbia University Press, 1985) and n. 1, p. 54; a further article has now been published by F Vos, '*Meishin hōgan* ni tusite', (*Tōhoku Daigaku*) *Nihon Bunka Kenkyūjo kenkyū hōkoku* 21 (1985), pp. 1–15. It is possible that the Cobo work was completed after a translation of the Confucian Four Books by Michele Ruggieri in 1591–92, the manuscript of which is now in Rome; Ruggieri is known to have translated one unnamed text as early as 1581, but this has not survived; *see* Paul A Rule, *K'ung-tzu or Confucius?* (North Sydney, NSW, 1986), pp. 6–7, and n. 35, p. 243.
16. Apart from the rapid survey by Pelliot cited in the preceding note, there is also a record of a visit to the libraries of the Peninsula compiled by Fang Hao under the title 'Liu luo yu xi, pu di zhong guo wen xian', now in his collected works, *Fang Hao liu shi zi ding gao* (Taipei, 1969), vol. 2, pp. 1, 743–92 (my thanks to Andrew Lo for reminding me who wrote this study). *See* also Lach, *Asia in the Making of Europe*, vol. 1 (Chicago, 1965) p. 747, n. 68, and pp. 779–80.
17. For Mendoza, *see* Boxer, 'Some Aspects of Western Historical Writing', p. 309, and p. 155 of Otto Berkelbach van der Sprenkel, 'Western Sources', in Donald D Leslie, Colin Mackerras and Wang Gungwu, eds, *Essays on the Sources for Chinese History* (Canberra, 1973) pp. 154–75.
18. *See* pp. lxxxvi–lxxxvii of C R Boxer, *South China in the Sixteenth Century*, in Hakluyt Society, Series II, no. CVI (London, 1953), a volume containing Mendoza's main sources in translation, and Lach, *Asia in the Making of Europe*, vol. 2, book 2, p. 53. Boxer, pp. xxxiv–xl, points to a Chinese geographical work already present in Madrid in 1574; Lach elsewhere (*see* n. 16, above) suggests that the main Spanish holdings that survive today were already formed by 1585.
19. Matteo Ricci's name hardly calls for any comment, especially since the publication of Jonathan D Spence, *The Memory Palace of Matteo Ricci* (Yale University Press, 1984); an interesting sidelight on Chinese studies and publishing in the Philippines may be found in P van der Loon, 'The Manila Incunabula and Early Hokkien Studies', *Asia Major*, new series, 12 (1966), pp. 1–45 and 13 (1968), pp. 95–186. For the rather tentative beginnings made in Chinese studies by Ricci's senior colleague Ruggieri, *see* Rule, *K'ung-tzu or Confucius?*, pp. 5–6.
20. *See* p. 353 of Ch'ien Chung-shu, 'China in the English Literature of the Seventeenth Century', *Quarterly Bulletin of Chinese Bibliography* (new series), vol. 1 (1940), pp. 351–84; his quotation is from a translation, published in 1577, of an Italian edition of an account by Galeote Pereira, later incorporated into Mendoza's work.
21. Zhang Yidong, on p. 58 of 'The earliest contacts between China and England', *Chinese Studies in history and philosophy* 1.3 (Spring, 1968), pp. 53–78, translated from *Li shi yan jiu* 5, 1958.
22. This is already mentioned in James Bromley Eames, *The English in China* (London, 1909) pp. 7–8; Chang, 'Earliest Contacts', reproduces two letters of 1583 and 1596 in English.
23. John Barrow, quoted by Stifler, 'Language students', p. 73, n. 53.
24. *See The Merchant Explorer: University of Minnesota Library, Minneapolis, Occasional Paper number 12* (April, 1972), p. ii.
25. Eames, *The English in China*, p. 11.
26. Chang, 'Earliest Contacts', p. 65. This may seem an unduly cynical judgement on Dittis, who certainly went out of his way to befriend Cocks. But one possible reading of the Cocks diaries suggests a man out of his depth; while Dittis may have been helpful, he was in all probability far more skilled than Cocks at looking after his own interests.
27. Lt Col Sir Richard Carnac Temple, ed., *The travels of Peter Mundy 1608–1667*, Hakluyt Society Series II, vol. XLV (London, 1919) vol. III, Part I, pp. 192 and 312, and *see* also pp. 178, 241. Spence, *Memory Palace*, p. 209, suggests that Ricci, too, had depended on black interpreters at first; Spence's references in his n. 19, p. 307, may be used to supplement those in the next note.
28. The presence of such slaves in Macao is well attested: C A Montalto de Jesus, *Historic Macao* (Hong Kong, 1902) p. 42 notes that the 900 settlers already present in 1563 included some Africans, mainly domestic slaves; Cesar Guillen-Nuñez, *Macau* (Oxford University Press, 1984) p. 8, reports that the wall across the isthmus joining Macao to the Chinese hinterland was said to have been constructed in 1573 to prevent thieving by black slaves from Macao in the Heung Shan area; he also describes the participation of African Macanese in the repulse of the Dutch attack of 1622 on pp. 16–19. For both these references I am indebted to my colleague Gervase Clarence-Smith.

29. Chang, 'Earliest Contacts', p. 65.
30. *The Travels of Peter Mundy*, vol. III, part I, p. 313. There seems to be, however, some possibility that Mundy was already aware of the trouble that some Chinese speakers had with the consonants of European languages, since the same observation is made (plainly without reference to Mundy's manuscript) in a Dutch source speaking of the late seventeenth century. By this time the Dutch would have had enough contact with Chinese for the observation to be 'common knowledge', but such 'common knowledge' might equally well date back to sixteenth-century Portuguese contacts with China. *See* J J L Duyvendak, p. 36, n. 3 of 'Les Études Hollando-Chinoises au 17me et au 18me Siècle', in *Quatre Esquisses Détachées Relatives aux Etudes Orientalistes à Leiden* (Leiden, n.d., [1931]) pp. 21–44.
31. *See* Rev. W Campbell, on p. 390 of 'The Past and Future of Formosa', *Scottish Geographical Magazine* August, 1896, pp. 385–99.
32. Eames, *The English in China*, p. 36.
33. *See* Xiang Da, on pp. 627–8 of 'Ji niu jin suo cang de zhong wen shu'; reprinted in his *Tang dai chang an yu xi yu wen ming* (Peking, 1957) pp. 617–52. The Bodleian also possesses some other materials reflecting Sino-British commerce of this period, specifically the visit of the vessel Flora to Canton in 1686: see J Edkins, *A Catalogue of Chinese works in the Bodleian Library* (Oxford, 1876) p. 43, item. 285.
34. J J L Duyvendak, 'An Old Chinese Fragment in the Bodleian', *Bodleian Library Record* 2.26 December, 1947, pp. 245–7.
35. Quoted on p. 305 of A F L Beeston, 'The Earliest Donations of Chinese Books to the Bodleian', *Bodleian Library Record* 4.6 December, 1953, pp. 304–13.
36. It is to be hoped that the very inadequate article by Beeston, cited in the preceding note, will one day be replaced by some observations on these matters by Professor P van der Loon: the information given here is from Beeston, together with what I understand, at second hand, to be Professor van der Loon's findings.
37. J J L Duyvendak, on pp. 314–16 of his 'Early Chinese Studies in Holland', *T'oung Pao* 32 (1936), pp. 293–344.
38. On Shen Fuzong, *see* Mungello, *Curious Land*, pp. 255–6; Beeston, 'Earliest Donations', p. 307, n. 4; Ch'ien, 'Seventeenth Century', pp. 382–3; and also references in the following note.
39. Beeston, 'Earliest Donations', p. 308; Duyvendak, 'Old Chinese Fragment'. For an eighteenth-century account of Hyde and his Latin conversations with Shen (whom he termed 'my brilliant friend Mr Michael Chin Fo Çum'), see Knud Lundbaek, *T S Bayer 1694–1738: Pioneer Sinologist* (London and Malmö, 1986) pp. 80–1; *see* also n. 140 on the latter page for some published letters by Shen to Hyde, and Hyde's account of Chinese games, based on Shen's information.
40. Stifler, 'Language students', p. 70, n. 8, based on his 'Observations and Conjectures concerning the Chinese Characters', *Transactions of the Royal Society*, III, pp. 285–291. The Bodleian also possesses a genealogical table presented by 'R Boyle' in 1671, which suggests that Hooke's mentor Robert Boyle (1627–91), who was known for his support for Orientalists, especially in connection with missionary work, shared his Chinese interests; *see* Edkins, *A Catalogue of Chinese Works*, p. 41, no. 270.
41. Ch'en Shou-i, 'John Webb: a forgotten page in the early history of Sinology in Europe', *Chinese Social and Political Science Review* 19 (1935), pp. 295–330, treats one British would-be sinologist perhaps best left forgotten, though Lundbaek, *Bayer*, p. 58, n. 64, commends his work as a good example of the speculation concerning the Chinese language then current in Europe.
42. The works in question were P Alvarez Semedo's *Imperio de la China* (Madrid, 1642), translated here from an Italian version under the title *The History of That Great and Renowned Monarchy of China*, and Martino Martini's *De Bello Tartarico* (retitled *Bellum Tartaricum* in this London publication), a treatment of the Manchu conquest of China first published in Antwerp in 1654 that had soon gone through more than a score of editions in various European languages. For Semedo and Martini, *see* Mungello, *Curious Land*, pp. 74–90 and 106–16 respectively.
43. Duyvendak, 'Les Études Hollando-Chinoises', pp. 31–32, mentions Dutch interpreters of Chinese in the Far East, though in 'Early Chinese Studies', pp. 298–305, he notes that J Golius (1597–1667), the Leiden savant most interested in things Chinese, was more or less incapable of reading the Chinese collection which he possessed. At all events the Dutch role in bringing Chinese materials back from the Far East (especially via Batavia, though we should not forget that they also controlled part of Taiwan) was crucial – even if the subsequent fate of those materials was sometimes a little unexpected: *see* van der Loon, 'Manila Incunabula', part two, p. 106, for an intriguing example.

44. Thus Mungello, *Curious Land*, p. 227; the Elector's purchases are discussed on pp. 208–9. For a lengthy eighteenth-century account of Müller and his work, *see* Knud Lundbaek, *T S Bayer*, pp. 61–76, a translation of Bayer's own introduction to his *Museum Sinicum*.
45. For Müller's catalogues, *see* p. 571 of Donald F Lach, 'The Chinese Studies of Andreas Müller', *Journal of the American Oriental Society* 60 (1940), pp. 564–75, and cf. Cordier, *Bibliotheca Sinica*, col. 1815, for Müller's catalogue of 1683. Col. 1813 suggests that the first published catalogue of Chinese books in Europe may have appeared in Amsterdam in 1605 – or so a source of the early eighteenth century would have us believe. The date and place are not impossible, in view of what has already been said of Dutch interest in Chinese books. Some more detailed information (which I have not been able to pursue) concerning Müller and the Elector's books may be found in a series of articles by Eva Kraft, listed in Lundbaek, *Bayer*, p. 66, n. 86. For the growth of the Elector's collection, *see* Mungello, *Curious Land*, pp. 244–46 and n. 98, and Lundbaek, *Bayer*, p. 76 and notes (which here also cite Eva Kraft's work).
46. Pentti Aalto, *Oriental Studies in Finland 1828–1918* (Helsinki, 1971), p. 18.
47. Such is the impression conveyed overall by Ch'ien Chung-shu's studies, 'China in the English Literature of the Eighteenth Century', *Quarterly Bulletin of Chinese Bibliography* (new series), II, 1–4 (June–December, 1941), pp. 7–48, 113–52, though given the Sino-British alliance operating at the time, Ch'ien contrives to be polite about it. That certain aspects of China were warmly praised in certain quarters in eighteenth-century England is beyond dispute: *see* Edmund Leites, 'Confucianism in Eighteenth-century England: National Morality and Social Reform', pp. 65–81 in *Actes du IIè colloque International de Sinologie: Les Rapports entre la Chine et l'Europe au temps des lumières*, (Paris, 1980). More disturbing, and more pervasive, is the evident willingness to rely on second-hand information, or even hearsay, rather than venture on any form of research into things Chinese.
48. For example, Raymond Dawson, *The Chinese Chameleon* (Oxford University Press, 1967), pp. 132–4, who gives an excellent summary of the change in attitudes at the start of the nineteenth century: it is, at any rate, undeniable that the rise of a new Protestant missionary endeavour at this time had profound consequences for our perception of China.
49. Eames, *The English in China*, p. 52.
50. Most useful is Ch'en Shou-i, 'Thomas Percy and his Chinese studies', *Chinese Social and Political Science Review* 20.2 (July, 1936), pp. 202–30; Ch'ien, 'Eighteenth Century', pp. 134–6, treats the matter more briefly, but lists the studies that had already appeared in the *Review of English Studies* in the 1920s.
51. For Prémare's translation, *see* Demiéville, 'Aperçu', pp. 68–9; for his position in the history of Jesuit scholarship on China, *see* Rule, *K'ung-tzu or Confucius?*, pp. 177–82.
52. Rule, *K'ung-tzu or Confucius?*, pp. 72–3, 116–23.
53. See the *Chinese Repository* 4 (1835), p. 252 and Lindsay Ride, *Robert Morrison: The Scholar and the Man* (Hong Kong, 1957), Appendix Two, pp. 45–8; Hubert Spillett (*see* below, n. 91), pp. x–xi.
54. Apart from Ch'ien's two-part article already cited above, something of the image of China as perceived in eighteenth-century Britain may be gleaned from Fan Tsen-chung, *Dr. Johnson and Chinese Culture* (The China Society, London, 1945). Cromwell Mortimer, Secretary of the Royal Society in the mid-eighteenth century, was a correspondent of the noted French Jesuit scholar Antoine Gaubil (1689–1759), suggesting that this debt to French sinology was incurred by some at least as the result of active interest rather than complete passivity: *see* Rule, *K'ung-tzu or Confucius?*, p. 189, and n. 1 to p. 183 (on p. 292).
55. Stifler, 'Language students', p. 47.
56. Stifler, 'Language students', n. 18, p. 71. The collection which reached Scotland was T S Bayer's: *see* Lundbaek, *Bayer*, p. 219.
57. Arthur Waley, 'Sir William Jones as Sinologist', *Bulletin of the School of Oriental and African Studies* 11.4 (1946), p. 842.
58. Eric Widmer, *The Russian ecclesiastical mission in Peking during the eighteenth century* (East Asian Research Center, Harvard University, 1976), pp. 103–4.
59. Widmer, *Russian ecclesiastical mission*, pp. 157–9. The German sinologist was none other than T S Bayer, subject of Lundbaek's monograph, already cited several times above. For Bayer's Russian career, see Lundbaek's chapter 3; for his contacts with the Jesuits in Peking, chapter 7.
60. Widmer, *Russian ecclesiastical mission*, pp. 160, 162–3.
61. Cordier, *Bibliotheca Sinica*, col. 1816; *see* Lundbaek, *Bayer*, p. 151 for the first Jesuit gifts.
62. Widmer's conclusion to his survey of eighteenth-century Russian sinology (*Russian ecclesiastical mission*, pp. 154–67) points out that the predominant concern of Russia at this time was (to

paraphrase somewhat loosely) 'westernization', so that China was perceived through French eyes, rather than directly.

63. *See* the summary history already in Stephanus Fourmont, *Linguae Sinarum Mandarinicae Hieroglyphicae Grammatica Duplex* (Lutetiae Parisiorum, MDCCXLII), p. 347. These books were a gift from the Kangxi emperor to Louis XIV: *see* p. 148 of J Witek, 'Jean-Francois Foucquet et les livres chinois de la Bibliothèque Royale' (in English!), *Acts du IIè Colloque International de Sinologie: Les Rapports entre la Chine et l'Europe au temps des lumières* (Paris, 1980) pp. 145–71, who gives a more detailed accounting for all acquisitions prior to 1722.
64. Demiéville, 'Aperçu', p. 72. Arcadius Hoang produced, it is true, no catalogue, but he did father a daughter, Marie-Claude Hoang, the first fruit of Franco-Chinese amity known to us.
65. On Jean-François Foucquet's books, *see* Witek's article, cited in n. 63 above; Rule, *K'ung-tzu or Confucius?*, p. 177, implies that Foucquet was wrongfully deprived of his own collection by the king.
66. The catalogue occupies pp. 343–516 of the *Grammatica Duplex*, a marked advance on the brief eighteenth-century lists of a Hyde or Müller.
67. *See* Jean-Pierre Abel-Rémusat, *Mémoire sur les livres Chinois de la Bibliothèque du Roi* (Paris, 1818), from whom the criticisms given here are drawn (cf. pp. 28, 30–2 and 36). His remarks on Fourmont's work were also reprinted in his *Mélanges Asiatiques*, vol. II (Paris, 1826), pp. 372–417.
68. Fourmount, *Grammatica Duplex*, p. 369.
69. Fourmount, *Grammatica Duplex*, p. 359.
70. The only exception that occurs to me is James Summers, *Descriptive Catalogue of the Chinese Japanese and Manchu Books in the Library of the India Office* (London, 1872), though the classification scheme he employs is rudimentary. Otherwise the catalogue by Kidd of the Royal Asiatic Society holdings, mentioned below, n. 119, does exhibit a classification scheme, but the lack of any Chinese characters makes it very difficult indeed to use.
71. Pierre-Martial Cibot, in a letter of 1767 quoted by Rule, *K'ung-tzu or Confucius?*, p. 193.
72. These men are discussed by Eames, *The English in China*, pp. 82–7, and also in Stifler's article.
73. Yves Hervouet, on p. 477 of 'Les bibliothèques chinoises d'Europe occidentale', *Mélanges* 1 (Paris, Université, Institut des hautes études chinoises, 1957), pp. 451–511.
74. Chinese sources on the Flint affair are translated in Lo-shu Fu, *A Documentary Chronicle of Sino-Western Relations* (Tucson, Arizona, 1966), vol. I, pp. 218–24; *see* also vol. II, n. 178: the name Liu Yabian derives from these sources. The English-language materials, treated eg. in Stifler, 'Language students', pp. 48–50, are much vaguer about Flint's Chinese helpers.
75. Stifler, 'Language students', pp. 49–51.
76. Cordier, 'Les études chinoises', p. 74–78, deals with Montucci. It should be said that French sinology, for all its supremacy over the rest of Europe, was at something of a low ebb at the end of the eighteenth and start of the nineteenth centuries, for obvious reasons.
77. Stifler, 'Language students', p. 51–3.
78. Fortunato Prandi, *Memoirs of Father Ripa*, new edition (London, 1861) pp. 158, 159; this addendum is also in the 1844 London edition, which I have not, however, had to hand. Ng Kwee Choo, *The Chinese in London* (London, 1968), p. 5, relies on a report on Asian seamen to date the beginnings of Britain's Chinese population to 1814, but as late as 1851 it was possible to charge two shillings in London for a chance to see a Chinese lady and her children: see Jerome Ch'en, *China and the West* (London, 1979) sixth plate between pp. 224–5. The first Chinese visitors to Britain came in 1588, according to Lach (*Asia in the Making of Europe*, vol. I, p. 742), or 1606, according to Chang I-tung ('Earliest contacts', p. 64), so the novelty obviously took some time to wear off.
79. *See* J L Cranmer-Byng, *An Embassy to China* (London, 1962) p. 319.
80. Stifler, 'Language students', p. 52.
81. Stifler, 'Language students', p. 53.
82. Stifler, 'Language students', p. 54.
83. Cordier, 'Les études chinoises', p. 67.
84. More precisely, the note on Manning reporting his death in the *Journal of the Royal Asiatic Society*, Annual Report, May, 1841, p. vii, suggests that he was drawn to the study of Chinese in a search for confirmation of certain ideas he had concerning Greek particles.
85. On Hager, *see* Cordier, 'Les études chinoises', pp. 68–74.
86. Manning is mentioned in Stifler, 'Language students', pp. 56–7, and also in Joseph Needham, *Within the Four Seas* (London, 1969), pp. 137–8; a fuller sketch may be found in Markham's preface to Manning's Tibetan journal, cited in the next note.
87. C R Markham, *Narratives of the Mission of G Bogle to Tibet and of the journey of T Manning to Lhasa* 2nd. ed. (London, 1879) p. 218.

88. The following account is based on E H Cutts, 'Chinese studies in Bengal', *Journal of the American Oriental Society* 62 (1942), pp. 171–4.
89. Stifler, 'Language students', p. 54.
90. The *Chinese Repository* 4 (1835), p. 254, quotes Marshman as having consulted a Chinese who knew no English in the preparation of his work: Marshman's report, dated 1813, does not make it clear whether this man had been involved in the project from the start or not.
91. The above is based on a catalogue of the British and Foreign Bible Society Chinese collection, viz. Hubert W Spillett, *A Catalogue of Scriptures in the Languages of China and the Republic of China* (London, 1975), pp. 1–6. The relationship between Marshman's Baptist associates at Serampore and the officially-sponsored Fort William College is explained in David Kopf, *British Orientalism and the Bengal Renaissance* (University of California press, 1969), pp. 71–80; *see* also, for the creation of the Chinese font used, p. 116. I am indebted to Professor Kenneth Ballhatchet for these references.
92. Twitchett, *Land Tenure*, p. 1.
93. Stifler, 'Language students', pp. 57–8.
94. Stifler, 'Language students', p. 54; cf. Twitchett, *Land Tenure*, p. 5.
95. J Marshman, *The Works of Confucius*, vol. I (Serampore, 1809). No further parts of this translation appeared.
96. *See* E H Cutts, on pp. 155–7, 162 of 'Political implications in Chinese studies in Bengal, 1800–1823', *Indian Historical Quarterly* 34 (1958), pp. 152–63.
97. Morrison's dictionary, *A dictionary of the Chinese language in three parts* (Macao, 1815–23), 'remained unsurpassed in Europe until the eve of the twentieth century', according to Twitchett, *Land Tenure*, p. 1; for his grammar, which had first appeared at Macao in 1811, but was also reprinted at Serampore in 1815, one year after a similar work by Marshman, *see* C Harbsmeier, *Wilhelm von Humbolts Brief an Abel-Remusat und die philosophische Grammatik des Altchinesischen* (Stuttgart, 1979), pp. 6 ff.
98. The *Mélanges Asiatiques* of Jean-Pierre Abel-Rémusat (1788–1832) contain a variety of notices on the works of Marshman, Milne and Morrison: cf. Volume One (Paris, 1825), pp. 1–50; Volume Two, pp. 132–216, 277–97.
99. This according to the entry under his name in Zhong guo she hui ke xue yuan jin dai yan jiu suo fan yi shi (comp.), *Jin dai lai hua wai guo ren ren ming ci dian* (Peking, 1981), pp. 322–3. I have not located the source of their information, but this handbook provides a generally reliable digest of information scattered throughout a large number of obituary notices, etc., and I have turned to it to provide a number of biographical details below.
100. The Anglo–Chinese College is treated briefly in Kenneth Scott Latourette, *A History of Christian Missions in China* (New York, 1929) pp. 214–5. The *Chinese Repository* 4 (1836), pp. 98–101, gives a detailed contemporary account.
101. *See* Alexander Wylie, *Memorials of the Protestant Missionaries to the Chinese* (Shanghai, 1867), pp. 45–6.
102. *See* David Collie, *The Chinese Classical Work Commonly Called the Four Books* (Gainesville, Florida, 1970, reprint of Malacca, 1828) and the 'Introduction' to the reprint, pp. vii–xvii, by William Bysshe Stein.
103. Prémare's work, *Notitia linguae sinicae*, had been composed in 1728, and was published in Malacca in 1831; *see* Demiéville, 'Apercu', p. 69.
104. J–P Abel-Rémusat, *Nouveaux Mélanges Asiatiques* I (Paris, 1829), pp. 332–3, in review of Morrison's *A View of China* (Macao, 1817).
105. *See* Margaret Medley, on pp. 99–100 of 'The Illustrated Regulations for Ceremonial Paraphernalia of the Ch'ing Dynasty', *Transactions of the Oriental Ceramics Society* 31 (1957–9), pp. 95–104.
106. *See* Summers, *Descriptive Catalogue*, p. iii.
107. *See Chinese Repository* 4 (1836), pp. 96–7.
108. J L Cranmer-Byng, 'Note on a Collection of Chinese Books Presented to the Royal Asiatic Society by Sir George Thomas Staunton in 1824', *Journal of the Hong Kong Branch of the Royal Asiatic Society* 1 (1960–1), pp. 124–6.
109. Robert Kennaway Douglas, *Catalogue of Chinese Printed Books, Manuscripts and Drawings in the Library of the British Museum* (London, 1877), p. v.
110. C F Beckingham, on p. 40 of 'A History of the Royal Asiatic Society, 1823–1973', in Stuart Simmonds and Simon Digby, eds, *The Royal Asiatic Society: Its History and Its Treasures* (London and Leiden, 1979), pp. 1–77. The donation of Manning's books to the library by his executors is noted in the *Journal of the Royal Asiatic Society* 6 (1841–2), Donations, p. xxviii.
111. *See* n. 106 above, and pp. 139–40 of Evelyn S Rawski, 'Elementary Education in the Mission

Enterprise', in Suzanne Wilson Barnett and John King Fairbank, eds, *Christianity in China: Early Protestant Missionary Writings* (Harvard University Press, 1985), pp. 135–51. The library is now in the possession of the University of Hong Kong: see Dorothea Scott, 'The Morrison Library, an early nineteenth century collection in the Library of the University of Hong Kong', *Journal of the Hong Kong Branch of the Royal Asiatic Society* 1 (1960–61), pp. 50–67.

112. See Twitchett, *Land Tenure*, pp. 4–6.
113. Twitchett, *Land Tenure*, pp. 3–4. The precise circumstances surrounding this appointment were actually somewhat complex: I hope to produce a fuller account of the episode on the basis of original materials at a later date.
114. Robert Thom, *Esop's Fables* (Canton, 1840) p. 1. of the Preface. Contrast also Kidd's salary as an academic with the £500 (later £1000) *per annum* paid by the E.I.C. to Robert Morrison for his services as a translator: *see* Ride, *Robert Morrison*, p. 11.
115. See Stifler, 'Language students', p. 54.
116. This development was reported in the Canton periodical, *The Chinese Repository* 7 (1838), p. 121.
117. See V V Barthold, trans. B Nikitine, *La Découverte de l'Asie: histoire de l'Orientalisme en Europe et en Russie* (Paris, 1947) p. 124 (and references, p. 128), 305.
118. See Wylie, *Memorials*, pp. 47–9; Kidd's tract is mentioned in Barnett and Fairbank, *Christianity in China*, p. 113.
119. James Legge, *The Chinese Classics*, Volume I Hong Kong University Press reprint, 1960, p. vii.
120. See Twitchett, *Land Tenure*, p. 4, quoting Samuel Kidd, *Catalogue of the Chinese Library of the Royal Asiatic Society* (London, 1838), p. 11. This, and Twitchett's other references to pp. 52 and 55 of the catalogue, are a little bit unfair to Kidd, who seems to have had at least half a notion of what he was about.
121. H Stanley, *Chinese Manual* (London, 1854), p. vi. This little work is a reproduction from manuscript 'by the new anastatic process' of a vocabulary of Chinese, evidently of Jesuit provenance.
122. Twitchett, *Land Tenure*, pp. 6–8.
123. For the Paris chairs, *see* Demiéville, 'Aperçu', pp. 78–85. Note, however, that Stanislas Julien is mentioned in J W de Jong's classic guide, *A Brief History of Buddhist Studies in Europe and America* (Varanasi, 1976), whereas Beal is not.
124. See S Couling, *Encyclopedia Sinica* (Shanghai, 1917), p. 396, and Barthold, *Découverte*, p. 151.
125. Technically, Klaproth's professorship was in Asian languages and literature: *see* Couling, *Encyclopedia Sinica*, pp. 275–6.
126. Julius Klaproth, *Verzeichniss der Chinesischen und Mandshuischen Bücher und Handschriften der Königlichen Bibliothek zu Berlin* (Paris, 1822), pp. 179–80.
127. Widmer, *Russian ecclesiastical mission*, p. 103.
128. Richard L Walker, 'August Pfizmaier's Translations from the Chinese', *Journal of the American Oriental Society* 69 (1949), pp. 215–23.
129. J J L Duyvendak, *Holland's Contribution to Chinese Studies* (The China Society, London, 1950), p. 21.
130. Legge, *Chinese Classics*, I, pp. vii–viii, though he forbears to mention any of his predecessors by name. My remarks on Legge have been kept deliberately to a minimum, since I understand that Norman Girardot is preparing a study of his life and work.
131. J Dyer Ball, revised E Chalmers Werner, *Things Chinese* (Shanghai, 1925), p. 147.
132. This was le Chevalier Charles Joseph de Harlez (1832–99), appointed at Louvain in 1871. See E Lamotte, 'Notice sur le Chevalier Charles de Harlez de Deulin', Académie Royale de Belgique, *Annuaire* 119 (1953), pp. 415–40.
133. See Edkins, *A Catalogue of Chinese Works*, p. 13, no. 72.
134. This collection has now been catalogued expertly by David Helliwell, *A Catalogue of the Old Chinese Books in the Bodleian Library, Volume Two*, Oxford, 1985. As his remarks on p. iii indicate, the accession of Wylie's 429 titles of Chinese origin more than doubled Oxford's holdings at a stroke.
135. Herbert A Giles, *A Catalogue of the Wade Collection of Chinese and Manchu Books in the Library of the University of Cambridge* (Cambridge, 1898), p. vi.
136. Quoted in Twitchett, *Land Tenure*, p. 8, from *JRAS* (N.s.), XX, 1888.
137. H A Giles, *Adversaria Sinica* (Shanghai, 1914), p. 347. For Wade's 'paltry contribution', *see* the appreciation and bibliography by Cordier in *T'oung Pao* 6 (1895), pp. 407–12. Some of Giles's feeling towards Sir Thomas may be explained by the fact that he had served in China as his subordinate.
138. Parker's appointment is noted in Dyer Ball, *Things Chinese*, p. 148.
139. The reader is mentioned (but not named) in *The Universities China Committee in London: Annual*

Proceedings, 1939–40, p. 5. These annual reports are cited below as *UCC Proceedings*. According to the *Scarborough Report*, dealt with below, only five students were taught in the ten years before the war by this reader in economics and commerce: see *Report of the Interdepartmental Commission of Enquiry on Oriental, Slavonic, East European and African Studies* London, HMSO, 1947, p. 13.
140. Hervouet, 'Les bibliothèques chinoises', p. 478, n. 1.
141. James Ludovic Lindsay, 26th Earl Crawford, *Bibliotheca Lindesiana: Catalogue of Chinese books and manuscripts* Aberdeen, 1895, p. ix.
142. *Ibid*, p. 42.
143. R K Douglas, *Catalogue... of the British Museum*, p. v.
144. Paul A Cohen, *Between Tradition and Modernity: Wang T'ao and Reform in Late Ch'ing China* (Harvard University Press, 1974), p. 72.
145. See Cohen's reference, *ibid.*, p. 290, n. 38, to Wang's published correspondence. Curiously enough, the British Museum had acquired a collection of the size indicated by Wang in 1847 which had been built up by Morrison's son, J R Morrison (1814–43): see Douglas, *Catalogue... of the British Museum*, p. v.
146. Beckingham, 'A History', p. 39.
147. It may be that the British Museum had some arrangement with the British Embassy in Peking. I note that the British Library copy of the *Tu shu ji cheng* was purchased from an unidentified Imperial Prince in 1877 after protracted bargaining between Mr Mayers of the British Embassy and what he called his 'book jackals' who succeeded in reducing the original asking price: see *The British Library India Office Library and Records Oriental Collections Newsletter* no. 39 (September, 1987), p. 2.
148. Scott, 'The Morrison Library', p. 62. On Neumann and his purchases, *see* also Herbert Franke, *Sinology at German Universities* (Wiesbaden, 1968), p. 8. This little work gives an excellent short history of Chinese studies of China.
149. Quoted in Hervouet, 'Les bibliothèques chinoises', p. 463, n. 1.
150. Liu Xihong *Ying yao si ji* (Changsha, 1981), p. 128. Liu was the more conservative colleague of the famous Guo Songtao; their visit took place in 1877.
151. Twitchett, *Land Tenure*, p. 8.
152. Twitchett, *Land Tenure*, p. 9.
153. Twitchett, *Land Tenure*, n. 20, p. 32.
154. Twitchett, *Land Tenure*, p. 9.
155. *Report of the Committee appointed by the Lords Commissioners of His Majesty's Treasury to consider the Organization of Oriental Studies in London* (HMSO, 1909), p. 142 (Minutes of Evidence).
156. *Ibid.*, p. 143.
157. Dyer Ball, *Things Chinese*, p. 137.
158. Giles, *Adversaria Sinica*, pp. 229; 1–19; and 27, 215, 300 respectively.
159. H Trevor-Roper, *Hermit of Peking*, London, 1986, p. 135.
160. Trevor-Roper, *Hermit of Peking*, p. 126.
161. The full story is told by Trevor-Roper, *Hermit of Peking*, pp. 122–61.
162. Herbert A Giles, *Supplementary Catalogue of the Wade Collection of Chinese and Manchu books* (Cambridge, 1915), p. v. For Luzac's catalogue and its link with Backhouse, see the MS note by G Haloun in the margin of the Cambridge University Library copy of this work; *see* Trevor-Roper, *Hermit of Peking*, p. 373.
163. Xiang Da, 'Ji Niu jin...', p. 618.
164. *See* Hervouet, 'Les bibliothèques chinoises', p. 501; p. 504, n. 3.
165. *See* Henri Maspero, trans. Frank A Kierman, Jr, *Taoism and Chinese Religion* (Amherst, 1981), pp. x–xviii.
166. The suggestion that Moule started systematic buying is made on p. 213 of E B Ceadel, 'Far Eastern collections in libraries in Great Britain, France, Holland and Germany', *Asia Major* (n.s.) 3 (1953), pp. 213–22; it is somewhat hard to square with accounts of Haloun's contribution.
167. *See* his obituary in *The Oxford Magazine*, 1933, pp. 666–7.
168. *See* Shu Chao Hu, *The Development of the Chinese Collection in the Library of Congress* (Boulder, 1979), p. 36 and notes. Hu's work provides a convenient sketch of American sinology with an emphasis on library resources.
169. The Yale collection was actually initiated in 1878 by a donation from Yung Wing (1828–1912), an alumnus who was the first Chinese graduate in the United States: see Hu, *Development*, p. 3.
170. According to L C Goodrich, on p. 68 of his 'Chinese Studies in the United States', *Chinese Social and Political Science Review* 15 (April, 1931), pp. 62–77, Carpentier's original grant was made in memory of Dean Lung, which makes this alleged donation a little odd.

171. The above account is based on Hu, *Development*, pp. 35–9 and p. 66, with some details from Goodrich (*see* preceding note).
172. The statistics are given on p. 75 of Serge Elisseeff, 'The Chinese–Japanese Library of the Harvard-Yenching Institute at Harvard University', *Harvard Library Bulletin* 10.1 (1956), pp. 73–93. *See* also the statistics for the Library of Congress in Hu, *Development*, pp. 92–3.
173. Apart from the surveys by Hu and Goodrich already cited in the preceding notes, the volume *Mei guo zhong guo xue shou ce* (Peking, 1981), published by the Chinese Academy of Social Sciences, also gives concise surveys, biographies and chronologies which I have found most useful in surveying the development of Chinese studies in the United States.
174. *See* Hu, *Development*, p. 133.
175. On Waley, see F A Johns, *A Bibliography of Arthur Waley* (New Brunswick, 1968) and Ivan Morris, ed., *Madly Singing in the Mountains* (London, 1970).
176. Thus George Weys, in review of the Ivan Morris volume, *Bulletin of the School of Oriental and African Studies* 34.1 (1971), p. 210.
177. Thus David Hawkes, in his obituary of Waley, *Asia Major* (n.s.) 12 (1966), pp. 143–7.
178. Xiang Da's report has been referred to already above. The quotation is from E R Hughes in *The Oxford Magazine*, 19 January 1939, p. 279.
179. *UCC Proceedings*, 1940–1, p. 78.
180. *See* p. 462 of C R Bawden, 'Ernst Julius Walter Simon', *Proceedings of the British Academy* 67 (1981), pp. 459–77.
181. Sir William Hornell, in *UCC Proceedings*, 1943–4, p. 9.
182. *See* P Demiéville and J Sauvaget, *La réorganisation des études Orientales en Grande-Bretagne* (Paris, 1950).
183. Demiéville and Sauvaget, *Réorganisation*, p. 4.
184. *UCC Proceedings* 1946–7, p. x; 1950–1, p. 15.
185. *UCC Proceedings* 1945–6, p. viii.
186. On Dubs, *see* L C Goodrich, in the *Journal of Asian Studies* 29.4 (1970), pp. 889–91; *UCC Proceedings* 1947–8, p. xi; Demiéville and Sauvaget, *Réorganisation*, p. 9.
187. *See* the report in the *Far Eastern Quarterly* 12 (1952), pp. 106–7, and W Seuberlich on p. 111 of J D Pearson, ed., *Papers on Oriental Library Collections* (Zug, 1971). *See* also Franke, *Sinology at German Universities*, for some further details.
188. Thus Keith Pratt, on p. 28 of the *Bulletin of the British Association for Chinese Studies*, 1982.
189. John K Fairbank, *China Perceived* (New York, 1976), p. 214.
190. Fairbank, *China Perceived*, p. 213.
191. A F Wright, on p. 253 of 'The study of Chinese civilization', *Journal of the History of Ideas* 21 (1960), pp. 233–55.
192. *See* D C Twitchett, 'Comments on the "Chinese studies and the disciplines" symposium: a lone cheer for Sinology', *Journal of Asian Studies* 24.1 (November, 1964), pp. 109–12; the symposium was in the preceding issue.
193. *See* John M H Lindbeck, *Understanding China* (New York, 1971), pp. 31, 59.
194. *See* Hu *Development*, p. 156, who quotes Luther Harris Evans, Librarian of Congress in 1945, on the drawbacks that had been revealed during the war as a result of the earlier policy of building up classical materials.
195. *See* e.g. Fairbank's remarks on the activities of Mary Wright (1917–70) on behalf of the Hoover Institution, in *China Perceived*, p. (x).
196. Sir Peter Parker, in his report to the Chairman of the University Grants Committee, 'Speaking for the Future' (dated February 1986; released May 1986), p. 2.
197. This date is recorded in the *Mei guo zhong guo xue shou ce* p. 8.
198. Lindbeck, *Understanding China*, p. 154.
199. Twitchett, *Land Tenure*, p. 35.
200. Eugene Wu, on pp. 144–5 of his 'Studies of contemporary China outside the United States', *Harvard Library Bulletin* 18.2 (1970), pp. 141–54.
201. Lindbeck, *Understanding China*, pp. 23–4.
202. Sir Peter Parker, 'Speaking for the Future', p. 68.
203. The fullest description of Chinese studies in recent years is given in the *Bulletin of the British Association for Chinese Studies* (1982), pp. 27–38, but this covers only the main university and polytechnic courses in Chinese.
204. G Rozman, ed., *Soviet Studies of Premodern China* (Ann Arbor, 1984), p. 11; *Mei guo zhong guo xue shou ce*, p. 8.

205. See Twitchett, *Land Tenure*, p. 7; for one Chinese professor of Chinese elected at University College in 1861, and also n. 13, p. 36.
206. See Twitchett, *Land Tenure*, p. 13; Bawden, 'Ernst Julius Walter Simon', pp. 474–5.
207. Cf. *Mei guo zhong guo xue shou ce*, p. 11, on the Contemporary China Institute and *China Quarterly*; the first Professor at Leeds, at the age of 63, was Owen Lattimore, who had already lived through some of the most dramatic episodes in America's postwar reappraisal of its relations with China.
208. John T Ma, *Chinese collections in western Europe, a survey of their technical and readers' service* (Zug, 1985), shows that individual collections at least twice as large as any in Britain exist in Paris and Leiden, and that our largest collections are also exceeded by the best in Germany (Bavaria) and even the second best in Paris; T H Tsien, *Current Status of East Asian Collections in American Libraries, 1974/5* (Washington, DC, 1976), shows that even a decade earlier a dozen American collections had already surpassed the holdings later reached in Britain at the time of Ma's survey. Tsien's statistics also make it clear that staffing levels in this country are often grossly inadequate by American standards.
209. One might add to this list early Protestant publications in Chinese, but apart from the work of the missionary cataloguer Hubert Spillet (1903–1984) mentioned above, this area remains almost totally unexplored. Contrast the recent publication in the United States of John Y Lai, comp., *Catalogue of Protestant Missionary works in Chinese* (Boston, 1980), based on the Harvard–Yenching holdings.
210. See p. 76 of Angus McDonald, 'The Historian's quest', in Maurice Meisner and Rhoads Murphey, eds, *The Mozartian Historian* (Berkeley and Los Angeles, 1976), pp. 77–8, for a succinct dismissal of both camps.
211. See e.g. the remarks of D C Twitchett, in his introduction, p. xv, to Henri Maspero, trans. Frank A Kierman, Jr, *China in Antiquity* (Amherst, 1978), and see Cohen, *Discovering History*, Chapter Four, especially p. 189.
212. Sir Peter Parker, 'Speaking for the Future', p. 1.
213. Fu Shang-lin, on p. 86 of 'One Generation of Chinese Studies in Cambridge', *Chinese Social and Political Science Review* 15 (1931), pp. 78–91.
214. W C Taylor, on p. 9 of 'On the present state and future prospects of Oriental literature', *Journal of the Royal Asiatic Society* 2 (1935), pp. 1–12.
215. Arthur Waley, *The Secret History of the Mongols and other Pieces* (London, 1963), p. 21, on Abraham–Hyacinthe Anquetil–Duperron.
216. Ainslie T Embree, on p. 7 of 'The Current State and Future Needs of Asian Studies', *Asian Studies Newsletter* 33.3 (February, 1985), pp. 7–10; this report, prepared by a committee of the Association for Asian Studies for the American Council of Learned Societies, reviews the progress made since the last such report in 1964.
217. See p. 14 of Allan Jackson, 'The Teaching of Chinese History in British Schools: an interim report', *Bulletin of the British Association for Chinese Studies* (1982), pp. 13–5.
218. Sir Peter Parker, 'Speaking for the Future', p. 52.
219. Arthur Waley, *Ballads and Stories from Tun-huang* (London, 1960), p. 237.

Charles d'Orban

The development of the Chinese Collections in SOAS Library

The School of Oriental Studies was founded 70 years ago in 1917,[1] the name School of Oriental and African Studies being adopted in 1938. However, to find the origins of the Chinese collections now held by the School's library we must look back 180 years to 1807 when the missionary Robert Morrison landed at Macao to begin his work for the London Missionary Society.

Born in Northumberland in 1782, Morrison holds an important position in the history of cultural contacts between China and the West. Among his achievements were the first Chinese–English dictionary (published in 1823), a translation of both the Old and New Testaments into Chinese and a Chinese grammar.[2] More significantly from our point of view, he saw the importance of educational projects which would spread knowledge about China and prepare missionaries and others for travel to China. In 1818 he established the Anglo–Chinese College at Malacca which was to act as a centre for missionary work in the Far East. In 1824 he returned to England bringing with him a library of approximately 15,000 Chinese volumes. It was his hope that these books would stimulate an interest in Chinese studies and that a university could be persuaded to establish a chair in Chinese language on receiving the library as a gift.

Morrison had some difficulty in persuading the authorities to admit the books free of duty,[3] a problem our libraries still face sometimes when ordering microfilm materials from abroad. However, with the help of members of Parliament and in particular through the efforts of Sir George Staunton, whom Morrison had met while acting as an interpreter to Lord Amherst's embassy to Peking in 1817, he was able to gain admission for his library. Despite the publicity which attended this incident, Morrison was unable to achieve his aim of founding a university chair in Chinese. Another of his educational projects, the foundation of the Language Institution (where Morrison himself taught Chinese for three months) collapsed within a few years of his return to China in 1826. Morrison died at Canton in 1834 and was buried at Macao.

In the mean time, Morrison's Chinese library had passed into the care of Sir George Staunton who, in 1837, was at last able to prevail upon University College, London to appoint a Professor of Chinese for a period of five years in return for the books.[4] In this way, Morrison's original intention was fulfilled even though it was after his death.

With the foundation of the School of Oriental Studies (to return to 1917), the nucleus of the School's library was formed by the collection of oriental books

owned by the London Institution, in whose former premises the School was to be
housed. The University Library and the libraries of University and King's College
transferred to the School their Oriental books in exchange for the Western books
from the London Institution Library.[5] It was in this manner that Morrison's
library finally came to rest in SOAS.

Morrison had the collection of approximately 15,000 Chinese volumes, which
contains some 800 titles bound in Western style. It was a good general collection
reflecting Morrison's (or his advisors') wide range of interests. Before his
ordination in 1807, Morrison had studied medicine and astronomy in London and
perhaps this explains the presence of medical and scientific works in the collection.
There are, surprisingly in view of Morrison's missionary work, quite a few
Buddhist and Taoist works, as well as the histories and philosophers one would
expect to find in a conventional collection. The collection consists mainly of
seventeenth and eighteenth century blockprints but it also contained most of the
100 or so Ming editions now held by SOAS. Morrison's own manuscript catalogue
of the collection is still in the Library's possession.

From King's College, the SOS Library received the printed books and
manuscripts collected by the orientalist and numismatist William Marsden. These
included some Chinese works and old travel books relevant to China. Two other
Chinese collections contributed to the newly formed library. In 1917 the library of
the China Association's School of Chinese, consisting of the standard classics and
manuals of instruction, were handed over to the School. Included with this
donation was one of the few complete sets of the encyclopaedia *Gu jin tu shu ji
cheng*.

The other collection is associated with the name of Mr F Anderson who was a
member of the Governing Body representing the London Chamber of Commerce
and later on Chairman of the Library Committee as well. Through him a donation
of 10,000 taels for the purchase of Chinese books was received. Of this, 5000 taels
represented a legacy to Mr Anderson from an old friend in China, Mr Yu
Binghan. Subsequently another friend of Mr Anderson's, Mr Jun Liangyue, added
a further 5000 taels as a permanent memorial to the first donor. Sir John Jordan,
British Minister in Peking at the time, arranged for some 12,500 Chinese volumes
to be purchased in China on the School's behalf. A framed inscription (dated 1923)
hanging in the Library still records the donation of the 'Anderson–Yu Ping
Han–Chun Liang Yue collection'.

With these various donations in its possession, the School's annual report for
1921–2 was able to declare, perhaps rather smugly, that the School 'now possesses
a Chinese library which has few rivals in Europe'. The next fifteen years or so
were certainly less eventful in the development of the Chinese collection although
it would have been in this period that large basic sets such as the Taoist Canon, the
Si bu cong kan and the *Si bu bei yao* were acquired. Although acquisitions of this
nature would have ensured that the library was reasonably well-equipped for
sinological work on ancient and medieval China, there is little evidence that
contemporary literature was being purchased. Moreover, it was at this time that
the great Japanese and American libraries were being built up. They were able to

take advantage of the dispersal of old Chinese collections during the period of warlord chaos and Japanese incursions, which meant that an enormous amount of material became available in the second-hand book market. This opportunity seems to have been missed by British collections, partly because of the lack of a well-formulated acquisitions policy and, no doubt, because of a lack of adequate funding.

This period of the collection's development can be seen as coming to an end in 1938 and coincides with the receipt of the library of Sir Reginald Johnston. The acquisition of this large and important collection did much to compensate for some of the missed opportunities of the previous fifteen years.

Sir Reginald Fleming Johnston (1874–1938) was for much of his career an administrator of the Weihaiwai district in Shandong province. The district was leased to Britain in 1898. Johnston was its Senior District Officer and Magistrate from 1906–18 and as Commissioner from 1927 oversaw the return of the area to Chinese administration in 1930.[6] Johnston is perhaps best-known for his role as tutor to the last of the Qing Emperors, Pu Yi from 1918 to 1925. When Pu Yi was placed under house arrest by the warlord Feng Yuxiang, Johnston arranged his flight to the refuge of the Japanese Embassy, for which he has been reviled ever since by the Chinese nationalist press and later the communists.[7] In the last phase of his career he was Professor of Chinese at SOAS from 1931–37.

After his death, Johnston's executrix, Mrs Elizabeth Sparshott, presented his library to the School. Consisting of over 16,000 volumes, it was considered to be one of the finest collections of Chinese and Far Eastern books in the country. Regrettably, Johnston had given instructions that his unpublished and personal papers should be destroyed after his death. The collection was rich in Buddhist materials and in the literature of the 1920s. Perhaps because of his unique position as Pu Yi's tutor, Johnston would appear to have had close links with other major Chinese literary and intellectual figures of the time. The library now possesses autographed editions of works by Hu Shi and Xu Zhimo with dedications to Johnston.

The next major figure in the development of the Chinese collection was Walter Simon (1893–1981).[8] A librarian at the University of Berlin from 1922–35, he developed a parallel career as a sinologist. Coming to Britain in 1936, he was offered academic hospitality at the School. He became a Reader in 1938 and in 1948 was appointed to a second Chair in Chinese, eventually retiring in 1960. He played a crucial role in the expansion of the Far East Department in the years following the war.

As early as 1937, Simon was recorded as giving expert advice in the purchase of books from the Far East. One of his lasting contributions to the library was to devise the classification scheme for the Chinese-language books which is still used in the Library. Simon was well-known for his use of mnemonic devices in teaching and his classification was based upon such a mnemonic device: subject headings were arranged in alphabetical order (biography, bibliography, classics, through to medicine, philology, religion, sciences, translations) and then assigned numbers from 9 to 900. It had been noted as early as 1928 that the Chinese library lacked any coherent form of arrangement on the shelves. In 1940, taking advantage of the lull in teaching (before a theatre of war had developed in the Far East), Drs Edwards and Simon reclassified the entire collection. At the same time, the Chinese lecturers Yu Daoquan (Yu Dawchyuan) and Xiao Qian (Hsiao Ch'ien) assisted by examining and regrouping the books. The subsequent growth of the collection has meant that Simon's classification scheme is no longer really adequate for the organisation of our Chinese books. But the task of reclassification into a new scheme would be enormous and so it is likely that use of Professor Simon's scheme will continue for a long time to come.

It was recognised that the destruction of books and printing presses in China during Japanese air raids was so great that many of the School's Chinese books had become rare and irreplaceable. Thus, with the help of the Dean and Chapter of Durham Cathedral, safe storage was found for them during the war.

However, Professor Simon's greatest contribution to the development of the collection was a visit made to the Far East from September 1948 to August 1949 for the purpose of buying books.[9] The University Grants Committee met half the total cost of £10,000. In Hong Kong he was able to buy many of the important books published by the Shanghai Commercial Press and the Zhong hua shu ju in the previous twenty years. Substantial purchases of modern literature were made. As old books were cheap in Peking, he was able to buy many *cong shu*, all the important encyclopaedias not already held in the School and books on the ancient script in which the library was significantly lacking. New gazetteers, important modern reference works, a complete series of the Harvard Yenching Indexes and modern periodicals dating from 1939 were also purchased. Manchu, Tibetan and Mongolian works were obtained and in Japan he was able to buy 'a fairly complete collection of Japanese Sinological contributions'.

These purchases meant that the library was in a good position to support the expansion in teaching and research which followed the implementation of the proposals of the Scarborough Report, published in 1947. As can be seen from the types of materials outlined above, the library was certainly now well-equipped for the study of pre-modern China in what one might call the traditional sinological mode. However, by the late 1950s and early 1960s the feeling was growing in the School that a better balance of posts could be achieved which would allow improved coverage of the living societies of Asia and the introduction of economics, politics and the social sciences into the School's teaching and research. The desirability of this shift of emphasis was confirmed by the publication of the Hayter Report in May 1961. This called for expansion in 'modern studies' (including history, geography, law, economics, social studies) and emphasised the concept of 'area studies'. Increased funds were to be made available for the purchase of the appropriate library resources.

The expansion of the SOAS Chinese collection to meet these new demands would not have been possible without the role played by the Contemporary China Institute. The CCI was established in 1968 to support advanced research and training in modern Chinese studies, to promote publications, and to find ways to disseminate knowledge of contemporary China to a wide audience.[10] After the exhaustion of an initial Ford Foundation grant of $325,000, SOAS assumed financial responsibility for the Institute. Of the original Ford grant, £10,000 was allocated for the acquisition of research materials which would supplement and complete existing SOAS Library holdings. A Materials Officer was appointed for this purpose until the termination of the post in December 1971. Materials were purchased from institutions such as the Library of Congress, Harvard University, the University of Michigan, the Hoover Institution, Columbia University and the Center for Chinese Research Materials (Washington, DC). Newspapers were purchased on microfilm. Gaps in SOAS Chinese periodical holdings for the previous twenty years were completed. Most of this was post-1949 material, although some relevant publications of the 1920s and 1930s were also obtained on microfilm.[11] The CCI collection was merged with the School's Library in 1972. It was at this time that the Library moved into its current premises, bringing the collections under one roof for the first time in 50 years.

One further individual bequest needs to be mentioned. In 1970, the widow of Mr H McAleavy presented her husband's library to the School. McAleavy had come to the School from the British Museum in 1954, initially as a member of the History Department and then as a member of the Law Department, holding the position of Reader in Oriental Laws from 1963 to 1969. His library consisted of 1250 volumes and parts, 1700 traditionally bound *ce* and 300 Japanese works dealing with China. There were also 40 other works in Manchu and Mongolian. The collection was noteworthy for popular literature of the nineteenth and early twentieth centuries and material on social life.

I have not yet paid tribute to the achievements of my predecessor, Mr John Lust. Despite his reputation for causing impromptu fire drills because of his habit of smoking a pipe in his office, he has contributed substantially to the development of the collection, having worked in the School as a Library Assistant from 1950 and then as Assistant Librarian and Principal Assistant Librarian from 1953 until his retirement in 1983. His *Index Sinicus* is well-established as a major reference tool and his bibliographical work has continued to the present with the recent publication of his descriptive catalogue of Western books on China published up to 1850.

The Chinese collection as it now stands consists of well over 100,000 volumes. There are perhaps some 3000 Chinese periodicals and newspapers including substantial holdings on microfilm. Approximately 500 current periodicals are taken. Its strength lies in the broad range of its coverage. Despite the shift of emphasis to contemporary China and the social sciences since the 1960s, traditional sinological interests have never been abandoned. At the same time, much of the material it holds dating from 1920s to the 1940s is extremely difficult to find elsewhere, especially in Europe.

The publishing explosion which has taken place in the PRC has, unfortunately, coincided with a very difficult period for British academic institutions. Nevertheless, despite these restrictions, the Chinese collection is still expanding at a rate which is rapidly consuming the allocated space in the library. Although new shelving space has been provided, one fears that it will barely last five years.

Changes in China and the requirements of those who conduct teaching and research on China continue to influence the development of the collection. A recent example is the revival of the Chinese legal profession in the 1980s. Because of increased teaching and research demand, a China Law Reading Room is now being set up where the major Chinese and Western Language reference works will be available side by side, along with the appropriate Chinese legal gazettes. Further changes and developments in the nature of the collection as a whole can be expected following the new posts in Chinese studies and the increased student numbers in the wake of the UGC response to Sir Peter Parker's report 'Speaking for the Future'.

Notes

1. The School received its Royal Charter as a College of the University of London on 5 June 1916 but the first students were admitted on 18 January 1917 and on 23 February the School was formally opened by George V. C H Phillips. See *The School of Oriental & African Studies, University of London: 1917–1967* (London, 1967) p. 14. For the events leading to the foundation of the School see *Ibid.* pp. 9–14 and P J Hartog, 'The Origins of the School of Oriental Studies', *Bulletin of the School of Oriental Studies* 1, pp. 5–22 (1917).
2. For a brief account of Morrison's life and work, see Lindsay Ride, *Robert Morrison: the Scholar and the Man* (Hong Kong, 1957).
3. Ride, *Robert Morrison*, p. 26.
4. D C Twitchett, *Land Tenure and the Social Order in T'ang and Sung China* (London, 1962), pp. 3–6.
5. The transfer is described in A Lodge, 'History of the Library of the School of Oriental and African Studies', W L Saunders, ed., *University and Research Library Studies* (Oxford, 1968), pp. 84–91.
6. P Atwell, *British Mandarins and Chinese Reformers* (Hong Kong, 1985). For biographical information on Johnston, see the entry by R Soame Jenyns in L C Wickham Legg, ed., *Dictionary of National Biography, 1931–1940*, (London, 1949), pp. 491–3.
7. There is an account of the unsympathetic portrait in Brian Power, *The Puppet Emperor* (London, 1986).
8. I am indebted to the obituary notice by C R Bawden, 'Ernst Julius Walter Simon, 1893–1981' *Proceedings of the British Academy* 67 (1981) pp. 459–77.
9. Bawden, *Simon*, pp. 468–70.
10. *Contemporary China Institute, Report, 1968–1978*, p. 9.
11. *CCI Annual Report, 1971*, p. 8.

Discussion

Comments on the paper on the Chinese collections in SOAS library included the remark that Henry MacAleavy, a distinguished scholar and benefactor of SOAS library, had spent much of his time when employed by the British Museum studying law, and preparing for his academic career, with the result that there are considerable gaps in the British Library's holdings of Chinese material from the 1950s. Professor Simon's collection ended up in the National Library of Australia; his son appears to have donated it through a tax incentive for the arts scheme.

On the question of losses from SOAS library through theft, Mr d'Orban said that SOAS suffered from being an open-access library and also from not implementing a policy of binding all Chinese books available for loan in the western style, which cut down the number of individual fascicules disappearing from cases. There had been severe depredations in early modern literature of the 1930s and 1940s and apparently systematic plundering of modern economic history (and rumour has it that these items are carried to Hong Kong for reprinting).

A question on whether the Parker report contained any recommendations on library funding was answered by Miss Burton, Librarian of SOAS, who confirmed that it did. By early 1988, funds not designated for new academic posts had already been allocated to relevant university libraries as a special grant. The future of non-post Parker money (including library support grants) was to be decided by a special sub-committee of the University Grants Committee.

SOAS's cooperation with Chinese libraries was mainly restricted to exchanges, largely of periodicals, and there were restrictions caused by imbalances in the exchanges. Pauline Haldane of the National Library of Australia raised the question of the exchange of duplicates, as the NLA successfully exchanges a number of duplicates with Taiwan.

Anthony Farrington

Chinese materials in the India Office Library and Records

Chinese language material in the India Office Library and Records (IOLR) is mainly confined to printed Buddhist texts of the late Ming and Qing. Since its foundation in 1801 the India Office Library's acquisitions policy was rarely ventured into the East India field and by 1895 had been narrowed to cover, outside the mainstream of India, merely a selection of works on other Asian countries which had Indian connections. China did not fall directly within the India Office's brief at the height of Empire in Asia and its distinguished succession of 'orientalist' librarians did not include a Sinologist.

The importance of IOLR's holdings lies rather in the India Office Records as a source for the history of Sino–British commercial and political relations. They are second only to the archives of the Foreign Office (held at the Public Record Office in Kew) and for the period before 1834 they constitute almost the sole source.

Background

The India Office Records consist of the archives of the East India Company 1600–1858, the Board of Control 1784–1858 (set up by Parliament to oversee the Company's affairs), the India Office 1858–1947 (the British government department responsible for the administration of India), and the Burma Office 1937–48. There are also the records of a number of agencies overseas which were linked officially with one or other of these four main bodies. Together they form part of the public records of the United Kingdom.

After India, Pakistan and Burma achieved independence in 1947–8 the records, unlike those of other British government departments, were not transferred to the Public Record Office but remained successively in the custody of the Commonwealth Relations Office, the Commonwealth Office and the Foreign and Commonwealth Office. Since 1982 they have been administered by the British Library on behalf of the Secretary of State for Foreign and Commonwealth Affairs.

The bulk of the material consists of original documents, amounting to some 200,000 volumes and files, and there are also extensive collections of maps and official publications. The whole is arranged in 49 classes which reflect either broad subject groupings or the administrative divisions and responsibilities within the East India Company's London headquarters and the India Office. The geographical scope is not confined to South Asia but covers all areas where the originating bodies had commercial, political or strategic interests, ranging from the South Atlantic to Japan. Material on China is scattered throughout most of the classes into which the records are divided, with the two main themes of commerce and politico-strategic interests.

The East India Company trading to China

The East India Company's royal charters, beginning with Elizabeth I in 1600 and renewed at intervals over the next two centuries, granted the monopoly of all British trade between the Cape of Good Hope and the Straits of Magellan, sailing east. China lay within these somewhat grandiose limits but it was almost a hundred years before effective trade began.

Almost from the time of its first factory or trading settlement at Bantam in Java in 1602, the Company emphasised the importance of China in its schemes for inter-Asiatic trade but had problems in realising them. Return cargoes for England could be obtained simply by purchasing goods in Asian ports or as the final stage in a port to port system of exchange in which Chinese silk, raw or finished, was a vital commodity which might obviate the need to carry bullion out of England. However, the Company had no direct access to China and for much of the seventeenth century, while on the one hand successfully penetrating the major seaports of the Indian sub-continent, in East Asia it struggled to obtain Chinese commodities on the peripheries of China. Ventures which can be so classified include the factory in Japan, 1613–23, and the attempt to re-establish it in 1673, the factory in Taiwan, 1672–85, the factory in Tongking, 1672–97 and various efforts in Thailand. For a few years between 1676 and 1682 ships were sent into Ming-held Amoy (Xiamen), though attempts at Canton in 1683 and 1689 failed.

India Office Records sources for these seventeenth-century would-be contacts consist of scattered 'commercial intelligence' correspondence in the series called *Original Correspondence*, 1602–1712, and *Despatch Books*, 1626–1753, (IOR: E/C 124 volumes) and in the minutes or 'consultations' kept locally by the various peripheral factories (IOR: G).

The barrier began to break down around 1700 and the Company gradually established a regular trading pattern at Canton. Each year East Indiamen from London, supplemented later by 'country ships' based in Indian ports, anchored in the Pearl River while the supercargoes, factors and merchants occupied a factory on shore for as long as it took to negotiate and lade the season's cargoes. In the 1770s the management of the Company's trade was placed under a Chief Council of Supercargoes which remained in China from year to year, withdrawing to Macao after the ships of each season left Canton. The Council was superseded in 1786 by a Select Committee of the senior supercargoes, which was responsible for affairs until the Company's monopoly was finally abolished in 1833. From 1834 British interests in South China were entrusted to a Superintendent of Trade, appointed by the British government and vested with consular as well as commercial authority. At this point the East India Company's direct rôle was over and that of the Foreign Office (plus Colonial Office involvement at Hong Kong) began.

The Company's records of its trade in South China are more or less complete from 1721, beginning as the diaries and consultations of the supercargoes of the individual ships of each season, in which they recorded details of sales and purchases and negotiations with merchants and officials, for the information of the Court of Directors in London. The archive of 315 volumes (IOR: G/12, R/10 & L/P&S/1) breaks down into nine main groups:

- Diaries and consultations of ships' supercargoes 1721–77: 42 vols
- Consultations of the Council and Select Committee 1775–1829: 110 vols
- Select Committee's secret consultations 1793–1834: 16 vols
- Commercial and financial consultations 1832–4: 6 vols
- Canton Agency consultations 1834–40: 6 vols
- Canton diaries 1779–1834: 72 vols
- Letters to and from China 1763–1834: 46 vols
- Minutes of the Secret Commercial Committee 1815–33: 3 vols
- Miscellanea and compilations: 14 vols

A somewhat confusing and disjointed narrative summary of this Canton material appears in *The chronicles of the East India Company trading to China 1635–1834*, Hosea Ballou Morse, 5 vols (Oxford, 1926–9), but enormous scope remains for a modern re-examination of the archive, with its wealth of statistical data on the export of Chinese products and the light which it throws on the mechanics of the first large-scale international trade. The scale of the Company's activities, centred upon tea, did, indeed, become staggeringly large for the period. The spread of the tea-drinking habit in Europe in the early eighteenth century was a rapid process, assisted by the greater availability of West Indian sugar. References to tea imports begin to appear in the Company's records from the 1660s – 222 lbs was brought to London in 1668 – and the first substantial quantities arrived in 1678. Despite high customs duties the profit potential soon became apparent – tea bought at Amoy (Xiamen) in 1697 at 2s 4d. per pound was sold in London in 1699 at 14s. 8d. per pound – and as early as 1704 the Company's instructions to its supercargoes make it clear that tea was then regarded as a commodity in general use in England. During the decade 1721–30, 8,800,000 lbs was imported, breaking down as 46.6% black and 53.4% green. In the decade 1751–60 this had increased to 37,350,000 lbs, an 85% increase in volume, divided into 66.3% black and 33.7% green. Following the reduction of customs duty to 12.5% in 1784 there was a demand explosion. In 1785 alone over 15,000,000 lbs was imported and during the last decade of the Company's monopoly sales averaged 30,000,000 lbs per year. Even at its lower rate the duty on tea was providing 10% of the total annual revenue of the British government and the profits of the trade were helping to finance the Company's administration in India.

The cultural counterpart of the new social habits associated with European consumption of tea (and to a lesser extent coffee and chocolate) was Chinese porcelain. Its value as a percentage of the Company's total investment at Canton was not of very great significance. In the logistics of the trade, porcelain provided the necessary heavy ballast upon which the tea cargoes were loaded and the

Company concentrated upon bulk purchases of average quality – fine pieces and special orders were the perquisite of the private trade of ships' officers and are little documented in the archive. Contracts were made in one season for delivery in the next, specifying shapes and types purely for the European market, with blue and white the most popular. Most must have come from the great manufacturers of Jingde zhen near Nanjing.

As examples of the detailed information, particularly statistical, which awaits the historian, Table 1 summarises English purchases at Canton in 1775, and Table 2 reproduces a 1775 porcelain order placed with one of the major suppliers – for a total of more than half a million pieces.

Table 1 Exports from Canton on the East India Company ships Morse, Lord North, Rochford, Grosvenor and Queen in 1775 (India Office Records: G/12/58).

Exports		peculs
Tea		
Bohea [black]		14,478.00
Hyson [green]		4,516.90
Souchong & Congou [black]		7,923.05
Porcelain		6,374.67
Silk		
raw		2,112.05
wrought	1,859 pieces	
Nankeen cloth		403.45
Tutenague		1,393.22
Fans	34,429	
Images	22	
Kittisols		2.08
Laquerware		21.88
Looking glasses	3	
Mats		13.15
Mother of pearl		25.43
Paper hangings	2,236 pieces	
Pictures		3.98
Cassia		1.86
Cassia flower		100.57
Cassia wood		66.58
Galingall		15.00
Rhubarb		6.15
Sago		323.83
Sugar		181.56
Sugar candy		152.21
Sweetmeats		4.50

1 pecul (100 catties) = $133\frac{1}{3}$ lbs

Table 2 Account of porcelain ordered from the Hong merchant 'Exchin' September 1775, for delivery in July 1776 (India Office Records: G/12/58 pp. 74–7).

		cost per piece taels	total taels
Blue and white, of four patterns			
64,000	cups & saucers	.032	2688
56,000	breakfast cups & saucers	.042	2352
28,000	half pint cups & saucers	.070	1960
7,000	chocolate cups & saucers, with handles	.050	350
2,100	teapots	.080	168
3,500	sugar boxes with covers	.130	455
7,000	milkpots	.050	350
14,000	coffee cups with handles	.025	350
7,000	custard cups	.050	350
7,000	sets of patty pans, 3 to a set	.150	1050
2,100	sauceboats	.100	210
350	one quart mugs	.150	52.5
350	one pint mugs	.120	42
350	half pint mugs	.110	38.5
350	quarter pint mugs	.100	35
5,600	waterplates, flat	.030	168
1,400	waterplates, deep	.030	42
35,000	plates	0.55	1925
7,000	soup plates	.065	455
28,000	half pint basins	.030	840
28,000	one pint basins	.040	1120
3,500	one quart basins	.080	280
3,500	three pint basins	.110	365
2,100	two quart basins	.180	378
1,050	three quart basins	.210	220.5
350	one gallon basins	.300	105
70	breakfast sets [slop basin & plate, sugar box & cover & plate, teapot, milk pot, 12 cups & saucers]	1.400	98
140	tea sets [12 coffee cups with handles, 1 middle size teapot, 1 larger, 12 cups & saucers, 1 slop basin & plate, 1 sugar box & cover, 1 milk pot & stand, 1 tea canister]	1.500	210
140	table sets, octagonal & oblong [16 dishes of 6 different sizes, 72 plates, 36 soup plates, 24 water plates, 6 tureens & covers & dishes, 24 side plates, 10 salad dishes, 4 sauceboats & stands]	19.000	2660

380,000 pieces   *19,257.5*

		cost per piece taels	total taels
Coloured, of two patterns			
12,000	cups & saucers	.042	504
28,000	breakfast cups & saucers	.052	1456
14,000	half pint cups & saucers	.090	1260
7,000	chocolate cups with handles	.060	420
2,100	tea pots	.130	273
3,500	sugar boxes with covers	.100	350
7,000	milkpots	.070	490
7,000	coffee cups with handles	.026	182
1,400	custard cups	.050	70
700	sets of patty pans, 3 to a set	.200	420
350	sauceboats	.120	42
350	one quart mugs	.110	38.5
350	one pint mugs	.090	31.5
350	half pint mugs	.070	24.5
350	quarter pint mugs	.050	17.5
2,800	waterplates, flat	.036	100.8
700	waterplates, deep	.039	27.3
14,000	plates	.080	1120
2,800	soup plates	.090	252
14,000	half pint basins	.035	490
14,000	one pint basins	.055	770
5,600	one quart bowls	.080	448
4,200	three pint bowls	.100	420
2,800	two quart bowls	.130	364
1,400	three quart bowls	.270	378
350	one gallon bowls	.330	115.5
70	breakfast sets	1.200	84
280	tea sets	1.800	504
70	table sets, octagonal & oblong	30.000	2100
171,320 pieces			12,752.6
	552,120 pieces at 32,010.1 taels		

The various series of consultations and correspondence also provide an insight into routine contact between the English and the Chinese, involving lengthy and often difficult diplomatic bargaining with port officials, principally the Hoppo or Collector of Customs. The habitual tension recorded in the Company's archive was the result of the commercial system at Canton and the conditions under which the Imperial Court was prepared to let Europeans enter China, coupled with inconsistent local administration, and the Chinese side of the constant negotiations routinely appears in English translation. In addition, the records include original papers of the two British government sponsored missions to China during the

Company period – Lord Macartney in 1793 (IOR: G/12/20 & 91–93) and Lord Amherst in 1816 (IOR: G12/195–197).

Political relations between China and the British Government of India

The second theme in the India Office Records is concentrated in the volumes and files of the Political & Secret Department, which partly complement Foreign Office and other series in the Public Record Office. From the second half of the nineteenth century, British India's borders gradually became contiguous with those of China along the enormous stretch from the North-west Frontier to Burma. Frontier security, trans-frontier trade and political intelligence on events beyond the frontier became standing concerns and as a result there is a mass of material, reported back to London, relating especially to Xinjiang, Tibet and Yunnan. The records also reflect the Government of India's general interest in the progress of Chinese development after the 1912 revolution, and end with significant documentation on cooperation with China during the Second World War.

The main series containing information are:

L/P&S/7 Political & Secret letters and enclosures received from the Government of India Foreign Department 1875–1911   253 vols

L/P&S/10 Political & Secret subject files 1902–31   (125 files relate to China)

L/P&S/11 Political & Secret annual files 1912–30   (800 files relate to China)

L/P&S/12 Political & External files and collections 1931–50   (464 files relate to China)

L/P&S/18 Political & Secret memoranda   (87 China items)

M/3–4   Burma Office annual files   (126 files relate to China)

As a sample only, Table 3 lists China-related papers in two volumes (IOR: L/P&S/7/64–65), covering September 1891 to March 1892, of the series of Political & Secret letters and enclosures.

Table 3 China-related papers, September 1891 to March 1892, in two volumes of the series of Political & Secret letters and enclosures.

L/P&S/7/64

pp 109–34. Secret No 165 of 30 Sep 1891
Papers on Russian and Chinese activities in the Pamirs, Aug–Sep 1891

pp 271–83. Secret No 172 of 14 Oct 1891
Trans-frontier journal for Sep 1891

pp 425–598. Secret No 182 of 14 Oct 1891
Papers on the delimitation of the Burma–China frontier, May–Oct 1891, inc:
Reports of Lt L E Eliott on exploration to the north and north-east of Bhamo district, May 1891

The Northern Trans-Salween states and the Chinese border, Lt H Daly (Rangoon, Jul 1891)
2 maps

pp 641–45. Secret No 184 of 14 Oct 1891
Russian activities in the Pamirs and report on Chinese defensive measures, Sep–Oct 1891

pp 781–809. Foreign No 189 of 28 Oct 1891
Attitude of and complaints by the Chinese community in Bhamo, Sep–Oct 1891

pp 1319–29. Secret No 198 of 2 Dec 1891
Trans-frontier journal for Oct 1891

pp 1355–75. Foreign No 34/182P of 3 Nov 1891
Chinese Agent at Bhamo and new Viceroy of Yunnan, Wang Wenshao, Jul–Nov 1891

pp 1399–1407. Secret No 204 of 9 Dec 1891
Trans-frontier journal for Nov 1891

pp 1483–1541. Secret No 212 of 16 Dec 1891
Russian activities in the Pamirs and reports from Yarkand, Sep–Dec 1891

pp 1647–67. Secret No 217 of 23 Dec 1891
Establishment of a British post near the Nampaung river on the Burma–China frontier, Oct–Dec 1891

L/P&S/7/65

pp 125–26. Secret No 9 of 20 Jan 1892
Forwards letter from George Macartney at Kashgar, Nov 1891, reporting Chinese reactions to the recent Russian expedition to the Pamirs

pp 548–81. Secret No 24 of 10 Feb 1892
Trans-frontier journal for Jan 1892

pp 759–69. Secret No 34 of 9 Mar 1892
Trans-frontier journal for Feb 1892

pp 801–42. Secret No 37 of 9 Mar 1892
Papers on the Burma–China boundary question, Feb–Apr 1892

pp 917–20. Secret No 41 of 16 Mar 1892
Forwards letter from George Macartney at Kashgar, Dec 1891, on Chinese reactions to the recent Russian advance in the Pamirs

pp 941–45. Secret No 44 of 16 Mar 1892
Establishment of a British post on the west bank of the Nampaung river, Jan 1892

pp 1039–74. Secret No 51 of 23 Mar 1892
Chinese apprehensions about British action in Hunza (Kanjut), Oct 1891–Mar 1892

pp 1091–1104. Secret No 54 of 30 Mar 1892
Destruction of a Chinese pillar on the borders of the Nantabet stream, and further papers on the Burma–China boundary, Dec 1891–Mar 1892

Finding aids

A summary list of the Canton archive, giving volume numbers and covering dates, was published in the *List of Factory records of the late East India Company*

(London, 1897), and a brief indication of other classes appears in *A guide to manuscripts and documents in the British Isles relating to the Far East*, ed. James Douglas Pearson (London, 1977). The forthcoming *Guide to source materials for Tibet, Bhutan and Sikkim* by Amar Kaur Jasbir Singh will cover one area of the 'political' material, but otherwise the only finding aids available are the typescript class lists of the India Office Records in the Catalogue Hall at IOLR. It is hoped that over the next five years these will be supplemented by a computer-derived subject index to some of the Political & Secret classes, and meanwhile work is well advanced on a *Guide to sources for Sino–British relations* which will cover all classes of the records over the whole period 1600–1950.

Archival cooperation

In 1985 a British Archival Delegation (which included a representative of IOLR and was accompanied by Dr Frances Wood of Oriental Collections) was received by the State Archives Bureau of China and visited the First Historical Archive in Beijing and provincial, local and agency archives elsewhere in China. A return delegation from China came to Britain in 1986. Both occasions gave opportunities for discussions on the exchange of microfilm, joint publications, training and exhibitions. Negotiations are now progressing on a programme to exchange microfilm of India Office Records holdings for First Historical Archive series, the latter to be deposited in Oriental Collections. The *Guide to sources* referred to above is designed to provide the basis for such an exchange.

India Office Library

The small collection of Chinese books in the Library began with items sent home as curiosities by Company servants at Canton, augmented after 1858 by Chinese Buddhist texts. James Summers's *Descriptive catalogue of the Chinese, Japanese and Manchu books in the Library of the India Office* (London, 1872) lists 170 books, mainly Chinese, and further details of 73 of them appear in an unpublished catalogue by Samuel Beal (IOR: Mss.Eur.D.453). In 1876 the Royal Society presented 29 Chinese printed books to the Library (manuscript catalogue by Beal, IOR: Mss.Eur.D.451), including some Jesuit works. Since 1895 the Library's acquisitions on Chinese Buddhism have been limited to translations.

The Library's Prints & Drawings include a number of 'Company' albums commissioned from Chinese studios at Canton and showing trades, crafts, costumes and furniture. The most interesting single item is the collection of sketches and drawings made by William Alexander, the draughtsman who accompanied Lord Macartney's mission to China (IOL: WD.959–961).

European Printed Books contain the standard late eighteenth and early nineteenth-century works on China, together with some valuable pamphlet literature on the Company's monopoly and its position at Canton.

Discussion

Questions arising included details of proposed exchanges with China and further questions on the content of the IOLR archives. On the proposed exchange of material with the First Historical Archive of China, it had already been agreed that the Chinese side would provide the same sort of lists as were being drawn up in the IOLR to help define the scope of the material available. It was assumed that the first listings would be on early Sino–British relations (as the IOLR listings were). As to the relative open-ness of the archive, it was important to remember that all dealings so far were with the archive that terminates with the Qing; there appeared to be no question as yet of exchanges with Nationalist or Party archives.

Mr Bloomfield mentioned discussions that he and Dr Martin, Director of the Public Record Office, had had with the Chinese authorities under the auspices of the International Council on Archives Programme for the Study of Resources for the History of Nations in Asia. The Chinese delegation had informed them that they were preparing inventories of the no. 1 and no. 2 archives and such was the interest in these that they planned to issue the breviate in English, this year.

The IOLR itself could be described as the classic 'closed archive' – there are no longer any accruals since British government in Asia is over. Everything in the archive is, however, open to the public. The only exception is the personal files of the European Officer cadre of the Indian Army which will be made available according to normal archival practice 50 years after death. There were some sensitive files emanating from the equivalent of the 'Special Branch' but these were returned to the Foreign Office when the IOLR became part of the British Library.

There is little of Chinese interest in the private paper collection apart from some Macartney and F M Bailey-related items. China disappears from EIC interest with the cessation of trade. The main 'China-watching' items are to be found in the Official, Political and Secret archive.

Some light is cast on the development of the Chinese Community in the UK, not in the Canton archive but in the field of shipping operations. In the 1790s, when the need for seamen became acute and the navy had to resort to 'pressing', in any season several hundred or as many as 2000 to 3000 Chinese seamen passed time between ships in the East End of London in the Limehouse area. These were the so-called 'lascars'. The Company had to make provision for Chinese seamen whilst they were waiting to go home and all sorts of charitable and welfare societies were established.

Raymond Kyang

Chinese collections at the British Library's Science Reference and Information Service

Introduction

Visitors coming to the Science Reference and Information Service (SRIS) to have a look at its collections will find the Library is divided into several sections, as most libraries are. Among them there is a section given over entirely to information on business and commerce with shelves full of market reports, trade directories, newsletters and journals. Then there is a large section devoted exclusively to patent literature or intellectual property, with boxes full of brochures with drawings and graphs and with language contents which are difficult to make sense of whether they are in English or Chinese. These are patent specifications. But inevitably the visitors will come to the largest collections of the Library which are journals and monographs on science and technology. What such visitors will not find is a corner in the Library entirely devoted to Chinese science and commerce, nor is there a room with only scientific literature from the United States or, for that matter, from the UK. If, out of curiosity, anybody takes a closer look at books and journals on the shelves, it will become apparent that books on similar subjects, mathematics, statistics, and computer science for instance, are gathered together with no separation by language. For every, say, ten books in English there may be one or two books in languages such as German, French, Russian, Japanese or even Chinese. So, altogether the arrangement of literature in SRIS is largely determined by subject and only very secondarily by country or language.

It may help to give a picture of a fairly common type of SRIS reader. Such a reader is usually attached to a research organisation in industry or to an academic body. The subject of his research may be on the role of the personal computer in office automation, on new applications of fibre optics in cable transmission, or simply on different types of pesticides. Whatever it is, the reader most likely has with him a handful of references he would like to consult. (If he doesn't, he will soon obtain these by using the many reference tools in SRIS such as subject indexes, abstracting publications etc.). He will then proceed to try to get hold of all the references available. If he is lucky and gets all of them, the chances are that the literature in front of him comes from many sources, and in more than one language. Obviously most of it will be in English but articles and chapters in German, Russian, Japanese or even Chinese are likely to be featured. He starts to sift to see which ones are useful. In the case of Russian, Japanese and Chinese, or maybe German, he is likely to have language problems. It is worth stressing at this stage that readers of scientific literature, unlike those of humanities, are as a rule not adept with languages other than their own. Fortunately for the reader, articles in Japanese and Chinese journals usually have helpful abstracts in English. These, together with the drawings and tabulated contents which are another common feature in such articles, go a long way towards enabling scientific research workers to get the gist of them. If the reader is really stuck, he can take advantage of the Library's linguistic aid service. Thus, the Chinese collections in SRIS are not just different in subject matter, from collections in the usual Sinological libraries, but are also used differently by readers.

When a reader comes to a sinological library looking for materials, say, on 'redology' (Hong lou meng) or for background materials to the cultural revolution, the chances are he is interested only in literature published in China, or maybe in Taiwan, and almost certainly in Chinese language material. He is unlikely to be much perturbed with missing some learned pieces published in Tokyo or New York. But if a reader comes to SRIS looking for literature on pesticides, it will be most surprising if he is only interested in Chinese brands and research. So, just as it is difficult to imagine sinological readers interested in materials other than Chinese, it is equally difficult to imagine SRIS readers interested exclusively in Chinese materials. One thing SRIS doesn't claim is that its Chinese collections exist to further specialised Chinese studies, though there are exceptions to which we will return. SRIS intends that its Chinese collections help to make increasingly significant contributions to the overall scientific and technological achievements of the world. The collection policy reflects this. For instance, we do not collect science at all levels, from the elementary to the latest high-tech with the intention of forming a kind of survey of the varieties of Chinese scientific experiences. Nether do we collect materials which introduce science to the general public. We cater neither for the interested public nor for science and engineering undergraduates using our materials to get their BSc degrees. Our targets are research workers in industry and post-graduates in academic institutions. We collect the following material for them in four main categories.

Business and commercial information on China

This may be the most pressing, if not the most important part of all information with regard to China. Since China re-opened its doors, practically every businessman and entrepeneur has contemplated setting up joint ventures or establishing an office in China. The library does not pretend to be able to give any advice on such matters. However, SRIS holds a core of 20 or so business journals, all predominantly in English which throw light on, for instance, the investment climate in China, the regional variations of investment possibilities, detailed case histories of actual investment, problems of bureaucracy, new laws and regulations governing taxes and foreign exchanges, statistics, etc. Furthermore, there is a collection of directories to help users to identify particular enterprises with whom they will want to initiate contacts. However, this part of Chinese collection in SRIS, important though it is, is comparatively small. Some other libraries, the library of the Sino-British Trade Council, for example, have a bigger collection in this field.

Patent or intellectual property

One of the buildings the SRIS now occupies used to be known as the Patent Office. Its history dates back to the last century and thus the collection of patent literature, known as specifications, has a fine and distinguished tradition in SRIS. China was a late-comer in this field, for it was only in 1985 that she became a signatory to the Paris Convention for the Protection of Intellectual Property. In the same year she started publishing patent specifications. The importance of patent literature cannot be over-stressed. According to surveys carried out throughout the world, more than 95 per cent of this literature has never found its way to other forms of publication. So, for scientists and engineers at the forefront of invention and innovation, access to patent specifications is mandatory. As yet Chinese patent specifications are still few in number (less than 10,000 having been granted at the time of writing). With patents come journals and other associated publications about patents. All these are well represented in SRIS.

Reference books and monographs

There is a good collection of reference books such as dictionaries and directories. General dictionaries (Chinese–English, English–Chinese), as well as more specific ones in subjects like physics, botany, electronics and most scientific disciplines, are represented. However, by far the largest and most comprehensive collection is on the flora and fauna of China. Books with titles such as *Plants of Jiangsu, Camellias of Yunnan, Medicinal Plants of Hebei, Mammals of Heilongjiang, Fossils of Xinjiang*, not to mention *Pandas of Sichuan* are quite typical. Books like these, apart from their intrinsic value, are written only in their country of origin. In their field they are practically the only source books of reference. Not long ago we had an enquiry from a researcher from Thames TV who was involved in a major series called *The Heart of the Dragon*. With the intention of taking another look at China from a different angle, natural history was taken as a focus for one programme. When she came to start research on the subject, to her dismay she could find no authoritative work in English less than 50 years old, and it was necessary to turn to Chinese sources. This example offers an exception to the general rule that readers coming to our Library are not primarily interested in materials from a national angle.

When it comes to books and monographs on less specific subjects from China, selection criteria are very stringent. Books in Chinese on electronics, chemical industry, lasers, mathematics and virtually all subjects other than those mentioned above, are, as a rule, not taken since books of that nature are invariably available in a far simpler language such as English. As scientists are not usually great linguists, it is pointless to duplicate such offerings in Chinese. However, books on the same topics consisting of a collection of papers presented in an international conference in China will be sought out, since papers submitted to such gatherings are usually original and many do not appear in any other publications. In addition they are, at least in the fields of science and technology, frequently cited in learned literature. As such they are, perhaps more than any other group with the possible exception of patents, the most sought after source of primary literature. In short, when selecting a monograph from China written in Chinese, the work has to be about a uniquely Chinese feature which is unlikely to be given treatment elsewhere in simpler languages, or is otherwise a collection of papers from an important conference, preferably international in character.

Periodicals

Perhaps the most prolific source of scientific and technological literature is learned periodicals. It is not surprising that periodicals constitute the largest volume of material in the SRIS collections, with the Chinese periodicals representing the largest, as well as the most important, part of all the SRIS Chinese collections.

As was mentioned before SRIS is a library (or an information service) for research workers. Thus following a policy similar to that employed in monograph selection, journal titles in popular agriculture, television, barefoot doctors etc., are not taken. The journals which are taken come mainly from sources such as universities and colleges, research institutes attached to Academia Sinica, learned societies and sometimes important ministries. These journals usually have two titles, one in Chinese and one in English. There are a small number, about 10 per cent, which are entirely in English and consist of selected translations, but by far the majority are in Chinese, and most of these give a brief summary in English or, failing that, a list of contents in English.

It is now nearly a decade since modernisation and reform became the official policy of the PRC. The quality of journals, in both content and production, has improved noticeably. Citations in Western learned publications have become increasingly frequent. As recently as 1981 one would be hard put to find any Chinese journals mentioned in authoritative publications like *Chemical Abstracts* or *INSPEC Institute of Physics, Electronics and Computer Abstracts*. Now nearly a hundred are represented. In SRIS we have close to 800 current titles which may seem an over-representation, but one important group of heavy users of SRIS are professional abstractors. It is mainly through their efforts that the increasingly important achievements of Chinese scientists gain a wider exposure. So it is our hope that more and more of their works in journals will find their way into eminent publications for dissemination to an ever widening scientific community.

Discussion

Mr R Foo-kune gave a brief illustrated talk on the collections of the British Library's Document Supply Centre. Early stages of plans to set up an Asian Information Service at SRIS was discussed. Japanese science, technology and business patents would form the main component, with Chinese and Korean. There were plans to expand cooperation with the Institute for Scientific and Technical Information of China (ISTIC) beyond exchange of journals, perhaps to abstracting and selected journal translations carried out in China and checked in London. Such projects were still in the very early planning stages. The Sino-British Trade Council already provides good expert information and has an office in China; it would perhaps be possible for SRIS to cooperate and supplement this work.

Rosemary Seton

Archives and manuscript collections relating to China in SOAS Library

It would be nonsense to pretend that archival and manuscript holdings at SOAS possessed any organic unity or, indeed, any very defined identity. They do not include the archives of the School itself, although the papers of several former members of the School have been deposited. They derive from a wide variety of sources, both individual and organisational, and, although some Government figures are included, are chiefly representative of mercantile and missionary interests. I sometimes reflect that the records of these latter groups must sit together rather uneasily on our shelves since the two groups so disliked and distrusted each other. Archives at SOAS relate to the Middle East, to South and South-east Asia, and to the continent of Africa as well, but our main strengths lie in the Far East and we have latterly been directing our collecting efforts to gathering primary source material relating to that area. I am glad of this opportunity of bringing together for the first time, for descriptive purposes, the many thousands of documents, letters, reports, printed ephemera and photographs, relating to China, which have been accumulating at SOAS in recent years. I shall now draw attention to some of the highlights of these holdings before going on summarily to describe them.

It is only comparatively recently that archives and manuscript collections have been acquired by SOAS Library in any quantity, mainly, of course, since the new Library building was opened in 1973. It was before that date, however, that some papers of considerable significance were acquired when the papers of a number of former members of staff of the Chinese Maritime Customs Service were deposited in the Library during the 1960s and early 1970s. These include correspondence between the first Inspector-General of the service, Sir Robert Hart and his London representative J D Campbell, papers of Edward Charles Macintosh Bowra and his son Cecil Arthur Bowra, and the official papers of Sir Frederick Maze who was Inspector-General from 1929 to 1943. These private papers had particular significance while the official archives in China remained closed. It is pleasing to be able to add that, as I understand it, the official archives of the Chinese Maritime Customs are soon to be made available for public consultation. In 1975 the archives of John Swire & Son were deposited. This firm had been established in 1832 by John Swire, a Liverpool merchant, but its expansion into the Eastern markets came in the 1860s under the direction of the son of the founder, John Samuel Swire. In 1867 an office, under the name of Butterfield and Swire, was opened in Shanghai to handle the sale of textiles in China. Later Swire interests included shipping, a sugar refinery and a dockyard as 'John Swire & Sons gradually changed the focus of its interests from the unprofitable produce trade to commission, shipping and other agency business.'[1] Most of the material which covers the history of the firm from about 1870 to 1947, comprises correspondence series created in and made up, either in bound letter books or loose leaf files by the London Office. The archive is by no means complete. There are many gaps and some whole record series are missing.

In 1883, a young Scot by the name of Charles Addis went out to China in the employ of the Hongkong and Shanghai Bank. He later rose to become senior manager of the Hongkong and Shanghai Bank in the London Office, a director of the Bank of England and, during the inter-war years, a leading adviser on monetary matters in London, Europe and America. Addis remained in the East until 1904, holding various appointments at Peking, where he was one of the earliest foreign bankers, and at Tientsin, Shanghai and Hankow. His diaries, letters and papers record not so much his daily routine which he perhaps found boring, as his vigorous participation in literary, sporting and philanthropic activities, although there is much to interest the economic historian because of the part Addis played in the China Consortium negotiations for which he received a knighthood in 1913. Addis corresponded with many of the notable 'China' personages of the day such as James Stewart Lockhart, Alexander Michie, J O P Bland and Timothy Richard. He wrote for *The China Review* and *The North-China Herald* under the *nom de plume* 'Quidnunc' and, despite an ambivalent attitude to missionaries, became a Director of the Society for the Diffusion of Christian and General Knowledge. Other individuals represented in the holdings include ambassadorial figures like Sir John Addis (one of the thirteen children of Charles Addis), and Sir John Pratt, who spent many years in the British Consular Service before becoming adviser to the Foreign Office on Far Eastern Affairs in 1925. His correspondence includes letters from his brother William 'Billy' Pratt, alias Boris Karloff.

By far the major quantity of archival material deposited in the Library documents the activities of several British Protestant missionary societies and allied organisations operating in China between 1807, when Robert Morrison first entered Canton, and 1951. These comprise the London Missionary Society, the Religious Tract Society and the Christian Literature Society for China, the Wesleyan Methodist Missionary Society, the Presbyterian Church of England and the Conference of British Missionary Societies, as well as the private papers of missionaries working for other missionary societies, notably the China Inland Mission. One of the major activities of Protestant Christianity in China was the translation and distribution of Christian literature and this theme is particularly well-documented in the SOAS holdings. It was a missionary of the London Missionary Society, Morrison's co-worker, William Milne who, in 1814, first made an application to the Religious Tract Society for funds to finance the production and distribution of tracts which could 'easily put on a Chinese coat' and 'penetrate silently even to the chamber of the emperor'.[2] His best known tract was *The Two Friends. A Dialogue between two friends, Chang and Yuen* which went through many editions. Another influential tract, *Good words to admonish the age*, was said to have been obtained by Hong Xiuquan, later leader of the Taiping rebels, when he attended the Canton examinations in 1832. A number of these tracts, in various editions, are to be found in the Library of the Council for World Mission (formerly the London Missionary Society) which was deposited in SOAS Library, along with the Archives, in 1973. Missionaries soon realised that the gathering of so many scholars at the various examination centres in China could provide the means whereby the Christian message could be spread most effectively amongst those who would become China's leaders, and from the 1830s they most diligently attended to this need, even though for many years such distribution was illegal.

However, the quality of the works to be circulated amongst this literary élite perplexed and concerned some. Amongst these was Alexander Williamson who addressed the Shanghai Missionary Conference in 1877 on this theme in a paper entitled *The Literati of China and how to meet them*. He poured scorn on the literary fare then on offer. He called upon his audience to imagine 'all the BAs in Scotland' assembled in Edinburgh to compete for the MA degree; or 'all the most cultivated men within the dominions of the Queen – all the keenest intellects and most aspiring minds of our country and colonies' met 'in some huge square in London to contend for the LL D degree ... [where] some Chinamen were to take advantage of the occasion and present them with a tract entitled James's "Anxious Enquirer" or with a translation of the Confucian classics rendered into easy English'. He deplored the fact that British missionaries 'should have nothing better to give to the descendants and representatives of the most literary nation the world has ever seen.'[3]

In 1887 Williamson founded the Society for the Diffusion of Christian and General Knowledge (later to become the Christian Literature Society for China) specifically to fulfil this need. He himself died in 1890 but was succeeded as General Secretary by the able and influential Timothy Richard and the Society continued its work in a manner worthy of its founder. A catalogue of the Society's publications (in the archives of the Christian Literature Society) in 1895 proclaimed that its books were 'particularly acceptable to mandarins and scholars and the coloured illustrations were highly prized by intelligent women and children.'[4]

It is interesting to note that some of the same students who were the targets of the missionaries' literary endeavours often took advantage of their attendance at the examination centres, voluntarily to seek medical treatment at nearby missionary hospitals. Their presence evidently provided a welcome break from routine. Dr John Dudgeon of the London Missionary Society's Peking Hospital, described how the streets at examination time suddenly filled with scholars wearing 'large spectacles with broad rims' and carrying 'little bags containing writing material and essay paper suspended from their necks'. He recorded his attempted treatment of one rather aged student who appeared during the MA examinations in October 1879 with a fractured collar bone. Treatment was suspended until the student emerged from his 'incarcerations in the examination stalls' but a permanent cure could not be effected due to the subject's advanced years and the fact that his 'writing habits prevented him' from resting his condition. Other students sought to throw off their addiction to opium by entering a missionary refuge. Dudgeon relates how one such young man, 'an opium smoker with harelip ... had both the physical and moral deformity cured.' His patient was so determined that the cure should be successful that after the operation he 'ceased to speak' though he had been 'most lively, interesting and talkative' beforehand.[5]

Medical work and the distribution of Christian literature only accounts, of course, for part of missionary work in China. Other topics referred to in the letters and reports sent to the London headquarters of the various missionary societies, and preserved in the archives, concern evangelisation, the building and growth of churches, the setting up of schools and colleges and the teaching carried on them, as well as missions specifically directed to women and work amongst various social groups and tribal peoples. In addition, however, missionaries often commented on what was going on around them and there are details about famines and other natural disasters as well as news about political developments, civil war, foreign invasions and, in more peaceful times, descriptions of everyday life in town and country. The objectivity of such accounts obviously varies, as do the descriptive abilities of their authors but all in all they constitute a valuable source of information and opinion to set alongside the official record. Detailed lists are to be found for most of the early and mid-nineteenth century records and these have been of great use to the many researchers who have consulted the archives. It remains a long-term ambition to provide lists to those private collections which remain unlisted and are thus unavailable to the scholar as well as to improve the listing of late nineteenth and twentieth-century material in the archives (which include useful photographic collections) in order to enlarge their accessibility.

List of archives and manuscript collections

ARCHIVES OF ORGANISATIONS

China Association
Founded in London in 1889 to represent the interests of those concerned with trade to China, Hong Kong and Japan. Records comprise annual reports, minute books, circulars, committee papers, bulletins and miscellaneous papers of the Association. Some documents dated 1948–49, chiefly comprising letters, cables and telegrams, have been retained by the Association.
116 volumes

Chinese Maritime Customs
This collection includes papers of the following members of the service:
See Papers relating to the Chinese Maritime Customs 1860–1943 (SOAS, London, 1973).

HART, Sir Robert, Inspector-General 1863–1906. Letters 1868–1911.
7 boxes

BOWRA, Edward Charles Mackintosh (1841–74) and Cecil Arthur Verner (1869–1947). Diaries, correspondence, family papers, photographs and press cuttings 1840–1966.
4 boxes, 7 volumes

AGLEN, Sir Francis, Inspector-General 1911–29, Correspondence 1921–26.
1 volume

MAZE, Sir Frederick, Inspector-General 1929–43. Personal and semi-official letters, letter-books, reports and circulars, 1882–1943.
63 volumes

The papers of Sir Frederick Maze are available on 23 reels of microfilm from Microform Academic Publishers, East Ardsley, Wakefield WF3 2JN.

Conference of British Missionary Societies
The Conference of British Missionary Societies (representing most of the Protestant missionary societies in Great Britain and Ireland) was founded in 1912. In 1977 the Conference merged with the British Council of Churches and is now known as the Conference for World Mission. The main record series relating to China are as follows:
China/Far East Committee 1930–53:   6 boxes
Subject Files 1890–1960:   72 boxes
Subjects include China missionary conferences 1890–1913, meetings of the National Christian Council of China and its committees; mission directories, China Mission Year Books 1910–39, records of various natural disaster and wartime committees; news bulletins; correspondence re. internees; documents on mission property in China; reports of medical institutions and schools and colleges; withdrawal of missionaries and the Church in China under Communism.

Papers less than thirty years old are not available for public consultation. The archives of the Conference of British Missionary Societies are available on microfiche from Inter Documentation Company AG, Postrasse 14, 6300 Zug, Switzerland.

Council for World Mission
(incorporating the London Missionary Society)
See C S Craig, *The Archives of the Council for World Mission* (SOAS, London, 1973)

Robert Morrison, who arrived in Canton in 1807, was the first LMS and the first Protestant Missionary in China. With the opening of the Treaty Ports in 1843, LMS Missions were established in Hong Kong, Amoy (Xiamen) and Shanghai. An LMS medical missionary, William Lockhart, was the first to reach Peking (in 1861). In that same year missions were also opened at Tientsin (Tianjin) and, in Central China, at Hankou. By 1923, there were six mission stations in Hupeh (Hubei) province, three in Fukien (Fujian), four in Hopei (Hebei) and establishments at Tsinan (Ji'nan), Shanghai and Canton and Hong Kong. By 1931 all the churches associated with the LMS had become part of the Church of Christ in China. Missionaries of note whose correspondence can be found in the archive, in addition to those mentioned above, include William Milne, W H Medhurst, Benjamin Hobson, James Legge, later Professor of Chinese at Oxford, Griffith John who opened a mission in Hankou, Arnold Foster who joined him in 1871, and James Gilmour who commenced his remarkable mission among the Mongols in 1870.

An LMS printing press was established at Malacca in 1818 before being transferred to Hong Kong in the mid 1840s. Another press was set up at Shanghai in 1847 but this ceased production when the American Presbyterian Mission Press was established there in 1860.

The main relevant records series are as follows:
COMMITTEE MINUTES (China) 1856–1939: 11 boxes
CORRESPONDENCE
South China 1803–1939: 19 boxes
Fukien (Fujian) 1845–1939: 25 boxes
North China 1860–1939: 39 boxes
JOURNALS: 1807–1896: 3 boxes
REPORTS: 1866–1939: 38 boxes
'Personal' and 'Odds' boxes, i.e. private and miscellaneous papers, include correspondence of Robert Morrison concerning the Oriental Language Institution in London and private letters and sermons of James Legge. 26 boxes
PHOTOGRAPHS
The work of both amateur and professional photographers is represented. Various buildings and places, occupations and events are depicted and there are individual and group portraits. 11 boxes

Correspondence, reports and subject files dated 1941–51 are due to be transferred by the Council for World Mission shortly. The Archives of the Council for World Mission are available on microfiche from Inter Documentation Company AG, Poststrasse 14, 6300 Zug, Switzerland.

The Library of the Council for World Mission was deposited in the SOAS Library together with the archives in 1973 and remains a separate entity within the Library. Its nucleus is the collection of Dr William Lockhart, medical missionary in China from 1838 to 1864. A catalogue was compiled in 1899 but many additions have been made since that date. It is disappointing to relate that most of the Chinese works originally in Lockhart's Library and catalogued by Goodeve Mabbs in 1899 are no longer there. The remaining western language materials, however, have a great deal of interest for the sinologist. In addition to early western books on China there are the *Reports* and *Chronicles* of the London Missionary Society, reports of various colleges, schools and hospitals in China and a series known as the China Pamphlets.

Methodist Church Overseas Division
(Incorporating the Wesleyan Methodist Missionary Society, the United Methodist Missionary Society and the Primitive Methodist Missionary Society)

The Wesleyan Methodist Missionary Society opened its first China Mission at Canton in 1852. It extended its work to Hupeh province (Hubei), Hankow (Hankou) (1862) and Hanyang (1863) and Wuchang (1865). In the early years of the twentieth century seven WMMS mission stations were opened in Hunan Province. The most eminent WMMS missionary in China was probably David Hill, who though independently financed, worked with the Society in Wuchang from 1865 to 1896 and in Shanxi during the famine of 1877. The redoubtable Samuel

Pollard of the United Methodist Church Mission introduced Christianity to the Miao people between 1887 and 1915.

The main records series are arranged as follows:

SYNOD MINUTES 1853–1950: 22 boxes

CORRESPONDENCE

Canton 1851–1905: 4 boxes
Hupeh (Hubei) 1905–1951: 17 boxes
Hunan 1907–1950: 8 boxes
Ningpo (Ningbo) 1939–1946: 2 boxes
North China 1933–1951: 3 boxes
South China 1905–1951: 13 boxes
South West China 1932–1951: 4 boxes
Wenchow (Wenzhou) 1933–1945: 3 boxes
Wuchang 1877–1905: 3 boxes
China General 1936–1938: 4 boxes

WOMEN'S WORK: Correspondence 1920–1951: 26 boxes

Biographical papers include a substantial collection of the journals, letters, papers and photographs of David Hill and also the diary and miscellaneous papers of Samuel Pollard (died 1915).

NOTES AND TRANSCRIPTS

Includes writings by Sister Gladys Stephenson and Samuel Pollard.

PHOTOGRAPHS: 3 boxes

The archives of the Methodist Missionary Society now known as the Methodist Church Overseas Division are available on microfiche from Inter Documentation Company AG, Poststrasse 14, 6300 Zug, Switzerland.

Presbyterian Church of England
(Foreign Missions Committee)

The Society's areas of activities in the Far East were South Fukien (Fujian), including Amoy (Xiamen) and Chuangchow (?Quanzhou, ?Zhangzhou), Kwangtong (Guangdong) and especially Swatow (Shantou) and Taiwan which they reached in 1864. Their pioneer missionary in China was William Chambers Burns who arrived there in 1847. Other missionaries of note were William Campbell who became a considerable scholar on Taiwan and Thomas Barclay who worked in Taiwan for sixty years from 1875. An English Presbyterian Mission was established at Swatow (Shantou) in 1880.

Correspondence, reports, printed material and photographs are arranged as follows:

Taiwan 1868–1959: 8 boxes
South Fukien (Fujian) 1863–1949: 16 boxes
Hakka 1880–1946: 7 boxes
Lingtung (?Lingdong, Hunan), Swatow (Shantou) 1867–1949: 15 boxes
Women's Missionary Association 1878–1961: 10 boxes

The archives of the Presbyterian Church of England have just been filmed and will shortly be available on microfiche from Inter Documentation Company (*see* above).

Royal Institute of International Affairs
(Chatham House, Far East Department)
Conference papers, research memoranda and miscellaneous papers, 1927–62.
72 boxes

John Swire & Sons Ltd
Founded in Liverpool in 1832, in 1870 the Head Office was moved to London. Business interests in the Far East included the China Navigation Company (1872), the Taikoo Sugar Refinery (1881), the Taikoo Dockyard & Engineering Company (1901), the Tientsin Lighter Company (1904) and the Orient Paint, Colour and Varnish Company (1934), all of which came under the direction of Butterfield and Swire, the Eastern Agents of John Swire & Sons.

Correspondence, accounts, legal documents and papers, 1868–1967 (papers less than thirty-five years old are not available for consultation).

See Elizabeth Hook, *A Guide to the papers of John Swire & Sons Limited* (SOAS, London, 1977).
251 boxes

United Society for Christian Literature
(Incorporates the Religious Tract Society and the Christian Literature Society for China)

The Religious Tract Society was founded in London in 1799 for the purpose of printing and distributing religious tracts and financed the production and circulation of tracts in China from 1814 onwards. The Christian Literature Society for China (Scotland) was founded by Alexander Williamson to support the work of the Society for the Diffusion of Christian and General Knowledge among the Chinese which, in 1905, became the Christian Literature Society for China. The Religious Tract Society joined with the Christian Literature Society for India in 1935 to form the United Society for Christian Literature Society and the CLS for China (Scotland) merged with this Society in 1942.

The main surviving records series are:
RELIGIOUS TRACT SOCIETY
Minutes 1799–1953: 122 volumes
Letter books 1824–1889: 45 volumes
Ledgers and accounts 1858–1952: 35 volumes
Annual reports 1830–1935 (with gaps): 25 volumes
RELIGIOUS TRACT SOCIETY (China)
(The RTS China merged with the RTS in London in 1931)
Annual reports:
Central China 1884–1915: 5 volumes
North and Central China 1916–1920: 1 volume
China 1920–1947: 7 volumes
CHRISTIAN LITERATURE SOCIETY FOR CHINA (Scotland)
Minutes and papers 1891–1942: 13 volumes
CHRISTIAN LITERATURE SOCIETY FOR CHINA

Annual reports:
Book and Tract Society of China 1885–1990: 6 volumes
Society for the Diffusion of Christian and General Knowledge 1893–1904: 13 volumes
Christian Literature Society for China 1905–1942: 38 volumes
MISCELLANEOUS PUBLICATIONS include:
Catalogue of the publications of the Society for the Diffusion of Christian and General Knowledge among the Chinese (Shanghai, 1895).

Collections of individuals

ADDIS, Sir Charles (1861–1945)
Served with the Hongkong and Shanghai Bank, chiefly in China, 1880–1904; London Manager of the Hongking and Shanghai Bank 1905–1921; Director of the Bank of England, 1918–32. His papers comprise diaries, correspondence, articles, miscellaneous papers and photographs dated 1881–1945 and have been catalogued.
  See Margaret Harcourt Williams, *Catalogue of the papers of Sir Charles Addis* (SOAS, London, 1986).
60 boxes

ADDIS, Sir John (1914–1983)
One of the thirteen children of Sir Charles Addis. Entered the Diplomatic Service in 1938 and was Ambassador to China from 1972 to 1974. His papers are not yet available for public consultation.
35 boxes approximately.

ALABASTER, Sir Chaloner (1838–98)
From 1855 to 1869 Sir Chaloner Alabaster was a Diplomatic Interpreter in China. He was Vice-Consul at Shanghai from 1869 to 1873 when he became Consul-General at Canton. The papers are dated from 1854 to 1898 and chiefly comprise his diaries though there are some miscellaneous papers.
13 volumes.

AYLWARD, Gladys
Worked as a missionary in Shanxi and Taiwan. The film *Inn of the Sixth Happiness*, starring Ingrid Bergman, is based on her life. Letters and a few personal effects.
1 box

BECKINSALE, Laura
Letters from Wuchang and Hankou where she was a missionary, describing events during the 1911 revolution.
1 box

CARPENTER, John Baker
Letters, papers and photographs of John Baker Carpenter who served with the Church Missionary Society in Fujian from 1899 to 1921.
1 box

EDWARDS, Dr Eva
Professor of Chinese, University of London, 1939-55. Scholarly papers.
4 boxes

EVANS, William
Chinese Protectorate Service 1882-1911. Letters 1883-1911.
2 boxes

MANN, Ebenezer and Mabel Mann worked with the China Inland Mission in Gansu Province from the early years of the century until their retirement in 1944. Letters and papers dated 1913-67.
1 box, 1 file

MCLEAN, David (1833-1908)
Manager of the Shanghai Branch of the Hongkong and Shanghai Bank from 1865 to 1873 when he was appointed Manager to the London Office. He retired in 1889. Letterbooks, 1862-1889 and typed transcripts.
13 volumes

PRATT, Sir John (1876-1970)
Served with the British Consular Service in China before becoming, in 1925, adviser to the Foreign Office on Far Eastern Affairs. He remained in this post until 1938. Author of *War and Politics in China* (London, 1943) and *China and Britain* (London, 1944). Most of his papers date from after 1941 (he was 'blitzed' three times) and include correspondence concerning his various publications, family correspondence including letters from his brother William 'Billy' Pratt (Boris Karloff), several files on his campaign against British involvement in the Korean War, articles lecture notes and press cuttings.
35 boxes

ROBINSON, A F
Salt Revenue Service. Papers, dated 1913-30, chiefly concerning the reorganisation loan of 1913.
1 box

SEWELL, William (1898-1984)
Went out to the West China Union University, Chengdu, with the Friends Foreign Mission Association, where he taught chemistry from 1924 to 1952. Was interned with his wife and children at Stanley Camp, Hong Kong from 1942 to 1945. Wrote *China through a College Window*, *Strange Harmony* and *I stayed in China*. Letters, diaries, reports, writings, photographs and printed ephemera.
7 boxes

SMITH, John H.
Journals kept by John Smith, Engine Room Artificer Navy, during voyages to the Pacific 1893 to 1896 and off the coast of China 1898 to 1901.
2 volumes

References

1 S Sugiyama, 'A British Trading Firm in the Far East: John Swire & Sons 1867–1914' in S Yonekawa and H Yoshihara, *Business History of General Trading Companies* (University of Tokyo Press, Tokyo, 1987), p. 2.
2 Quoted in 'Notes on the origins of the work of the RTS (London) in China' by an unknown author, written in 1948. SOAS: Archives of the United Society for Christian Literature, vol. 398, p. 1.
3 Rev A Williamson, 'The Literati of China and how to meet them', a paper read before the Shanghai Missionary Conference, Glasgow, n.d., SOAS: Archives of the United Society for Christian Literature, vol. S/USCL/111.
4 *Catalogue of the Publications of the Society for the Diffusion of Christian and General Knowledge among the Chinese* (Shanghai, 1895). SOAS: Archives of the United Society for Christian Literature, vol. S/USCL/109.
5 *Report of the Peking Hospital for 1878 and 1879* (Shanghai: American Presbyterian Press, 1880). SOAS: CWM Library o.5. Pam–vol. 64., p. 44.

Discussion

It was noted that photographs of China not from the Missionary societies were in the care of the Art Librarian, Miss Yasumura. There was considerable demand from picture researchers for pictorial material on China and perhaps the China Library Group might consider undertaking a directory of photographic archives, as the Middle East Library Group was preparing to do. There are a certain number of photographs in the Prints and Drawings Department of the Victoria and Albert Museum; virtually none in the British Library. The Salvation Army was in the process of preparing its new headquarters in Judd Street which would soon house its archive.

On the question of preservation, the SOAS archive photographs were about to be moved into an air-conditioned strong room and complete listing would also prevent over-handling. Further preservation measures were being considered.

Helen Wallis

Chinese Maps and Globes in the British Library and the Phillips Collection

For the sixteenth-century European the name of Cathay conjured up visions of the oldest and richest empire in the world and prompted hopes of profitable trade. The interest in China first inspired by Marco Polo's travels in the thirteenth century is reflected in the collections which the British Library inherited from the British Museum and which the India Office Library and Records received from the East India Company.

Our Chinese holdings of maps and atlases are divided between 'departments' (to use the familiar though now outmoded term). Oriental Manuscripts and Printed Books, now Oriental Collections, holds a wide assortment of cartographic material spanning many centuries. From the earliest times, as Howard Nelson has pointed out in his various accounts of these collections, the Chinese have appreciated the value of an exact knowledge of the Empire's geography. The earliest reference to map-making dates from the fifth century BC. This is a record of the route taken by the mythical emperor, the Great Yu, as he moved across the empty landscape, laying down China's mountains, rivers and plains. The *Yu gong* (Tribute to Yu) is part of the *Shu Jing*, the 'Classic of History'. One of a pair of steles (maps engraved on stone) from 1137 found at Xi'an illustrates the *Yu gong*, *Yu ji tu* (Map of the tracks of Yu), and it is of special interest because of its square grid, which the Chinese used over many centuries as their cartographic reference system. (A rubbing is at 15406.a.74/l.) The earliest reference to the use of a grid appears in the 'History of the Later Han Dynasty' in a biography of Zhang Heng of the first century AD.

The earliest specific reference to a map dates from 227BC, when a would-be assassin gained an audience with the emperor Qin Shi Huang di, the first emperor of a united China, to present him with a map whose case concealed a poisoned dagger. No maps of this early period were believed to survive, however, until in 1974 Chinese archaeologists discovered two Han maps in one of the three tombs at Mawangdui in Hunan Province. These pre-date by some 1,300 years the earliest extant Chinese map previously known and are the earliest surviving manuscript maps on silk in the world. Facsimiles with text are held in the Map Library.

The stone engravings of 1137 at Xi'an were followed by three more engraved in 1244 which are now preserved in the Confucian temple at Suzhou. One dating from 1229 is a town plan of Suzhou, the second city of the empire under the Song, and is notable in showing the town 50 years before Marco Polo visited it. A rubbing is held in OC (15406.a.5.), and a photograph of this is displayed in the

Map Gallery exhibition, 'The city in maps'. The Oriental Collection's other rubbings of the Xi'an and Suzhou stone engravings comprise a map of China and the Barbarian Countries, based on an original c.1045, engraved at Xi'an in 1137 (15406.a.74/2) and a celestial planisphere of 1193 by Huang Shang, engraved in 1247 (15406.a.5/2). This latter was made for Huang's pupil, the future Ningzong emperor, who reigned from 1195 to 1224, and has been described by Needham as the most famous of Chinese celestial maps.

Chinese achievements in astronomy and in celestial mapping gave China pride of place for the antiquity and continuity of her records. The earliest star chart from any civilization (if generalized fresco painting from the classical world is excluded) is the manuscript map found by Sir Aurel Stein in the great library of early Chinese and Central Asian manuscripts at Dunhuang on the edge of the Gobi desert, and is now in OC (s.3326). Dating from approximately 940AD, it derives from the work of three great astronomers of the fourth century BC, as interpreted and conflated by the astronomer Chen Zhuo of the sixth century AD.

In cartographic techniques China also leads the field. The steles at Xi'an and Suzhou provided what W M Ivins has described (in reference to the European invention of printing) as 'the exactly repeatable picture'. The oldest printed map known is a map of West China in the *Liu Jing Tu* ('Illustrations of objects mentioned in the Six Classics'), edited about 1155AD. The facility for producing maps in multiple copies thus became available 300 years earlier than in Europe. With the long tradition of map-making and the ready use of maps this provided an ideal medium to record both ancient and current geography, as well as to meet administrative needs. The great world map of Zhu Siben, drawn between 1311 and 1320, is now lost, but it was the basis of the so-called 'Mongol atlas', the *Guang yu tu*, first published in 1555. This remained until the nineteenth century a standard work in Chinese geography. A copy (1799) of the edition of 1579 is in OC (15261.e.2.).

Other notable works are the gazetteers and the many general and local topographies which were illustrated with maps. An encyclopaedic work, including physical geography and maps, was undertaken for the Kangxi Emperor by the scholar Chen Menglei in the later years of the seventeenth century and published at Peking in 1726 under the title *Gu jin tu shu ji cheng*. (15000.VII.ch.53–64). Of the many administrative atlases in the collections, that of Jiangxi province, of the eighteenth century is a notable example (Add. MS. 16356). From the same period, there are examples of geomancers handbooks explaining natural configurations in terms of good fortune, illustrated with maps and diagrams (15257.a.12, 15111.e.18 etc.).

The importance of hydrology and hydrography for the physical and economic management of China's great rivers and canals is reflected in the many fine strip maps preserved on long scrolls. On display in the King's Library is a manuscript of the Yellow River, 'Wang Shigu quan huang tu', by Wang Hui, 1704 (but probably a copy of c.1800; Or.13990). The Grand Canal, one of the world's greatest achievements in hydraulic engineering, was begun in the fourth century BC. The short early sections were joined up during the Sui dynasty (589–618AD) to form a continuous inland waterway from Peking to Hangzhou. A manuscript scroll of the eighteenth century depicts its course of more than 1,000 miles from north to south (OC Or. 2362).

Map rolls covering coastal areas mapped for administrative and military purposes were made from the sixteenth century onwards. The prototype was Zheng Ruozeng's large work, the *Zhou hai tu bian* ('Illustrated Seaboard Strategy'), 1562, which was illustrated with maps. A later model was the geographical treatise by Chen Lunjiong entitled *Hai guo wen jian lu*, a record of information and observations regarding the countries of the seas, published in 1744. Two fine panoramic coastal charts of the later half of the eighteenth century are in OC (Or. 13844, (1) and (2)). A similar coastal roll of about 1840, in traditional style, 32ft × 1ft 2in, came to the Map Room of the British Museum (now the BL Map Library) in a collection of maps and sketches put together for General Sir Hugh Gough, Commander of the British Expeditionary Force during the Chinese War of 1841–3 (Maps 162.o.2.). A second coastal roll of the same period has historical notes of western concessions, added later (Maps 162.o.3.).

Another important genre results from the custom of preparing maps and plans for the Emperor on his tours and military campaigns. Visitors in 1985 to the exhibition at the Berliner Festspiele in West Berlin, 'Palast-museum Peking, Schätze aus der Verbotenen Stadt' (Treasures from the Forbidden City) will recall the magnificent scrolls illustrating the southern journeys of the Kangxi Emperor (who reigned from 1662 to 1722). On exhibition in the King's Library is an Album by Qian Weicheng of the Fifth Journey of the Qianlong Emperor, eighteenth century, and the volume has the library stamp of the Emperor himself (OC Or.12895).

The Map Library's collections supplement those of OC in the field of Chinese cartography, as well as including many maps and atlases of China made by westerners. Some of the finest pieces came to the British Museum in King George III's Topographical Collection. One notable item is a view of the Canton waterfront painted *c.*1760. It is the work of a Chinese artist, but was probably commissioned by a European merchant. The detail extends even to the pot plants on the boats and in the houses. Of special interest are the 'factories' (warehouses) of the foreign traders, now a formidable presence in this single open port (Map Library, K. Top. CXVI.23). The exhibition at the Royal Pavilion, Brighton, 'The China Trade 1600–1860', held in 1986, showed this and related pieces to fine effect.

These collections of our two departments are further complemented by those in the Department of Manuscripts, comprising maps and views by Chinese and by Europeans. The Cotton collection (one of the three Foundation Collections of the British Museum) includes, for example, one of the earliest English maps of China, inscribed 'From Madrid. Ao 1609', and presumably drawn by an English agent using Spanish sources (Cotton MS. Aug. I.ii.45). The English East India Company, chartered in 1600, had been concerned to develop trade with China from its beginnings, and from 1685, when the port of Canton was opened, shared its facilities with other European traders. Early Chinese material in the East India Company's collections came through important gifts from John Reeves in 1825 and J G Ravenshaw, in the name of his son Edward C Ravenshaw in 1828. In 1825 Reeves, an officer in the Company's service in Canton, presented a Chinese map of the greater part of Asia and European Russia, partly in Chinese and partly in Manchu, engraved and printed in about 1761. The Chinese maps in the India Office, now IOLR, were catalogued by R K (Sir Robert) Douglas in his annotations to the *Catalogue of maps etc. in the Map Room of the India Office*, 1878 (pp. 504–510). Other items or collections to note include the 'Compleat Geography of the whole Empire of China . . .' copied from the original charts used at the Imperial Court of Peking, 1712 to 1716, put in order by A E Van Braam Houckgeest (MS.K.Top. CXVI.6.). A collection of 352 maps of China, and Japan, chiefly from standard blockprints, brought together by the German traveller Julius Klaproth, and with his manuscript notes, c.1830, is in Oriental Collections (Add. MS. 11,705). An atlas containing maps of parts of China and Tartary, with Klaproth's annotations, nineteenth century, is Add. MS. 11706.

I have left to the end the *pièce de résistance*, a major group of items which illustrate one of the most remarkable cartographic achievements of any age, namely Jesuit map-making in China. The organisers of this colloquium kindly granted me permission to include in my survey the Chinese maps in the collection of Sir Thomas Phillipps Bart, owned by Mr Philip Robinson and his brother the late Mr Lionel Robinson. The maps derive from the Jesuit College of Clermont (from 1682 the College Louis-le-Grand) in Paris. The College was suppressed in 1762, and its collection was purchased in 1764 by the Dutchman Gerard Meerman, to be sold in 1824 to Sir Thomas Phillipps, the great collector and bibliophile. A note in Sir Thomas's hand describes the material as 'the original papers of the Jesuit Verbiest, the astronomer in China'.

Our British Library holdings, combined with the maps of this private collection, make London one of the two greatest centres for Chinese Jesuit cartography, the other being the Vatican Library in Rome. I express here my appreciation to Philip Robinson for giving his permission for me to encompass both collections. The loan of many items from the Phillipps Collection in 1974 was the occasion of our British Library exhibition 'Chinese and Japanese Maps', accompanied by a catalogue published by the British Library Board, 1974. A selection of materials from this collection and from the British Library's holdings was taken to Berlin in 1985 to form a major part of the display in the cartographic gallery of the exhibition 'Europa und die Kaiser von China', a complement to the 'Treasures from the Forbidden City', in the great hall and galleries below.

Chinese Jesuit cartography assimilated the scientific and geographical knowledge of Renaissance Europe with the traditional skills of Chinese cosmography and map-making. Father Matteo Ricci SJ, founder of the China Mission in 1583, was the pioneer of this remarkable school. A fine example of his woodcut world map published in 1602 is in the Phillipps collection, one of three extant copies. A later edition hangs on the wall of the Map Room in the Royal Geographical Society.

Although Ricci's first world map, 1584 in date, does not survive, an indication of how traditional Chinese map-makers reacted to it is provided in a printed world map of 'Liang Zhou a man from Si, an Education official of Wuxi County'.

Entitled 'A comprehensive map (delineating) heaven and earth and the myriad countries (of the world) and ancient and modern affairs', and dated 1593, the map is, in effect, an administrative map of China for mandarin officials, but the author explains that having seen the drawings of the Xi tai scholar (i.e. Ricci) and the European engraved maps, he realized that the world was extremely large and combined all these 'utilising both the knowledge of the Chinese and that of foreigners'. Western countries are arranged round the margins, from Canada, Anian and America (top right) to Brazil, Magellanica, the lands of Tall Men (Patagonians), Short Men, and Hairy Men, and the Kingdom of Women (Amazons) (bottom right). These countries are shown as small islands surrounding the nucleus of the Chinese empire.

The unique exemplar of this map is in the Phillipps Collection. It became a model for maps of the 'Chinese dominions or universe'. A derived version, woodcut, was made about 1743, with reference to 'Liang's old map', and examples of this are held both in OC (15406.a.28.) and in the Phillipps collection. 'A universal map of the Chinese Empire under the Da Qing or Tartar Dynasty, by Chu Siling', published probably at Peking in 1819, is a smaller scale derivative, and still consigns western countries to the margins. The Map Library's copy (Maps 162.b.4.) has manuscript annotations in Russian. We learn from a note on the map, and from J D Cochrane's *Narrative of a pedestrian journey through Russia and Siberian Tartary* (London, 1824), p.506, that the Director of the Kiakhta Customs Port presented it to Cochrane on 3 February 1823, and he in turn passed it to the British Museum.

Ricci's successor in the China mission, the Sicilian Father Nicolo Longobardi (1559–1654), and his colleague, the Portuguese Father Manuel Dias (1574–1659), carried on the work of cartographic instruction. Their large painted terrestrial globe made in 1623, believed to have been made for the Emperor and to come from the Imperial Palace, was acquired from China by Sir Percival David just as the Second World War broke out and was presented by Sir Percival and Lady David to the Map Rooms of the British Museum in 1962. One of the treasures of the Map Library (Maps C.6.a.2.), it ranks with Father Ricci's world map among the two or three most important relics of early Chinese Jesuit cartography.

Other Fathers followed in the tradition. Father Francesco Sanbiasi's world map, manuscript, c.1648, is in the Phillipps Collection. The Belgian Father Ferdinand Verbiest made his woodcut double hemisphere world map in 1674. An example is preserved in the Phillipps Collection, while the Map Library has pulls from the blocks made for a Korean edition printed at Seoul by order of the King of Korea in 1860 (Maps 183.p.4.2.).

The Celestial maps of Father Verbiest and of his predecessor as head of the China mission, Father Johann Adam Schall von Bell, are also preserved in the Phillipps Collection. We do not know as yet if the description of the collection as from Verbiest is true, or whether this was the only European name which Sir Thomas could identify.

Another outstanding seventeenth century item from the Phillipps Collection is the manuscript map of China, c.1652, by the Polish Jesuit and sinologue Michael

Boym (1612-1659). His concern was to bring knowledge of Chinese philosophy and science to Europe. Three manuscript maps of China by Boym are known. One is in the Vatican, the second disappeared from Paris in the Second World War, and the one in the Phillipps Collection is believed to be the original. For the first time names are given in Chinese characters and in romanized form.

Regional maps from the Phillipps Collection include one of Sunjiang prefecture, manuscript, drawn between 1661 and 1725, and one of Guangdong province, published in c.1739, otherwise unknown.

The reign of the Kangxi Emperor (1662-1722), to whom, in his youth, Verbiest was tutor, was a period of intense cartographic activity, especially in topographical survey. The Kangxi map of China, five metres long, completed between 1716 and 1718, engraved on copper by Father Matteo Ripa at Peking in 1719, is preserved in King George III's Topographical Collection (K. Top. CXVI.15.). Some years later the Qianlong Emperor commissioned a new survey from the Jesuits to complete the work of their predecessors. The Portuguese Fathers Rocha and Espinha carried out the work between 1756 and 1759, and Father Michael Benoist edited the cartography for a woodcut edition of 1769, followed by a copper engraved edition in 1775. The Qianlong map (or atlas) is regarded as one of the finest surveys of its day. Examples are held in the King's Topographical Collection Maps Tab. 1.b.(1-4).

It is appropriate also to include in this survey Lord Macartney's embassy to China, 1793-4, by which Great Britain sought to establish relations with the Qianlong Emperor, a new advance towards the 'happy meeting of minds', western and eastern, in which the Jesuit Fathers had been so successful. The embassy's progress is illustrated in the fine watercolours of William Alexander, of which one volume (with maps) is preserved in King George III's Topographical Collection (K.Top. 8.tab.c.8.). Other collections of Alexander's Chinese watercolours are in the India Office Library and Records and in the Department of Prints and Drawings of the British Museum and the Victoria and Albert Museum. (There are further holdings in Maidstone Museum and Art Gallery.) Whether the Jesuit surveys and other Chinese pieces came into George III's collection as a result of the embassy, as gifts from the Emperor, has still to be established.

A Chinese tapestry (ke si), preserved in the National Maritime Museum, depicts two presentation pieces from George III to the Emperor, an astronomical planetarium and a celestial globe brought to China by Macartney (although the craftsman evidently had not seen the embassy or the gifts, as he depicts the astronomical pieces of Father Verbiest made for the Peking observatory in 1673-4). The work is inscribed with a poem composed by the Emperor himself for the occasion.

The military and commercial activities of the British in the nineteenth century and the collecting policies for modern mapping have brought a wealth of further materials. In the Map Library we have recently added to our nineteenth and twentieth century collections of topographical maps an Atlas of false colour Landsat Images of China, compiled by the Institute of Geography, Academia Sinica, 1:500,000 and published by the Science Press in Peking, 1983, three volumes. We also have a useful exchange with the cartographic institutions at Wuhan.

Finally, I will allow the Qianlong Emperor the last word by quoting his poem, which sums up nicely the ideals behind the cultural exchanges which have brought us some of the rarer items in these collections.

Formerly Portugal undertook the task of bringing tributes.
Now England follows suit with all sincerity.
Truly the work and virtues of our ancestors have echoed far beyond the seas.
Though the gifts may be commonplace enough our heart commends the giver.
Strange things indeed we prize not, nor do we listen to boastful claims.
Yet mindful of the great distance journeyed We shall repay a hundredfold.
For in such wise do sage-kings preserve the plenitude of their prosperity.

Appendix

CATALOGUES
1. *Catalogues of Maps, Prints, Drawings, etc. forming a Geographical and Topographical Collection attached to the library of ... King George the Third*, 1829.
2. *Catalogue of King George III's Maritime Collection*, about 1850. (MSS and printed charts; dictionary arrangement; reproduced by the 'carbonic process', not published. Copies in Map Library, Reading Room, and Department of Manuscripts.)
3. *Catalogue of the Manuscript Maps, Charts, and Plans, and of the Topographical Drawings in the British Museum*, 3 vols (London, 1844–61). (Vols 1 and 2, 1944; vol. 3, 1861; reprinted 1962.) Compiled by John Holmes and R H Major; classified arrangement. Each volume includes material in the collections to the date of its publication. Manuscript material in the King's Topographical Collection is included in all three volumes, but that in the King's Maritime Collection is only in vol. 3. Accessions of maps in the Department of Manuscripts after 1861 are entered in the periodically printed *Catalogue of Additions to the Manuscripts.*
4. *The British Museum Catalogue of Printed Maps, Charts and Plans*, photolithographic edition up to the end of 1964 (London, 1967); *Ten-year Supplement 1965–1975* (London, 1978).
5. *British Library cartographic materials* [microfiche catalogue covering accessions from 1975].
6. *Catalogue to the Chinese Collection*, Oriental Collections (Chinese Section). Card index; pre-1965 holdings are on microfiche, the rest are on card.
7. W Simon and Howard G H Nelson, *Manchu Books in London. A Union catalogue* (the British Library, London, 1977).
8. *Catalogue of Manuscript and Printed Reports, Field Books, Memoirs, Maps, etc., of the India Surveys, deposited in the Map Room of the India Office* (London, 1878) – especially pp. 504–510.

EXHIBITION CATALOGUES AND ASSOCIATED BOOKS AND PRODUCTIONS

Yolande Hodson, Howard Nelson, Helen Wallis, *Chinese & Japanese Maps. An exhibition organised by the British Library at the British Museum, 1 February – 31 December 1974* (London, 1974) – section on Chinese map-making.

Howard Nelson, 'Chinese maps. An exhibition at the British Library,' *China Quarterly* April 2–May 1974, pp. 357–62.

—'Maps from old Cathay', *Geographical Magazine*, vol. XLVII (1975), pp. 707–8.

Helen Wallis, 'Missionary cartographers to China', *Geographical Magazine*, vol. XLVII (1975), pp. 751–9.

Patrick Conner, *The China Trade, 1600–1860* (Brighton, 1986).

Europa und die Kaiser von China (Berliner Festspiele, Berlin, 1985).

OTHER WORKS

Andrew S Cook, 'Maps from a Survey Archive: the India Office Collection', *The Map Collector*, no. 28 (1984), pp. 27–32.

Pasquale M d.Elia *Recent discoveries and new studies (1938–1960) on the world map in Chinese of Father Matteo Ricci SJ.*, Monumenta Serica, vol. XX (1961), p. 161.

Yolande Hodson, 'Maps of the Orient at the British Library', *The Map Collector*, no. 28 (1984), pp. 12–15.

Joseph Needham, *Science and Civilization in China*, vol. III (1959).

J V Mills, 'Three Chinese maps', *British Museum Quarterly*, vol. XVIII, no. 3 (1953), pp. 65–7; (two coastal charts and the 'Qianlong map'.)

Philip Robinson, *'Phillips 1986' The Chinese Puzzle*, Collector's Piece VI, reprinted from The Book Collector (London, summer 1976).

Helen Wallis and E D Grinstead, 'A Chinese terrestrial globe, AD1623, *British Museum Quarterly*, vol. XXV (1962), pp. 83–91; and Wallis (1965), pp. 4042.

Helen Wallis, 'The influence of Father Ricci on Far Eastern cartography,' *Imago Mundi*, vol. XIX (1965), pp. 38–45.

—'A Banquet of Maps. An account of the map collections of the British Library,' *Map Collector*, no. 28 (1984), pp. 3–10.

—'Die Kartographie der Jesuiten am Hof in Peking', *Europa und die Kaiser von China* (1985), pp. 107–113.

My thanks are due to Frances Wood (Oriental Collections), Howard Nelson (previously in Oriental Manuscripts and Printed Books), and Andrew Cook (India Office Library and Records); also to Mr Philip Robinson for kindly giving permission for the inclusion of the Phillipps Collection.

Discussion

In the subsequent discussion, it emerged that a listing of Chinese maps is proposed, which would draw together those in the Map Library, Oriental Collections and the IOLR, not only helping to trace locations but demonstrating how the whole collection fits together. Maps in the Map Library are listed first in the Printed Catalogue (including items catalogued up to 1964) and then in the 10-year supplement listing acquisitions up to 1975, subsequently on microfiche.

Frances Wood

Curiosities of the British Library Chinese Collection

The treasures of the British Library's Chinese collection are well known to scholars, thanks mainly to the published catalogues of Lionel Giles, Arthur Waley, Edouard Chavannes and Henri Maspero which have listed most of the material brought back from Dunhuang and its environs by Aurel Stein in the early years of this century. Whilst the woodslips from the Dunhuang *limes* are amongst the earliest items in the British Library's collection, it is not perhaps so widely known that Chinese items were included in the library's founding collections. Some of these items are of more than curiosity value and the story of their collection and conservation is part of the history of sinological librarianship in Great Britain.

The 'founding collections' were those of the British Museum (founded in 1753), of which the library was a significant part until the passing of the British Library Act and the establishment of the British Library in 1973. The British Museum's Chinese manuscripts and printed books then became part of the British Library's Department of Oriental Manuscripts and Printed Books which has recently been re-entitled 'Oriental Collections'.

The founding collection with most Chinese items was that of Sir Hans Sloane (1660–1753), an Irish doctor who had 'treated such diverse patients as Samuel Pepys and Queen Anne, and who had been largely responsible for the development in this country of the practice of innoculation against smallpox and the popularisation of milk chocolate'.[1] Appointed personal physician to the Duke of Albermarle, Governor of Jamaica, in 1687, Sloane decided to accept the appointment partly because he had already begun to collect natural and artificial 'curiosities' and natural history specimens. On his return from Jamaica, he brought back some of his pets: a yellow snake, an iguana and a crocodile, all of which perished *en voyage* and presumably turned into 'specimens'. Sloane's collection grew to incorporate Etruscan, Egyptian, Roman and Assyrian antiquities, and Dürer and Holbein drawings. Discarded items which made their way into his ex-servant Mr Salter's collection of curiosities, on view at 18 Cheyne Walk, included 'the Queen of Sheba's fan and cordial bottle, Robinson Crusoe's and his Man Friday's shirt, the Four Evangelists cut on a cherry stone ... and Pontius Pilate's Wife's chambermaid's sister's hat'.[2] Sloane's visitors included Voltaire, Benjamin Franklin (who also praised Mr Salter's collection), Linnaeus and the composer Handel who annoyed Sloane by placing a hot buttered muffin on a valuable book. Handel is said to have attributed Sloane's annoyance to his famous parsimony and the waste of the butter ('If it had been a biscuit, it would not have mattered ...'[3]).

Buttered or not, books and manuscripts (50,000 volumes including 3,516 of manuscripts, and 347 volumes of drawings and illuminations) formed the heart of Sloane's collection and the heart of the British Museum which was set up in something of a hurry after Sloane left the collection to the nation on his death. Then, as now, money had to be begged from an unwilling government; the Chancellor of the Exchequer did not think he had enough money for 'knick knackeries' and resorted to a public lottery which raised nearly £100,000 despite being 'more corrupt than had been feared . . .'[4].

Sloane's own collection has been dispersed throughout the various departments of the Museum and Library and whilst only three 'Chinese' items are listed in the manuscripts' inventory kept in the Department of Manuscripts, Prevost's manuscripts' inventory of 1854 lists six, and one Mongolian item; the current inventory lists seven but other relevant material, such as Hyde's orientalia, some of which Sloane purchased has to be sought in the general index of manuscripts, kept in the Department of Western Manuscripts.

The majority of the items with Chinese connections amongst the Sloane manuscripts are grammars or parts of grammars; *Dictionarium Chinense*, the Dutch-Latin-Chinese dictionary of 1628 by Heurnius[5], a seventeenth-century Spanish *Vocabulario de lengua mandarina*, a fragment of Bayer's Chinese–Latin dictionary, the bulk of which is preserved in Leningrad; and religious miscellanea reflecting contemporary preoccupations. Sloane 3401 is a copy of the woodblock edition of Verbiest's 1671 *Typus eclipsus lunae* . . . with Chinese and Manchu text, here preserved rather archaically in scroll format. This provides a tantalising link with the Hyde collection, part of which was purchased by Sloane on Hyde's death, part of which appears to have entered the Royal Library. Thomas Hyde (1639–1703) was the foremost orientalist of his day and served as 'interpreter and secretary in oriental languages' to Charles II, James II and William III, as well as being Chief Librarian of the Bodleian. In the manuscript list of his books and papers preserved in the Sloane collection (Sloane 3323, ff. 270–272), item 9 is described as 'Phases lunares in the Tartar and Chinese languages, viz an account of an eclipse . . . printed by Father Verbiest, late professor of astronomy at Pekin in China, 1671. This tho' a small book is a great rarity being the only thing of its kind in England'. It seems likely that it was Hyde's own copy of the Verbiest volume that entered the Royal Library (ex. Reg.16.B.IX) for it bears an inscription in Hyde's own hand which is almost identical with the description in the Sloane list. It is ironic that Sloane, who was to buy many of Hyde's own papers, should also possess a copy; both are now in the British Library, demonstrating that from the beginning there were at least two 'of its kind in England'.

Other papers of Hyde's appear to have made their way into the collection of his royal masters; Reg.16.B.III is entitled *Miscellanea orientalia* on the spine and has a blue paper, inscribed in Hyde's hand 'several manuscript papers', with a scrawled number at the bottom: (Hyde) Royal 16.B.III. It includes the first (printed) page of Verbiest's *Elements linguae Tartaricae*, with marginal notes mentioning Father Couplet, the Jesuit missionary to China who provided Hyde with his very own Chinese tutor. This was one of the earliest Chinese visitors to the West, Michael

Shen Fuzong, a convert who accompanied Couplet to Europe when he returned to 'enlighten' the Pope on the matter of the Chinese rites. Couplet, who had gone out to China with Verbiest in 1659 and was killed by a box during his return to China in 1692, presented Shen Fuzong to Louis XIV in France and later took him to England. In Oxford, Shen Fuzong catalogued the Bodleian's Chinese books and taught Hyde Chinese through the medium of their only common language, Latin. Amongst Hyde's papers acquired by Sloane (Sloane 853) are envelopes and scraps of paper covered in Chinese characters and Latin translations; diagrams of the geomantic compass and abacus; variant forms of numerals and other bits and pieces. During his stay in Oxford, Shen Fuzong attracted the attention of James II, although it is difficult to say whether they actually met. When James visited Oxford in September 1687 'for the purpose of overawing the fellows of Magdalene College',[6] he asked Hyde about the Chinese cataloguer: 'He was a little blinking fellow was he not?'

There are one or two Chinese items in the other two major founding collections; the Cottonian and Harleian, surprising since these were not wide-ranging magpie gatherings but, in the case of Cotton, for example, a collection devoted to English history and literature, including two Magna Cartas, the Beowulf manuscript and the Lindisfarne gospels. There is also a small, fat leather-bound volume containing some medical prescriptions and a series of stories of gangsters and crimes; an example being that of the man who lost his money and his house, and when arrested for failing to pay his taxes, hit the policeman with a fan. These short accounts are written in a poor hand but the whole is splendidly bound and entitled *Liber parvus sinensis*, and must have entered the collection before 1700. Similarly, amongst the more noble manuscripts, characters and rolls of the Harleian collection assembled by two Earls of Oxford, is Harleian 344–347, grandly entitled *Libri sinici de rebus mercatoriis*, which consists of advertisements for various tea merchants in the Xiamen area and a couple of 'log books' of the most diverse business which dealt in white sugar, tea, occasional articles of furniture, gold leaf, thread and bullion, silks and cottons of all sorts, with a careful register of letters received and sent.

Apart from the few items from the founding collections, the eighteenth century was not one of the Museum's great periods for the acquisition and care of Chinese material. Books and manuscripts continued to arrive in the library but there was no specialist to catalogue them and such was the crisis that a visiting portrait-modeller from China was invited to 'examine' the Chinese books in the library in December 1770. Chitqua, or Chetqua, was described in 1770, in a letter to Josiah Wedgwood:

He intends to stay here some years, is in the Chinese dress, makes portraits (small busts in clay, which he colours) and produces very striking likenesses with great expedition. I have paid him three visits and had a good deal of conversation with him; for he speaks some English and is a good natured, sensible man, very mild in his temper and gentle in his motions. His dresses are chiefly of satin and I have seen him in crimson and in black ... He has been with the King and Queen, who were much pleased with him and he is to take portraits of the Royal Infantry. He has ten guineas apiece for his little portraits which are very small.[7]

In artistic circles, Chitqua enjoyed considerable success; invited to the Royal Academy dinner, he was also included in Zoffany's group portrait of the academicians, *Life School in the Royal Academy*, 'peeping over the shoulders of Benjamin West and Jeremiah Meyer'.[8] In contrast with Zoffany's straightforward depiction, Sir William Chambers whose fame and fortune depended on Chinoiserie, wrote in the second edition of his *Dissertation on Oriental Gardening* of how the whole world:

... knew Chet-Qua and how he was born at Quang-chew-fu, in the fourth moon of the year twenty-eight; also how he was bred a face-maker, and had three wives, two of whom he caressed very much; the third but seldom for she was a virago, and had large feet. He dressed well, often in thick sattin; wore nine whiskers and four long nails, with silk boots, callico breeches and every other ornament that mandarins are wont to wear; equalling therein the prime macarones, and scavoir vivres, not only of Quang-chew, but even of Kyang-ning or Shun-tien-fu. He likewise danced a fandando, after the newest of Macao, played divinely upon the bag-pipe and made excellent remarks.[9]

Not only was poor Chitqua subject to such orientalising but, when asked to 'examine' the library's collection, it seems to have been assumed that Chinese and Japanese were one and the same to him. He managed brief descriptions of a number of Chinese books, including simple illustrated primers, and correctly described the *Tian zhu jiao yao* as a work on 'Christianity in Chinese'. This volume, incidentally, was dated to approximately 1790 by Douglas in his printed catalogue of 1877, but as Chitqua visited the library in 1770, Douglas was, for once, being over-cautious. Chitqua seems to have spent more time on Japanese books than Chinese, inspecting the whole of the Kaempfer collection (assembled in Japan, 1691–92 by a German physician, the collection was later acquired by Sloane), which seems to have meant nothing to him. A manuscript on Japanese–Dutch trading relations is described as 'A letter from the Emperor of China to the Emperor of Russia', and a collection of illustrated dramas of the bedchamber was said by Chitqua to be episodes from the rather quieter life of Confucius. The temporary consultant returned to China soon after, not without difficulty, for he was thrown off the first ship he boarded, the sailors for some reason feeling he would bring back bad luck to the ship. He wore European clothes on his second attempt and returned to Canton, where the Gentleman's Recorder announced his death in May 1797, from poisoning.

The nineteenth century was the period in which the library developed at its fastest rate; Panizzi's grand Reading Room emphasised the function of the library as the heart of the Museum, for the Museum departments were, in building terms, assigned to its periphery, and Panizzi also presided over grand cataloguing projects as well as promoting a more serious acquisitions policy. In 1843, when the Museum had been offered a collection of Chinese titles by the French bookseller M Molini, Panizzi made an impassioned plea on behalf of the Chinese collection, calling up comparisons of the type made nearly 150 years later in the Parker report.[10] The report of the Trustees' meeting on 5 July 1843, when Panizzi pleaded for 3,721 francs to purchase 1,186 'cahiers' (presumably *ce*), contains his description of the then tiny collection:

The British Museum possesses perhaps 300 Chinese volumes ... They were mostly presented by Mr Hill [sic] ... Should the Trustees purchase the works now offered, the collection of Chinese works in this library would then begin to be respectable; the works now offered supply important deficiencies and are precisely such as one should wish to add to those already in the Museum. Mr Panizzi has used the word *respectable* with reference to the collection of Chinese works in the British Museum supposing those now offered to be purchased as expressing its importance when spoken of in comparison with the great libraries of Paris, Vienna and, Mr Panizzi believes, Berlin. Even then the British Museum would be inferior to them, but the comparison would not be humiliating as it would be at present. The Russian government having an eye to their political intercourse with China have spared no pains in collecting the most numerous and valuable library of Chinese works known out of China. In England, there is no *public* institution to which scholars can apply for assistance in the pursuit of their Chinese studies. If assistance is to be looked for from any quarter Mr Panizzi thinks it ought to be from the British Museum and that efforts should be made to place it even in this respect not merely on a par, but above similar institutions in other countries.

The Trustees succumbed to Mr Panizzi's persuasion and whilst it is difficult to identify the works offered by M Molini, for the book-lists have not, apparently, survived, a number of the rarer works of fiction listed by Liu Ts'un-yan,[11] including the *Hua guang tian wang nan you zhi zhuan* (1571) and the *Guan yin chu shen nan you ji*, of a similar date, bear the date stamp for 1844, suggesting that they may have formed part of M Molini's collection.

As printed materials were not generally kept as collections (though manuscripts often were in the early days) it is difficult to identify specific volumes except by inscription and by stamp. Different stamps were used at different periods of the Museum's history and the combination of a stamp and other textual evidence can help to identify individual volumes lost in the anonymous mass. A book stamp associated with the founding collections in a copy of the crudely printed guide to Pu tuo shan (*Nan hai sheng jing Pu tuo shan zhi*) suggests that this particular volume is probably that sent to Sloane by James Cunningham in 1703 when he was serving as physician to the East India Company Factory in the Zhou shan archipelago which includes the Buddhist island of Pu tuo. Apart from the interest of connecting Cunningham, whose name is still associated with a number of Far Eastern plants, with the Sloane collection, the association helps to date the otherwise undated work which could conceivably be late Ming.

The Chinese books, part of what was to become the Department of Oriental Manuscripts (1866) and the Department of Oriental Printed Books and Manuscripts (1892) were catalogued by Sir Robert Kennaway Douglas, first Keeper of the Department (1892–1908). Douglas' catalogue, published in 1877, with a supplement in 1903, has a number of drawbacks but was a pioneering work in its time. He used 'the Orthography adopted by Morrison in his dictionary' because, he explained, '... it is one most generally known amongst Chinese scholars and also because it is the one best suited for English readers ...',[12] and he arranged works eurocentrically by alphabetical order of author's name. The result is that the catalogue would be quite unusable today, were it not for the inclusion of Chinese characters. The catalogue has a certain charm, as Douglas invariably translated titles rather quaintly: *Tian ce hua chun quan ben* is rendered as 'The Heaven-sent flowery petticoat'; *Wen zhang you xi* as 'Rambles in polite literature'; the *Yu zhi sheng jing fu* as 'A Poetical Eulogium on the city of Moukden', and so on. Douglas was occasionally over-diplomatic, translating *Ni jiao xi ying ji li ce* as 'Notes on England' rather than, as Hervouet suggested, 'Plan for getting rid of the English'.[13] H A Giles, who had a horribly sharp tongue, described Douglas's catalogue as 'a monument of immature scholarship'[14] whilst Pelliot commented more mildly on the Supplement. Certainly, a major fault of Douglas's was his tendency to conflate date of preface and date of edition.

If the nineteenth century was not a great era of bibliography, it was certainly a great era of collecting by various means. Douglas refers in the preface to his *Catalogue* to Panizzi's 'Mr Hill', giving his correct name as 'Mr Fowler Hull of Sigaur in the East Indies'. This early donation remains somewhat mysterious; the *Book of presents* (11 November 1826) records the accession of 'A collection of books and mss., in the Sanskrit, Chinese and other Oriental languages, bequeathed by the late Joseph Fowler Hull Esq., who died at Sigaur in India, in December 1825' and the Officer's Reports gives a fuller account:

In consequence of Mr Hull's legacy to the British Museum, Mr Baber with two attendants of the library proceeded to Uxbridge to take possession of the Books bequeathed and to superintend their packing up and careful removal. By this valuable legacy the Printed Books department has been enriched by the addition of about six hundred volumes in the following languages, Sanskrit, Hindi, Bengalee, Hindustanee, Bruj, B'hak'ha, Hebrew, Arabic, Persian, Armenian, Syriac, Athiopic, Chinese.

Mr Fowler Hull remains a shadowy figure, unconnected, apparently, to the East India Company and not mentioned in Indian almanacs for the period, he may, with his linguistic interests, have been a missionary. Even his place of death is somewhat obscure: was it Sigaura, Bilaspur, Central Provinces, Sigur of the Nilgiri area in Madras, or Sigaura in Mysore? The books were sent to his solicitor's office in Uxbridge and, as with all these early collections, were separated by language, so clues may yet be found through the chance discovery of an appropriate date stamp.

Some methods of collection, like Mr Fowler Hull's generous donation, were more fragrant than others. Douglas also describes the books presented by Queen Victoria which had been 'taken during the War in China of 1842' and the Library's copy of the *Zhi guo lun*, an essay by the Qianlong emperor in his own hand, wrapped in yellow silk and boxed in red carved lacquer, was purchased from the French General Montauban who had been active in the destruction of the Summer Palace in 1860. The collection of Morrison Junior was purchased by the Foreign Office after his death and presented to the Museum by the Foreign Secretary, Lord Aberdeen, in 1846. Notable items in the Morrison collection are a series of coastal maps, presumably of interest to the Foreign Office. It is clear that members of the British Legation in Peking occasionally bore the British Museum's Library in mind, for the acquisition of the *Tu shu ji cheng* in 1877 took place after protracted bargaining over several years between the Museum and an unidentified 'imperial

Prince', though the good offices of Mr Mayers of the British Embassy in Peking and what he called his 'book jackals'. The price was brought down from £2,000 to £1,500.

The Museum's acquisition of such *shan ben* in the nineteenth and early twentieth centuries was haphazard rather than systematic, but, as its reputation grew, it attracted gifts and donations of items of great rarity and historical value. There is a semantic problem in the description of some categories of Chinese 'rare' or antiquarian books. The usual Chinese term is *shan ben* and the connotations of *shan* are 'good', 'fine',[15] words which traditional and traditionalist bibliographical historians of China find it almost impossible to apply to, for example, crude popular editions which, as they did not attract the attention of bibliophiles in the past, may be far more rare than a fine edition of the 'Four Books'. The preferred term for crude or 'bad' editions or items is *hanjian ziliao*, literally 'rare materials', implying that they have historical or social significance and virtually require a context, whilst a *shan ben* can stand alone. Whilst the enigmatic Backhouse collected *shan ben* in the form of *nei fu* or 'palace editions' for the Bodleian, the British Museum's only piece of Backhousiana (apart from his extraordinary memoirs which were deposited in a number of libraries throughout the world) is the *Diary of Jing-shan*, deposited with the Museum by Backhouse's luckless collaborator, Bland. For forty years, scholars disputed the authenticity of this initimate record that had come to light so opportunely. Now regarded as a fake,[16] it must be considered as *hanjian ziliao*, or *ziliao* at least.

Other groups of *hanjian ziliao* include the papers of General Charles George 'Chinese' Gordon (1833–1885), Commander of the anti-Taiping 'Ever-Victorious Army' in 1863 and 1864. As a result of Gordon's negotiations and differences of opinion, his papers, deposited by his family in 1881 and 1887, include many letters from Li Hongzhang and several of the Taiping leaders, as well as such items as Prince Kong's list of presents.

A small block-printed scroll *Ying yi zuo luan* ('The English barbarians create havoc') of *c*.1841, depicting HMS *Nemesis* about to suffer its eponymous fate, could also be considered in this category, as may the large collection of often crudely-printed illustrated woodblock editions of popular novels which have been partially listed by Liu Ts'un-yan.[17]

The most important collection is undoubtedly that from Dunhuang and the surrounding areas, made by Stein on his three expeditions. The Dunhuang materials are well-known through catalogues, although there is still much work to be done on the uncatalogued fragments. One of the most exciting things about the Dunhuang collection is that it provides apparently endless research opportunities. Early scholars were interested in the collection as a whole; later, economic and social historians began to sift through and more recently, the emphasis has shifted to an interest in paper and book formats.[18]

In a recent article in the *Bulletin of the China Society of Library Sciences*,[19] Li Zhizhong of the Rare Book (*shan ben*) section of the National Library of China, basing his thesis on a number of differently 'bound' tenth-century booklets in the British Library Dunhuang collection, suggests that the prototypes of all the major later binding formats can be found in the tenth century or earlier. His description of s.5444 as a 'whirlwind binding' is perhaps pushing the concept to the extreme but s.5366, for example, has a thread binding that is uncannily modern in appearance and calls into question the accepted view that this format arose in the Ming, some four hundred years later. Li's article is quite challenging; he does not seek to answer the question raised by this time warp, nor whether thread bindings in tenth-century Dunhuang might be quite unconnected with developments in metropolitan China during the Ming; and he does not discuss paper quality in close relation to format. All the examples he cites, whether prototype butterfly, wrapped-back, whirlwind or thread binding, are made from thick strong, coarse paper inscribed on both sides, very different from the fine yellow papers of the Tang and the thin, often fragile paper of later periods which was printed on one side only and folded for greater strength. These aspects have yet to be examined, as does the extraordinary fact that 70 per cent of the booklets that Li Zhizhong presents as prototypes of new binding styles appear to have been written by the same octogenarian who describes in his colophons how he copies Buddhist texts from editions printed in Sichuan. His manuscripts comprise the possible whirlwind binding, butterfly binding and some very convincing thread binding, all produced during the two years 905 and 906. He deserves further investigation. Did he do his own binding? In the past, most have followed the slow evolutionary theory of development from the inconvenience of the scroll to the improvement of the whirlwind binding which, since it did not completely solve the scroll problem was supplanted by the butterfly binding which, in turn, tended to split at the spine until the spine was wrapped; the process of perpetual improvement ending in the stable *xian zhuang* or thread-bound book of the Ming and Qing. All this is challenged, apparently, by the extraordinary ingenuity of one old gentleman, another footnote to Dunhuang researches.

The great Dunhuang collection was not the only one acquired in the early years of the twentieth century. The oracle bone collection, built up by purchase in Wei xian, Shandong from 1904–06 by Couling and Chalfant, was sold in 1911 and dispersed to the British Museum, the Royal Scottish Museum and the Carnegie Museum in Pittsburg with a few samples sent to the Field Museum in Chicago.[20] Frank Herring Chalfant was a missionary with the American Presbyterian Mission, North, serving in Shandong until an accident at Qingdao in 1911 left him partially paralysed. His collaborator, Samuel Couling, was a British Baptist missionary in China from 1884 until 1908 when he resigned following a dispute over educational policy. He wore a Chinese blue gown and artificial queue for missionary work, and was said to look 'like an understudy for Gandhi'.[21] After his resignation, he went to Shanghai and supported himself and his family with some difficulty by writing (the *Encyclopaedia Sinica* amongst other things) and tutoring. The sale of the collection must have helped.

In recent years, though a number of *shan ben*, including pre-Ming editions of Buddhist works, have been acquired, more items of the *hanjian ziliao* category have been added to the collection. This is partly because of economic strictures but it also reflects changes in the publishing world, in library practice and in public relations. The vast number of reprints, better and closer links with other libraries, and the proliferation of microforms have given professional sinologists better access to the contents of more books. For European non-professionals, popular, illlustrated material, with historical and social significance, may well mean more than a beautiful edition of an untranslated work. Thus, recent acquisitions have included a collection of modern photolitho *nianhua* prints from Shanghai (*c.*1930), some with strange subjects in peculiar colours but which nevertheless continue the old woodblock New Year Print tradition at a distance; some of Zheng Zhenduo's 1940s reproductions of earlier illustrated works, photographs and postcards of Peking in the 1910s and some actual woodblocks to illustrate the techniques used in the country where printing first developed; educational toys in a collection which happens to house the world's earliest printed book.

References

1. Edward Miller *That Noble Cabinet: a history of the British Museum* (London, 1973).
2. Ibid.
3. Ibid.
4. Ibid.
5. J J L Duyvendak, 'Early Chinese studies in Holland' in *T'oung Pao*, XXXII (Leiden, 1936).
6. W D Macray, *Annals of the Bodleian Library*, 2nd ed. (Oxford, 1890). For more on Shen Fuzong, see also Professor Barrett's paper in this collection, p. 15.
7. W T Whitley, *Artists and their friends in England* (London, 1928).
8. Ibid.
9. Hugh Honour, *Chinoiserie: the vision of Cathay* (London, 1961).
10. *Speaking for the future: a review of the requirements of diplomacy and commerce for Asian and African languages and area studies* (The Parker Report), (University Grants Committee, London, 1986), see references in Professor Barrett's and B C Bloomfield's papers in this collection, pp. 39–43, pp. 4, 7.
11. Liu Ts'un-yan, *Chinese fiction in two London libraries* (Hong Kong, 1967).
12. Robert Kennaway Douglas, *Catalogue of Chinese printed books ... in the library of the British Museum* (London, 1877).
13. Yves Hervouet, 'Les bibliothèques chinoises de l'Europe occidentale' in *Mélanges ... L'Institut des Hautes Etudes Chinoises*, 1 (Paris, 1957).
14. H A Giles, *Adversaria Sinica*, II (Shanghai, 1914).
15. For an up-to-date definition of *shan ben*, see Ji Shuying's paper in this collection, pp. 161–9.
16. Hugh Trevor-Roper, *Hermit of Peking* ... (Harmondsworth, 1976).
17. Liu Ts'un-yan, *Chinese fiction in two London libraries* (Hong Kong, 1967).
18. *See* Jean-Pierre Drège's paper in this collection, pp. 171–4.
19. Li Zhizhong, 'Zhongguo shu shi yanjiu zhong de wenti (2)' in *Tu shu guan xue tong xun*, 2 (Beijing, 1987).
20. Roswell S Britton, *The Couling-Chalfant Collection* ... (Shanghai, 1935).
21. Samuel Couling, *Encyclopaedia Sinica* (reprint), (Hong Kong, 1983).

Paper and the book in China

Zhang Gong

Painters of the Tang period in Dunhuang and Turfan*

From the impressive scale and high level of achievement of Dunhuang wall paintings it is clear that in the fourth to tenth centuries there was a large body of artists in the area who possessed consummate artistic skills. Because the profession of artist was despised in feudal China, official records retain hardly any mention of this artist class. Today when people stand in this treasure-house of far eastern art, they are overwhelmed with admiration but almost completely ignorant about its creators. This paper attempts to investigate the changing social status of the Tang period painters (618–905) in the Hexi area of North-west China, on the basis of historical records from Dunhuang and Turfan along with other fragmentary historical references.

In the kingdom of Karakhoja in the early Tang period, painters in the Longyou area formed part of the wider class of craftsmen, and were called 'painting artisans'. A document from Turfan, *Tang he hao ren deng jiang ren ming ji* (names of artisans, first section) first lists the names of 13 tailors, leather workers and carpenters and then lists painters 'Shi X cai; Lian Mao huang; Su Shanshou; these are painters.'[1] Another document, *Tang Xi zhou du du fu zhu si, ding, cang ku deng pei yi ming ji*[2] also reveals artists in line 2: '[beginning missing] 1. X Saizi, copper worker; 2. X Haihui, bowmaker; 3. X X Hai, painter [end missing]'.

Both name lists were made by contemporary official authorities. The first can be dated to c.693 AD and is a list of artisans awaiting summons to state labour (*daiyi*) while the second is after 640 AD and is an official list of artisans fulfilling state labour service. The difference between the two lists shows that in the first, Shi and others are artisans waiting to do their service, and in the second X X Hai has already fulfilled his service; this has been 'certified by the examiner'.

The artisan class, including painters in Karakhoja and Hexi in early Tang China were the descendants of the 'hundred craftsmen' of the sixteen kingdoms and Northern Wei periods (fourth to sixth centuries) in these regions. In the Northern Wei period, the 'hundred craftsmen' were considered 'despicable families' of the 'low-class people';[3] they lived together grouped by profession;[4] professions were hereditary;[5] and status could not be changed from one generation to the next. Craftsmen had to fulfil 'service' for the official authorities, and were craftsmen-slaves dependent upon feudal officials. In the mid-sixth century the status of the hundred craftsmen changed. In 531 AD the Northern Wei court issued an edict:

*Translated from the Chinese by Beth McKillop.

'The hundred craftsmen now are raised to the category of people [*min*] but must carry out service as before.'⁶ In 551 AD another edict proclaimed: 'Apart from craftsmen and shepherds, workers, other categories of slaves are allowed to take the status of ordinary people [*baihu*]'.⁷ So, all those artisan households including painters who were originally classified as low-class families were for the first time removed from the status of artisan-slave and took on the status of 'people'.

At the Taifusi in the northern Qi period there was an official in charge of painting cave temple paintings.⁸ Officials in the kingdom of Karakhoja often carried out work on contract for Wei and Qi and perhaps the Hexi painters in Karakhoja who mainly carried out government service by painting in Buddhist cave temples did so under the jurisdiction of the 'cave temple official'. The second document mentioned above lists 'men fu' and 'cang zi' and other service undertaken by *ding* and *zhong* males alongside painters' service. This demonstrates that in the Zhenguan period of the Tang (627–650), painters from Hexi had the same social status as ordinary householders.

The craftsmen classes including painters in the Tang had thus attained the same social status as ordinary households, but in the early part of the Tang, vestiges of craftsmen's earlier dependent relationship on the feudal officials survived. One significant instance is that the Tang authorities continued to exercise close control over the hereditary transmission of some craftsmen's professions. As early as the Yanxing period of the Northern Wei (471–476) the authorities formally permitted craftsmen to change professions and to become farmers.⁹ Between the Sui and the Tang periods (late sixth to early seventh centuries) quite a few artisans made their living mainly from farming, while at the same time maintaining their family profession, thus combining art and agriculture; a considerable number of craftsmen continued to make their living mainly through their inherited professions. These two groups of artisans both maintained the tradition of hereditary transmission of crafts. They were different from households which had been farmers for generations and therefore continued to occupy a specially important place in fulfilling the artistic side of state service required by officials, unlike the farming families which mainly rendered tax to the state in the form of ordinary '*dingyi*' tax. The Tang code specifies *ding* tax and artisans tax as 20 days,¹⁰ the only difference being that they were fulfilled in different ways, originally without distinction in the time required. But the Tang code also specified that in a family of craftsmen 'once someone is classified as a certain kind of artisan he may not change to other branches',¹¹ so the family profession could not be changed. This meant that craftsmen were more closely dependent on the authorities than ordinary farming households.

This can be seen as an important reason for the continuation in Tang society of the traditional practice of despising artists and technicians. The social status of all Tang craftsmen including painters is revealed as being more humble and lower than most ordinary households. The treatment and attitude of the great early Tang painter Yan Liben graphically illustrate this pattern. According to the *Jiu tang shu* in the biographies section, Yan Liben's father Yan Bi was famous in Sui times as a painter and Yan Liben soon learned the family trade, becoming well-known as a painter. One day the emperor Taizong (r.626–649) went out boating and called on Yan Liben to make a picture 'calling outside the pavilion, "painter Yan Liben"' to summon him into his courtyard. At that time Yan Liben had already become a noble gentleman, the assistant to a fifth grade high official, and upon hearing himself referred to as a painter he 'blushed furiously' and brooded over the incident for a long time afterwards. He saw his status as a kind of slavery, 'nothing could be worse', and he warned his son 'not to follow this useless profession'. Yan Liben hated being called a painter and regarded painting as a profession with no future. This certainly shows the chasm separating a famous painter from ordinary painters doing state service, and also demonstrates the low esteem in which Tang painters, regarded as servants, were held.

The motive for the Tang court's strict control by legal decree over the mobility of craftsmen was to ensure that there were enough craftsmen and artists to build and maintain royal palaces and official *yamen* at various levels. In the early Tang, fairly heavy official demands were made of painters and other artisans. Whether they worked for the official authorities, or were called out by civil or military *yamen*, they had to work for long periods without being allowed to go home.

In the mid-eighth century, Du Huan saw two Chang'an artists in the Caliphate of 'Abbasid (Dashi), Fan Shu and Liu Ci, starting to paint there.[12] These two were perhaps the Chang'an painters who had been conscripted into the army and were taken prisoner on the Talas River in 751AD after Gao Xianzhi was defeated by the Arabs. These two Chang'an painters who ended up in the Caliphate of 'Abbasid and had to live so far from home exemplify the sad fate of Tang painters carrying out government duties.

The gradual easing of the close dependence of painters on officialdom in Tang times and the improvement in painters' social position are both connected to the developing commodity economy and hired labour relations at that time. Compared to the '*Liuganjiang*' system of the Zhou and Sui periods (557–618) in which each artisan spent two months a year on government service,[13] the Tang rules allowing 20 days labour service per year and the change of profession from one generation to the next generally made it more common for artists to arrange their working patterns freely. Apart from farming and doing government duty, artists also hired themselves out and painted for wages, as had been happening for many years – there are plenty of records of such practices in the history books. In the Tang period, and particularly in the mid-Tang, the development of the commodity economy and the rise of Buddhist monasteries meant that many more painters were hired and some even made their living from hiring themselves out to paint pictures. According to historical records, the Zen Abbot Yan of Bingzhou in the early Tang period 'sought out painters all over the land' to paint Avalokiteśvara and Mahāsthāmaprāpta Bodhisattva figures for his monastery.[14] In the Wu Zetian period (684–701) monks at Yuehua temple also summoned painters looking for work to paint for their temple.[15] In the Kaiyuan era (713–742), in Jiangzhou, painters were hired at Dayun temple 'to paint seven Avalokiteśvara figures'.[16] These hired artists all painted for temples, showing that Tang temples and monasteries were an important arena and breeding ground for a whole group of talented artists to demonstrate and develop their artistic abilities. All kinds of

Buddhist stories and figures were painted by artists of the Tang. The exquisite mural paintings in the Dunhuang temples took shape under these circumstances.

In Tang times, the Hexi area was at the eastern edge of the Silk Road, on an important route between east and west, and was on the path through which Buddhism entered China from India. From the Kaiyuan period to the end of the Tang era into the Five Dynasties (713–c.950), as trade flourished and temples blossomed, the area from Khotan to Dunhuang already boasted a large group of highly accomplished hired painters. In this area, employment for painters varied according to the scale of the work they undertook and may be described as short, medium and long-term projects. According to 'Accounts of the monastery in Khotan'[17] between 713 and 742, this monastery 'paid 80 *wen* to the painter Yena for his services to paint banners'. The Khotanese painter Yena was hired to paint dragons and phoenixes and when the painting was done he was paid by the monastery, thus ending the relationship between employer and employee. This is an example of the simplest kind of employment: short-term. Used for small projects lasting a few days, the formalities were fairly straightforward: sometimes the employer sought out painters and at other times painters looked for jobs.[18] Employer and painter would make a contract based on the painting and the payment for the job.

Another kind of work pattern is described in Dunhuang manuscript S.4642, dating from the mid-tenth century and recording grain rations. 'Two piculs and five *sheng* of flour given to the painter ... eight pecks of flour for the painter ... two *sheng* of oil for the painter.' The first two examples mention two piculs, five *sheng* and eight pecks of flour, equivalent approximately to three months supply for a hired painter. This allows us to imagine that the painter was employed for at least three man-months and his project was a fairly big one. We can regard these painters being employed for a few weeks or a few months as medium-term labour. In the Kaicheng period of Wenzong's reign in the Tang dynasty (836–841) in Chang'an, the Japanese monk Ennin hired the master painter Wang Hui of Yongchang fang to paint Womb-realm Maṇḍalas and Diamond-realm Maṇḍalas: 'the fee was agreed ... five Womb-realm Maṇḍalas 50 strings of cash, five Diamond-realm Maṇḍalas 6,000 *wen* plus expenses for materials'[19] Compared with the Khotanese painter Yena's 80 *wen*, Wang Hui got 1,200 for each Maṇḍala which is 150 times as much. This startling difference in the two men's fees arises because the Maṇḍala are extremely complex, large-scale pieces which require a high level of skill, while painting dragons and phoenixes on a banner is fairly easy and commands a lower wage. Wang Hui's painting of the diamond-realm Maṇḍala took him from the 22nd day of the 12th month of 840AD until the 8th day of the 2nd year of Kaicheng, 47 days altogether, so it should be considered medium-length. From S.4642 we also know that, at least in the Dunhuang area, all painters being hired for a fairly long period would have provisions and materials (silk guaze, colours, oils, etc.) supplied by the employers. If the painters supplied materials themselves the employers then had to add in extra recompense. Ennin agreed with Wang Hui to pay '6000 *wen* on top of the cost of silk gauze' showing that the textile for painting on was accounted separately.

When Dunhuang temples hired painters, the work sometimes lasted for a few months or even a year or more. Compared to short and medium-term work contracts, employer–employee relations in long-term jobs were closer and more stable. Long-term employment always occurred when the project concerned was on a large scale, more complex in theme and required more time. According to the Dunhuang document P.2032, dating from 884, 'Jingtu temple prepared its accounts in the following way: Nine piculs of rice for the painter and his assistants. Three pecks of white flour and two *sheng* of oil, four pecks of rice, blue and red colours for the walls... Five pecks of rice; green colour for the painter... Two piculs, three pecks and five *sheng* of rice, wine, for when the walls of the bell tower are being prepared, to be given to the painters and sculptors and the monks helping them as they work ... Five pecks of rice, and green colour for the painter.' Although we do not know the number of people employed at the temple or how long for, it is clear that since one payment to the painter's assistant was more than nine piculs of grain, this was equivalent to the ration for one worker for nine months. Fairly large quantities of colours, flour, oil and so on were bought for the painter to use as materials, showing that the painting was on a large scale. And since quite a lot of red and blue and green were ordered, it looks as if they were used to paint murals inside the temple.

From the huge number of Buddhist wall paintings which survive at Dunhuang, from the imaginative composition and the fineness of the colours, it is obvious that the work could not have been carried out in a short period by ordinary painters. It was definitely achieved through long-term employment of a larger number of top-grade masters. It is very likely that most long-term hired painters were taken on to work on wall paintings for temples. Temple paintings were a major tool of religious propaganda, making enormous demands on the painters' technical skills; so the selection of long-term workers was serious, considered matter. In the time of Wu Zetian (684–701) when Yunhua temple took on painters to paint wall paintings, the temple monks would 'look over the brushwork' – in other words, inspect some sample paintings by the artist-candidates before making a final decision. The painters seeking employment who were accomplished painters were keen to 'push the price up' or demand a higher fee from the employer.

In Longyou (Gansu province) temples also took a great deal of care when engaging long-term hired painters. Because the paintings done by long-term employed painters were important and significant, the painter and the employer went through a lengthy period of mutual inspection and repeated weighing up, arriving at a full understanding of each other so that during the period of employment the relationship between the two parties was close and stable. The Jingfu temple at Dunhuang not only paid the painter's wages, it also offered wine when 'ash paste' was being applied to the walls of the bell tower,[21] to show that the temple was a caring employer and perhaps to encourage the artists to put their best efforts into the painting. This exceedingly generous treatment of painters by employers demonstrates that in the late Tang, employed painters' social status had changed very noticeably from the artist-artisan stratum closely dependent on officialdom and required to perform state labour. Under the arrangements between employer and employee the close physical and personal dependence of the past had been relaxed. From the mid-Tang onwards, Longyou temple wall paintings were usually done by countless talented painters working as hired artists.

Notes

1. *Tu lu fan chu tu wen shu*, vol. 4, p. 16.
2. *Tu lu fan chu tu wen shu*, vol. 6, p. 89.
3. *Wei shu: Gao zong Ji; 8th month of 468AD*: 'it is commanded that royal family, masters, nobles and ordinary people must not marry the hundred craftsmen.'
4. *Wei shu: Hun zi lin fu zi xian zhuan.*
5. *Wei shu: Shi zu ji*: 'The skills of the hundred craftsmen, ... are learned by following the father's profession.'
6. *Wei shu: Qian fei di ji.*
7. *Bei ji shu: Wen xuan di ji.*
8. *Sui shu: Bin guan zhi.*
9. *Wei shu: Gao zu ji.* In the fourth month of 472AD 'merchants and craftsmen were permitted to follow agriculture at the same time as practising their trade.'
10. *Tong dian juan 6.* Foodstuffs: 'all farmers and craftsmen to render 20 days work, plus 2 days in intercalary years.'
11. *Tang liu dian juan 7* 'gongbu' note.
12. *Tong dian juan 193*, 'bian fang dian', note.
13. *Sui shi Shi huo zhi.*
14. *Song Gao zong zhuan juan 18, Tang Yan chan shi zhuan.*
15. *Yuan shi zhi juan 1.*
16. *Tai ping guang ji juan 111, zeng dao xuan.*
17. Ikeda On, *Chugoku kodai sekicho kenkyu*, p. 349.
18. *Song Gao zeng zhuan juan 18 Tang yan chan shi zhuan.*
19. Ennin *Ennin's diary ...*, tr. Reischauer (New York, 1955).
20. *Xuan shi zhi juan 1.*
21. That is, applying mud-paste to walls in preparation for painting.

Song Jiayu

The evolution of the Tang household records and census system reflected in Dunhuang manuscripts*

In order to control and govern its citizens, the Tang dynasty (618–907AD) adopted strict census laws, based on the population records of earlier dynasties. From household records and census documents discovered in Dunhuang and Turfan it has been established that each local administrative area carried out regular periodic population investigations and registrations in the early Tang. But the historical record is not clear about whether this practice continued into the later Tang period. Some late Tang documents relating to population questionnaires and registrations, discovered at Dunhuang, show that the system was still upheld, up to a certain point, but the form of the household returns and census documents changed and it is often difficult to distinguish between documents of this kind. I shall now summarise the results of my research into these documents over the past few years.

Notable features of household returns and census documents in the early Tang period

In the *Shi huo zhi* of the *Xin tang shu*, Ouyang Xiu wrote: 'There was a return for each village (*li*) and at the year's end all the people had to state their ages and landholdings, making a local record ...'. In 1074AD, Lü Huiqing memorialised: 'according to the census regulations, land and dwellings should both be verified.'[1] According to Niida Noburu's findings, Lü Huiqing was referring to a census regulation of the Tiansheng period (1023–1031AD) and the Tiansheng period ordinances were amended versions of the Tang ordinances, so it is reasonable to suppose that in essence this followed the Tang code.[2] Thus it seems that the household records required at periodic intervals by the Tang authorities demanded information on the household numbers and land held. In the 1960s, Chinese archaeologists discovered a large number of official and private Tang period documents in the Turfan area. Among the most significant documents are

*Translated from the Chinese by Beth Mckillop.

household records from between the Zhenguan and Zaichu periods (627–689AD) from Astana and Karakhoja graveyards. They verify the account in the historical record quoted on p. 114 above.[3]

These household records fall into three main categories:
1. Names, sex and age of head of household and household members, and state of health (for example, aged male, able-bodied male, middle-aged male, etc.).
2. Land (number of *mou* belonging to or worked by the household).
3. Head of household's affirmation (for example: 'If anyone discovers that what I have said is untrue, I beg to be punished for disobedience to imperial command'). The Tang law code (*Tang lü shu yi*) chapters 1 and 2 notes: 'the village head's duty is to record the population, gather in the household records and make the census.' This shows that household records were gathered for district officials every three years when they compiled the census. The village heads had the task of collecting them. (The Tang regulations stipulated 'Every hundred families were organised into a village, with one village head to regulate them.') But in the household registers of the Zhenguan and Zaichu periods discovered in Xinjiang, all the household records in one village are in the same handwriting and all are joined together to make a scroll which shows that, in reality, they were actually written by the village heads in place of the heads of households, then joined into a scroll and submitted to the county authorities. On the evidence of these household returns, petty officials at village and county level compiled census returns according to the Tang regulations on the basis of this information. The many Tang census documents discovered at Dunhuang and Turfan were compiled on the basis of household records of this kind.

The earliest known Tang census to survive is one found in the Turfan area, from Xizhou, dating from between the Zhenguan and Yongzheng periods (627–655AD).[4] The latest such document is from Dunhuang county, Xuanquan Nayihe village, and dates from 770AD, and although it is usually called a household register, it is in fact a census return (British Library s.513). What these two census documents have in common is that they are fundamentally organised into two parts, by names (population) and fields (land records). The name part records heads of household and family members' sex, age and fitness, health and status. The land part shows how much land should be allocated to each household, how much has been given out and the amount due, as well as currently held, inheritable (*yongye*) and personal share (*koufen*) land – its state, position, area and extent. Further, the name part makes copious individual notes against each name: recording births, deaths, movements and fleeings. Changes in people's health, tax position and so on are also noted. In the Zhenguan period (627–649AD), such notes on census records were fairly simple, but by the Kaiyuan and Tianbao periods (713–755AD) they had become more detailed.[5]

Household records of the later Tang

Census laws changed somewhat by the late Tang. The most important change was the move away from the three yearly interval rule. At the same time, changes developed in the content and form of both household reports of population and landholdings and in official census compilations. One group of documents of this type survives from Dunhuang.

In the period of Turfan's occupation of Dunhuang (781–85AD) the local authorities continued to enforce the Tang law code, and to demand that households submit records. British Library s.3287 verso is a document of this kind. In *Dun huang zi liao* no. 1 this document was named 'an incomplete record of Jifu'.[6] In these records, the first part is the list of names, sex, age, and changes in family members. The second part is the family head's affirmation, for example: 'All this is a true record of the facts, if it is discovered to be false may I be severely punished.' When these documents are compared to the early Tang household records from Turfan they appear to be very similar, apart from the absence of landholding records. The form of the document is *die* (official document) or *zhuang* (report), just like the earlier ones. This shows that they were compiled as household registers. Likewise, since this was the period of occupation by Turfan, household register questionnaires followed Turfan tax laws and left out land records.

After Dunhuang was returned to Tang rule in Dazhong 6 (852) the local authorities again required household registers to be carried out. But now the information required was different. Some documents which originally made up one scroll are now scattered between London, Paris and Leningrad.[7] (Ikeda and Yamamoto have both written on the 852 census.[8]) The first part of the 852 census documents consists of the names, sex and age of family members. The second part contains land records: the total land for each household, its disposition and extent. The third part is the household head's affirmation: 'The information given here is all correct.'

These are exactly the same as the household records of the early Tang period. They are also in the form of *die* and *zhuang*. The 852 household records show that when families reported their numbers and land holdings, there was no mention of able-bodied males or other distinctions of age and health, nor of inheritable land, personal share land or other kinds of landholding. This reveals that the Tang census law (*huling*) about distinctions between types of person by health, and distinctions between different types of landholding, had ceased to be enforced by the late Tang. However, the population still had to report family size and landholdings, if in a more simplified form.

Late Tang census records

The Dunhuang manuscripts which relate to late Tang household registrations have been given different titles by various scholars. Until now, though, no one has regarded them as containing population records. Following my argument above, the household reports of 852 are in fact household records (*shoushi*). By analogy with early Tang period household records and their relationship to census records, we can make deductions about the 852 documents. For example, British Library s.6235 (household register of Tang Junsheng, dated 852) reports family members and landholdings in the following manner:

household (hu)	Tang Junsheng	age 37	wife	Asu	Age 20
brothers	Junyi	age 35	xx		Age xx
father	Moya	age 63	wife	Aji	Age xx
land 47 mou[9]					

Another Dunhuang manuscript (P.4989 in the Bibliothèque Nationale) with similar information, similarly presented, confirms this impression. It has incomplete records of the members of three households and their landholdings – 20 lines in total.[10] A comparison of the format and content of P.4989 and S.6235 shows that they are of the same type. The records of Zhang Xiaoshun are as follows:

Household (hu)	Zhang Xiaoshun	age 30	wife Achen	age 25
daughter	Youxiu [?]	age 2		
and 10 mou[11]				

As discussed earlier, in the case of Tang Junsheng's household record, we can affirm that P.4989 is also a population record. The only difference between these and early Tang population records is that they are less detailed. If our argument is correct, then BN. MS P.3384 and Luo Zhenyu collection MS *Sha zhou Gui Ming ming hu* (an 891 population record) also fall into the category of population records, or source material for compiling population records. These manuscripts demonstrate major differences from early Tang population records:
1. The formula household (hu) x x x [Name] must imply 'householder' (huzhu), though the term itself does not appear.
2. Population and landholdings are listed separately, although names and land are listed in consecutive order and not in separate lines for each name and each piece of land.
3. The name list omits state of health (ding, zhong) and makes no notes.
4. The land is listed as a lump figure of actual current land held with no annotation of land received, due, inheritable land or personal share land.
5. In landholding records, the character *xi* is used to mean a large unit.
This all demonstrates that late Tang population records were very much simplified compared to early Tang records, and although there are still a few references to 'allocated land', 'requested land', etc., these are no longer affirmed as part of the equal field law and they do not serve as quotas limiting the amount of land held. The population records refer to 'land allocated', 'district allocated land', 'requested land', etc., which may arise from the late Tang practice of requesting from the authorities permission to take over unfarmed land.

Conclusions

To sum up, the most important purpose of Tang household returns and population records was to register population and land holdings. By the late Tang, household returns and population records had changed substantially in form and content. The abolition of the equal field law and the direct taxation system (*zu yong diao fa*), the implementation of the two tax laws and changes in the actual pattern of land occupation were important factors leading to changes in household returns and population records.

Notes

1. *Xu zi zhi tong jian chang bian*, ch. 254.
2. *Torei shui* (Tokyo, 1964), preface.
3. *Tu lu fan chu tu wen shu* (Beijing, 1981), vols 4, 6 and 7.
4. *Tu lu chu tu wen shu*, vol. 6.
5. See Ikeda On, *Chugoku kodai sekicho kenkyu* ('Research into ancient Chinese census records'), notes abstracted in the Chinese journal *Zhong guo shi yan jiu*, 1981:6, 'Tang dai hu ji shang de tian ji yu jun tian zhi' ('Land records and the equal field system in Tang census documents').
6. Also discussed by Ikeda, *Chugoku kodai sekicho kenkyu*, notes, p. 519 and in T Yamamoto *et al.*, *Tunhuang and Turfan documents* (Tokyo, 1980), vol. 2, p. 98.
7. British Library S.6235 verso, Bibliothèque Nationale P.3245 verso; L I Chuguevskogo and L N Men'shikov *Kitaiskie dokumenty iz Dunkhuana: faksimile;* (Moscow, 1983–), vol. 1.
8. See Ikeda, *Chugoku kodai sekicho kenkyu*, pp. 569–70 and Yamatoto, *Tunhuang and Turfan documents*, pp. 100–01.
9. Details of the land boundaries omitted [translator's note].
10. See Ikeda, *Chugoku kodai sekicho kenkyu*, p. 105 and Yamatoto *Tunhuang and Turfan documents* for further discussion of this manuscript.
11. Details of land boundaries omitted [translator's note].

Yanwen Liu and David Arrandale

An Introduction to the Dunhuang manuscript, *Shi yao zi yang*

This paper concerns the lost Tang Dynasty book, *Shi yao zi yang* ('Samples of Characters Essential for the Present Day'),[1] which has been partially recovered from two Dunhuang manuscripts, S.5731 and S.6208.[2] The value of the book for the study of the standardisation of writing and speech sounds in the Tang Dynasty is also outlined.

The recovery of the *Shi yao zi yang* from the Dunhuang manuscripts

The *Shi yao zi yang* was one of the Chinese character books, analogous with *Yan shi zi yang* ('Yan's Samples of Characters') and *Gan lu zi shu* ('Samples of Characters for Officials'), compiled in order to standardise writing in the Tang period. All copies of the original text were lost long ago, and there is now no way of identifying the author. To my knowledge, the second volume is still extant, though incomplete, in the Dunhuang manuscripts S.5731 and S.6208.

There are short descriptions of the content of these two manuscripts in the *Descriptive Catalogue of the Chinese Manuscripts from Tunhuang in the British Museum*[3] by Dr Lionel Giles and in *Dun huang yi shu zong mu suo yin* ('General Catalogue of Dunhuang manuscripts')[4] by Liu Mingshu. These descriptions are as follows:

S.5731, Lionel Giles: *Shi yao zi yang*
Samples of characters essential for the present day. A list of characters ... arranged more or less according to rhymes or phonetics. Each is followed by one or more characters giving a rough clue to the sense, and in many cases the explanatory term is followed by a number (varying from 1 to 6, with one 8) of doubtful import ... most of the lower portion torn away ...

Liu Mingshu: *Shi yao zi yang*, Volume 2
Section 3 and section 4 are extant.

S.6208 [a manuscript in 5 fragments], Lionel Giles:
1. Dictionary or phraseology ... Beginning mutilated. With one small fragment. The following categories remain: [food and drink category, fruit category, ginger and bamboo shoot category, mat category, cloth category, seven-things category, wine category] ...
2. Part of a list of characters with brief explanations, and 3 smaller fragments. Title at beginning: [Xin shang lue gu jin zi yang zuo qi shi yao bing yin zheng shi Volume 2].[5]

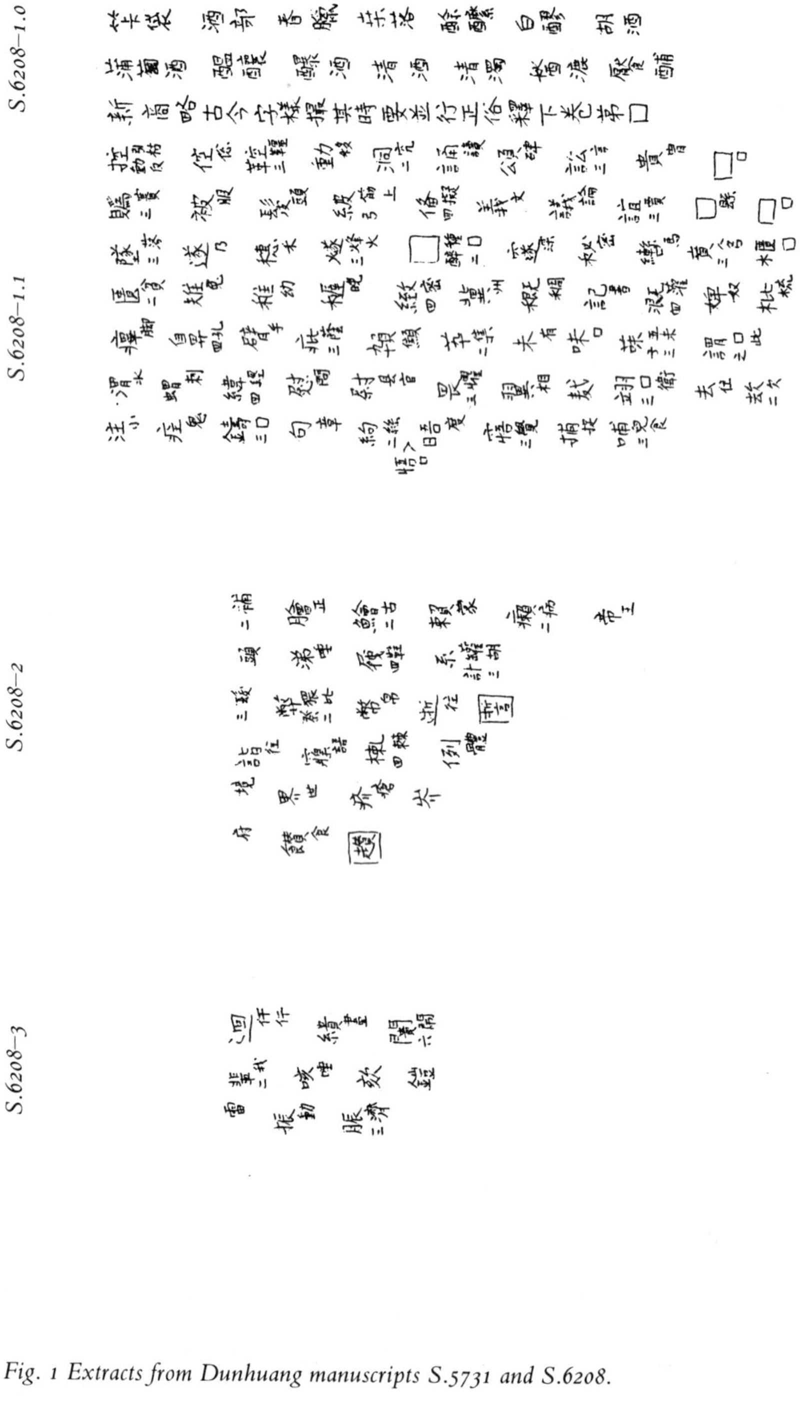

Fig. 1 Extracts from Dunhuang manuscripts S.5731 and S.6208.

S.5731

S.6208-4

Liu Mingshu: *Xin shang lue gu jin zi yang zuo qi shi yao bing yin zheng shi*, Volume 1 and Volume 2

The beginning of volume 1 mutilated. The following categories remain: music category, food and drink category, fruit category, mat category, seven-things category and wine category. Volume 2 consists of a list of characters.

From the above quotations, we can draw the following conclusions from the viewpoints of Giles and Liu. Liu considers that S.6208 contains both volume one and volume two of *Xin shang lue gu jin zi yang zuo qi shi yao bing xing zheng su shi*; while Giles believed that S.6208 includes only volume two, and he described the first part of S.6208 as a 'Dictionary of Phraseology'.

Although Giles mentioned 'a list of characters' in S.5731 and in the second part of S.6208, neither he nor Liu realised that S.5731 and S.6208 were originally the same manuscript nor that *Shi yao zi yang* and *Xin shang lue gu jin zi yang zuo qi shi yao bing xing zheng su shi* are two different titles for the same book.

Our own conclusions are as follows: Firstly, S.5731 and S.6208 were originally one manuscript. Of the surviving five fragments, one fragment was given the number S.5731, and four given the number S.6208 by Sir Aurel Stein. On the largest fragment of S.6208 there is a title, *Xin shang lue gu jin zi yang zuo qi shi yao bing xing zheng su shi*, volume two. The text on either side is different. For convenience, we will call the text on the right side the first part of S.6208; and we will call the text on the left and of the other small fragments, the second part of S.6208. S.5731 and the second part of S.6208 together form a portion of a book with the title *Shi yao zi yang* or *Xin shang lue gu jin zi yang zuo qi shi yao bing xing zheng su shi*. Furthermore, *Shi yao zi yang* and *Xin shang lue gu jin zi yang zuo qi shi yao bing xing zheng su shi* are two different titles for the same book.

In addition, the first part of S.6208 must be part of another kind of character book arranged according to categories of activities. It is definitely not the first part of the *Shi yao zi yang*.

To prove our conclusions and give detailed descriptions of recovery of the *Shi yao zi yang*, it is necessary to deal further with the content of S.5731 and the second part of S.6208. To begin with, we will designate the first part of S.6208 as S.6208–1.0, while the subsequent parts are numbered S.6208–1.1, S.6208–2, S.6208–3, and S.6208–4 respectively. The original text of these four fragments and part of S.5731 is shown on pp. 120 and 121.

First, let us look at S.6208–1.1. We see that a series of large characters are written in each line, and each character is followed by one or more small characters giving a brief explanation and, in certain cases, these are followed by the *fan qie* pronunciation.[6] It is worth noting that the order of these large characters is not haphazard. On the contrary, they are arranged according to strict rules which can be divided into three levels. The first level is 'tone', namely, characters are first listed in 'tone order'. We know that there are four tones in ancient Chinese: the first, or even tone; the second, or rising tone; the third, or falling tone, and the fourth, or abrupt tone. We find that all the large characters in S.6208–1.1 are classified into the third tone, i.e. the falling tone. The characters are first listed according to their tones, then, for those characters with the same tone, they are ordered by their 'rhymes'. The rhyming order is the second level. We can find that the characters in S.6208–1.1 are all arranged according to the rhyming order given by the *Qie yun*.[7]

The last level, namely the third level of order, is the 'initial consonant'. The characters beginning with the same initial consonant are listed together, if they are in the same tone and in the same rhyme. In other words, homonyms are listed in groups. There is also a number in each group denoting the number of characters having the same tone, same rhyme and same initial consonant.[8]

Basing our approach on the above analysis, we can know the content, the stylistic rules and layout of S.6208–1.1. Now we turn our attention to the remaining three fragments of S.6208. S.6208–2 and S.6208–3 are two small fragments, consisting of altogether only eight broken lines, with less than six characters in each line; while S.6208–4 is a larger piece of 13 half lines. Although these three fragments have been badly mutilated, they are perfectly consistent with S.6208–1.1 both in content and style (*see* p. 120 for more details). In brief, all their characters are in the falling tone and are also listed in the order of priorities: rhyme, initial consonant. Each large character is followed by one or more small characters giving a simple explanation, sound, and the number of homonyms. Obviously they and S.6208–1.1 come from the same manuscript. On the basis of the rhyming sequence in the *Qie yun*, it can be shown that the correct order for the four relevant fragments of S.6208 is: S.6208–1.1, S.6208–2, S.6208–3, and S.6208–4.

Now that we have an insight into the second part of S.6208, we are able to deal with S.5731. In the middle of S.5731, there is the title, *Shi yao zi yang*, Volume 2, Section 4. On the left are listed all abrupt tone characters; on the right are listed all falling tone characters. Since abrupt tone characters have been indicated in Volume 2, Section 4, falling tone characters must be in Volume 2, Section 3. Both sections have the same style of compilation as S.6208–1.1, –2, –3, –4. When we were examining the falling tone part of S.5731 and S.6208–4 in accordance with rhyming order given by the *Qie yun*, we suspected that the broken lines 2–14 in S.5731 might connect with the broken lines 1–13 in S.6208–4. This is the case. We found that all the joins in the broken lines fit together and coincide perfectly. 'Rise' is the large character at the end of line no. 5 in S.5731, its gloss 'water' properly lies at the beginning of line no. 4 in S.6208–4; 'hinder' is the large character at the end of line no. 6 in S.5731, its gloss 'obstruct' properly lies at the beginning of line no. 5 in S.6208–4; and so forth.[9] As a result, all the broken lines in S.6208–4 connect with S.5731 without any gaps.

Thus we can conclusively demonstrate that S.5731 and S.6208 were originally the same manuscript, and that the *Shi yao zi yang* and the *Xin shang lue gu jin zi yang zuo qi shi yao bing xing zheng su shi* are the same book. Though the two titles appear to be different, their basic meaning is the same. Both imply that the book deals with sample characters, which were important at that time. It is probable that *Shi yao zi yang* is an abbreviated form of *Xing shang lue gu jin zi yang zuo qi shi yao bing xing zheng su shi*.

So far, we have put Section 3 and Section 4 of Volume 2 of the *Shi yao zi yang* in their proper order. Another question, which has not been addressed, is whether S.6208–1.0, (the first part of S.6208), is Volume 1 of the *Shi yao zi yang*. The answer must be negative, since S.6208–1.0 is not a list of sample characters. It has neither individual large characters nor small characters as notes, and it only gathers together some disyllabic words arranged according to categories of activities. Subtitles in the text include: fruit category, music category, mat category, and cloth category, etc. With regard to its content and style, it is totally different from the second part of S.6208. It seems more fitting to take it as a separate book containing miscellaneous collections of Chinese characters. From the contents of Volumes 3 and 4, we would infer that Volume 1 of the *Shi yao zi yang* should contain even tone and rising tone characters in Section 1 and Section 2 respectively. We hope that we can, in the near future, discover the missing Volume 1 and other parts of Volume 2 from fragmentary manuscripts which have not been catalogued by Dr Giles.

The research value of the *Shi yao zi yang*

There is no doubt that the recovery of the *Shi yao zi yang* will be of great value to us in our research work on standardisation of Chinese characters and speech sounds in Tang times. It is well known that Chinese characters have a long history of more than three thousand years. The use of unified characters in the vast territory of China with its large population would have been impossible without continual efforts to standardise the writing system. As early as the Qin dynasty (221–206BC), Qin shi huang di standardised the writing system and *xiao zhuan* characters were used throughout the country. The early Tang Dynasty was also faced with the arduous task of standardising writing. At that time, China had suffered nearly three hundred years of civil war during the Eastern Jin Dynasty (317–420AD), and the Northern and Southern Dynasties (420–581AD). The resultant disruption, along with the migration of the minority nationalities from the outlying districts to the interior of the country, had made the use of Chinese characters extremely confused. According to historical records, Tang Tai Zong issued an imperial edict ordering one of his ministers Yan Shigu to check the Five Classics.[10] In the course of this work, Yan had made out a list of model characters, known as *Yan Shi zi yang*, which was then circulated and copied among the people. Unfortunately, no copies appear to have survived. The rediscovery of the *Shi yao zi yang* will obviously supply important reference material for the study of standardisation of characters in the Tang period. It seems that the *Shi yao zi yang* focuses on distinctions between homonyms. There is a large number of homonyms in Chinese characters. For example, the sound *song* may have three different meanings: 'to read aloud', 'to sing praises', or 'to bring a case to court', if written with different characters.[11] As these three characters have the exactly same pronunciation, people may tend to use them interchangeably. Therefore, the *Shi yao zi yang* gives clear explanations of the use of each character. This is one aspect of standardising Chinese characters. Another important aspect is to distinguish the standard forms of Chinese characters from their popular forms. The partial title of this book *Bing xing zheng su shi* indicates that differentiation between running-hand, standardised and common forms of Chinese characters was also a significant component of the book. Unfortunately, only one instance was preserved.[12]

The *Shi yao zi yang* also provides us with valuable reference material for the study of pronunciation in Tang times. Great changes in Chinese pronunciation have taken place, both from ancient times to medieval times (from the third to the ninth century) and from medieval times to modern times. It is evident that Chinese characters are not alphabetic and do not themselves indicate sounds and changes in sounds. This fundamental aspect of Chinese characters causes difficulties in the study of the history of Chinese pronunciation. However, Chinese phoneticians have discovered some laws for variations in Chinese pronunciation. Among them is the law that, in ancient times, all Chinese characters in the rising tone with voiced initial consonants are today pronounced in the falling tone with voiceless initial consonants. Thus, two questions are left open. How exactly did this change come about? Did it go through two stages, with characters in the rising tone with voiced initial consonants first changing to the falling tone, and then developing voiceless initial consonants?

Up to now, the instances showing the change from 'rising tone with voiced consonant' to 'falling tone with voiced consonant' have been very few. There are eight examples in the *Shi yao zi yang*.[13] These examples indicate that some of the Chinese characters in the rising tone with voiced consonants had already become falling tone with voiced initial consonants at that time.

There are also other examples, which reflect the fact that several rhymes were combined into one.[14] All these examples serve to illustrate the value of the *Shi yao zi yang* for the study of pronunciation of Chinese characters. In short, verifying it from the Dunhuang manuscripts has been worth while.

Last but not least, is the question of the date when the *Shi yao zi yang* was written and the date of its transcription. The only clue is that a few fragmentary notes referring to the purchase of grain were written on the back of S.5731. These include a date, '6th year of Qian fu', namely 880AD. This means that the *Shi yao zi yang* on the front of S.5731 was transcribed earlier than 880, and its composition was obviously much earlier than 880.

Notes

1. 時要字樣
2. Stein numbers for Dunhuang manuscripts are adopted in this paper.
3. This is a full and systematic catalogue of Dunhuang manuscripts formerly kept in the British Museum (now in the British Library), published by the Trustees of the British Museum, London, 1957.
4. *Dun huang yi shu zong mu suo yin*, second edition (Zhong hua shu ju, Beijing, 1983).
5. 新商略古今字樣撰其時要並行正俗釋下卷. Incidentally, Dr Giles mistook '引正經' for '行正俗'.
6. Sometimes a number is also included in small characters, which indicates the number of homonyms.

7. There is, however, a doubt what rhymes 翼, 越 and 翊 should belong to.
8. For example 控, 倥, 箜 are homonyms listed in one group and the number is three. This kind of number puzzled Dr Giles.
9. Rise: 漲; water: 水; hinder: 妨; obstruct: 礙.
10. The 'Five Classics', namely, 'The Book of Songs', 'The Book of History', 'The Book of Changes', 'The Book of Rites', and 'The Spring and Autumn Annals'.
11. These Chinese characters are: 誚, 頌, 訟 respectively.
12. 贈正　贈古
13. The examples are: 勘, 挂, 婢, 蕩, 舅, 受, 湛, 厚.
14. For instance, the 送 rhyme and the 宋 rhyme are combined, as are the 真 rhyme and the 至 rhyme.

Andrew Lo

Dice, dominoes and card games in Chinese literature: a preliminary survey

Sources

This paper is a preliminary survey of the main sources for understanding dice, domino and card games of the Ming and Qing period. The sources that I have come across can be divided into four categories: monographs and manuals in Ming-Qing collectanea (*congshu*), anecdotal writings, scenes in Ming-Qing fiction, and modern studies of these games.

MONOGRAPHS AND MANUALS IN COLLECTANEA

Ming-Qing monographs on these games are difficult to come by these days, and I have managed to find two in rare book collections in Taiwan. Luckily, one function of collectanea is to preserve short works that may get lost easily, and on checking the indispensable *Zhong guo cong shu zong lu* ('A Bibliography of Chinese Collectanea'),[1] we find that three collectanea have preserved most of the manuals in question. They are:

1. *Shuo fu* ('Sayings within a City wall'), compiled by Tao Zongyi (1316–1403) before 1366, and the *Shuo fu xu* ('Sequel to Sayings within a City wall'), with preface dated 1647.

2. The *Tan ji cong shu* ('Sandalwood Table Collectanea') compiled by Wang Zhuo (1636–1699+) and Zhang Chao (1650–1707+) in 1695–1697.

3. The *Zhao dai cong shu* ('Collectanea of this Glorious Age') compiled by Zhang Chao and others from the period 1697–1844. There is a major study by Chang Bide on the *Shuofu*,[2] and in a previous paper, I have introduced a history of the compilation of the last two.[3]

ANECDOTAL WRITINGS

I cannot claim to have combed the vast amount of *biji xiaoshuo*, but three works proved indispensable for an understanding of these games. They are:

1. Wang Shihan's (1707–1780, *jinshi* degree 1733) *Ye xi yuan qi* ('On the Origin of Card Games').[4]

2. Jin Xueshi's *Mu zhu xian hua* ('Idle Talks on The Game of Swineherds') compiled in the late eighteenth century.[5] (The swineherd's game refers to gambling.)

3. Li Dou's *Yang zhou hua fang lu* ('The Decorated Boats of Yangzhou'), with preface dated the twelfth month of 1795.[6]

MING-QING FICTION

In the third category – Ming-Qing fiction, such works contain a wealth of scenes where these games are played out. It is impossible for me at this stage to comb through each Ming or Qing novel, but intuition tells me there is a wealth of material to be found in fiction of the late Qing period. For example, each of the three sequels to *Hong lou meng* ('Dream of the Red Chamber') that I mention later on contains scenes where these games are described. There are at least seven more nineteenth-century sequels to *Hong lou meng* to work through.

MODERN STUDIES

In the last category, Stewart Culin's works on games published in the late nineteenth century and onwards contain valuable information on games played then and provide a useful reference point.[7] Yang Yinshen's *Zhong guo you yi yan jiu* ('Chinese Games and Skills') published in 1946 contains much information on how some of our games are played.[8]

Manuals and scenes in Ming and Qing fiction

Having introduced some of the main sources, I would like to devote the rest of the paper to the manuals and scenes in Ming and Qing fiction.

MANUALS ON DICE

Manuals on the type of dice with six faces and pips date from the Song to the Ming period.[9] These are relatively simple to understand and describe games ranging from the use of one die to six dice. The use of dice with board games such as backgammon (*shuanglu*), etc., is another category of research that will provide much pleasure. Here, however, we shall focus on two other related families of games, one belonging to the domino family, and the other belonging to the card game of three or four suits.

But before we go any further, I would like to clarify some terminology. First, the Chinese term 'pai' can refer to a card or a tile. That is, a 'pai' can be made of paper, ivory or bone. Second, most paper, ivory or bone 'pai' will either have the pip markings of the domino family or markings of the four suits. In other words, when a manual or a scene in a novel simply mentions the word 'pai', we still do not know exactly which game is played. Clues such as pips or suit markings are required; better still, sometimes the exact name of the game is mentioned.

Fig. 2 A domino scene in Jinpingmei Cihua.

MANUALS ON DOMINOES

Scholars trace the invention of the domino game to the second year of the Xuanhe period (1112).[10] but as with the history of card games, it is only in the Ming period that we begin to have information on how the games are played. The following is a list of extant manuals:

1. Qu You's (1347–1433) *Xuan he pai pu* ('Manual of Xuanhe Period Dominoes') lists names of 66 combinations of dominoes. Each combination is also accompanied by a line of corresponding imagery from a Tang poet.

2. Gu Yingxiang's (1483–1565) *Pai pu* ('Manual of Dominoes')[12] lists names of sixty combinations, each accompanied by a corresponding line of imagery from a Tang or Song poet. Gu Yingxiang is a famous mathematician of the Ming period.

3. Zhang Qiaosou's *Ying pu* ('The Glume Manual')[13] describes a game of 64 dominoes, different from the game of 32. This game contains blanks, and corrects the notion that western dominoes have blanks and Chinese ones do not.

4. Qiyunzi's *Pai tong fu yu* (preface 1639) is a rare work in the Library of Congress Collection.[14] I have yet to consult it.

5. Jin Xingyuan's *Xuan he pu ya pai hui ji* ('A Miscellany on the Xuanhe Period Domino Game') with preface dated 1757 survives in the Fu Sinian Library, Taiwan, and contains much information on the game.[15]

MANUALS ON CARDS

1. Pan Zhiheng's (1556–1622) *Ye zi pu* ('Manual on Cards')[16] and *Xu ye zi pu* ('Sequel to Manual on Cards')[17] are the earliest extant manuals on card games. I have yet to decipher the section on the *madiao* game.

2. Feng Menglong's (1574–1646) *Pai jing* ('Classic of Cards')[18] and *Ma diao jiao li* ('Rules of the Madiaojiao Game.)[19] concentrate on the *madiao* game. The texts are also difficult to decipher.

3. Li Suiqiu's (1602–1646) *Yun zhang jing* ('Classic of Deploying Cards in one's Palms')[20] represents a Cantonese claim to scholarship in gambling. The work is a philosophical reading of the forty-card game.

4. Wu Weiye's (1609–1672) *Ye gong zhuan* ('Biography of Lord Ye')[2] is a pseudobiography of a card.

5. Li Shiyu's (1622–?) *Si shi zhang zhi pai shuo* ('On the Forty Paper Cards')[22] renders a philosophical interpretation of the card game.

6. Li Yesi's (1622–1680) *Ma diao shuo* ('On the Madiao Game')[23] is a fanciful reading of the game which tries to argue that the game predicted the fall of the Ming, and reading *diao* to mean 'lament', argues that the game laments the ministers Ma Shiying (1591–1647) and Ma Jixiang (died 1661).

7. Shouan jushi's *Ma diao pu* ('Manual on the Madiao Game') is a Qing period manuscript in the National Central Library collection.[24] It gives a very detailed description of the game, but parts I have yet to decipher.

8. Finally, there is Zheng Xudan's *Hun tong tian pai pu* ('Manual of a Card Game by a Fellow Traveller in Primordial Heaven')[25] which describes a new game invented by the author, combining principles of the *madiao* card game and the *tianjiu* domino game.

I have been complaining about the difficulty of reading some of the above texts, and I am sorry to say, I fare no better in trying to comprehend some scenes describing these games in Ming-Qing fiction. That being the case, I think if I first locate some of these scenes in fiction, then the two types of sources (manuals and fiction scenes) should throw light on each other, and I can then proceed with a full-length study of the subject. The following then is a list of 22 titles in Ming-Qing fiction which contain these scenes.

	TILES/CARDS WITH PIPS	CARDS/TILES WITH 3 OR 4 SUITS
1 c.1592 *Jin ping mei ci hua*[26]	p. 466 *mopai*	p. 1,370 *dou pair*
2 1661 *Zhao shi bei*[27]		*juan* 4 *madiao*
3 Seventeenth century *Xing shi yin yuan zhuan*[28]	p. 781 *gupai*	p. 781 *zhipai*
4 1722+ *Wu se shi*[29]		*juan* 7 *zhipai*
5 1722+ *Ba dong tian*[30]		p. 109 *juepai*
6 c.1760 *Hong lou meng*[31]		p. 647 *doupai (shihu?)*
7 c.1760 *Lin lan xiang*[32]	p. 463 *Xuanhe pai*	
8 1777 *Qi lu deng*[33]	p. 156 *da kuai, da tianjiu* p. 317 *gupai hu*	p. 317 *hun jianghu, madiao*
9 1785 *Zhong Kui ping gui zhuan*[34]	p. 646–7 *gupai*	
10 c.1799 *Hou hong lou meng*[35]	p. 273 *dianzipai*	p. 273 *madiao*
11 1799 *Xu hong lou meng*[36]	p. 373 *doupai*	
12 1819 *Hong lou meng bu*[37]	5/9b–10b *dianzipai* (= *huahu?*); *tianjiu*	

	TILES/CARDS WITH PIPS	CARDS/TILES WITH 3 OR 4 SUITS
13 1832 *Jing hua yuan*[38]	p. 514 *huahu*	p. 168 *madiao* p. 514 *shihu*
14 1849 *Pin hua bao jian*[39]	vol. 1, p. 162 *gupai*	vol. 2, p. 194 *madiao*
15 1868–78 *Hong gui chun meng*[40]		p. 170 *shihu*
16. 1878 *Qing lou meng*[41]	p. 297 *zhipai (huahu?)*	
17 1892 *Hai shang hua lie zhuan*[42]	p. 95 solitaire	p. 185 *penghe = maquepai*
18 1903 *Hai shang fan hua meng*[43]	p. 76 *wahuapai, paijiu*	p. 170 *penghe*
19 1905 *Er shi zai fan hua meng*[44]	p. 161 *paijiu*	
20 1906–10 *Jiu wei gui*[45]		p. 624 *penghe*
21 1908 *Jiu wei hu*[46]	p. 9 *laohe (= tongqi?)*	p. 46 *maque* p. 79 *penghe*
22 1910 *Jin shi nian zhi guai xian zhuang*[47]		p. 38 *penghe*

Towards the latter half of the list, there is more than one episode in each novel which contains these scenes, and here I only list some examples. Some of these games I have yet to comprehend fully, while some I have identified from clues. One particular term worth mentioning is *penghe*. This is used more often than the term *maquepai* to refer to mahjong, but it is also used to refer to other games of both families.

For the curious who plan to look up the page references for these games, I can promise much humorous reading. To give a few examples, the *Zhao shi bei* ('Cup that Reflects the World') contains a scene where a master *madiao* player lectures on Feng Menglong's 'Classic of Cards' in the Academy of Madiao.[49] In the novel 'Zong Kui Vanquishes the Demons', the Gambling Demon has six sons and one daughter named after domino combinations.[50] The *Hai shang fan hua meng* ('A Dream of Shanghai Splendour') contains a scene which describes various methods of cheating, and one involves training to recognise the value of a bamboo tile from the patterning of the bamboo fibres on the back – by the light of a single lampwick.[51] In the same novel, a foreign player, Mr Dallas, emerges to join in the game of *penghe*.[52]

Finally, I would like to sketch out some of the literati activities connected with these games. Under the category of wine games (*jiuling*), which deserves another full-length study, the quoting of lines associated with dice or domino combinations is a major opportunity to display one's talent. Lines from the play *Xi xiang ji* ('The Western Wing') and *Mu dan ting* ('The Peony Pavilion') are used to describe various dice combinations,[53] and we have already mentioned lines from Tang-Song poets used to describe domino combinations. Again, the whole phenomenon of 'writings done in jest' (*xiwen*) remains to be clarified,[54] but for our cards and dominoes, we have already mentioned Wu Weiye's pseudo-biography of a card; and in Jin Xingyuan's compilation mentioned before, there are two plaints written with names of domino combinations,[55] but the tour de force is certainly the two-act play *Xuan he xi zheng ji* ('Dominoes March West') written in the eighteenth century,[56] composed entirely of the names of domino combinations.

To end on a sobering note, in contrast to the decadence portrayed in some novels at the turn of the twentieth century, we may mention the work of Tan Renfeng (1860–1920) entitled *Shi sou pai ci* ('Domino poems by the Old Man of Rock').[57] This work contains 49 *ci*-poems describing major events in China from 1895–1913 illustrated with corresponding domino pieces.

References

1. Shanghai tushuguan, comp., *Zhong guo cong shu zong lu* (Zhonghua shuju, Shanghai, 1961), vol. 2, pp. 951–2.
2. Chang Bide, *Shuo fu kao* (Wenshizhe chubanshe, Taipei, 1979).
3. Andrew Lo, 'Amusement Literature in Some Early Qing Collectanea', paper presented at a Conference on Chinese Cultural History, Princeton University, May 13–15 1987.
4. Wang Shihan, *Ye xi yuan qi*, in *Cong mu wang shi yi shu* (Qiantang Wangshi edition, Changsha, 1886).
5. Zhang Chao et al., ed., *Zhao dai cong shu* (Shikaitang edition), *bieji*, part 43.
6. Li Dou, *Yang zhou hua fang lu* (Guangling guji keyinshe, Jiangsu, 1984).
7. Stewart Culin, *Chinese Games With Dice And Dominoes* (Smithsonian Institution, United States National Museum, Washington, Government Printing Office, 1895); Stewart Culin, *Games Of The Orient* (Charles E. Tuttle Co., Tokyo, 1958), (original edition published 1895); Stewart Culin, 'The Game of Ma-Jong: Its Origin And Significance', *The Brooklyn Museum Quarterly* (New York, 1924).
8. Yang Yinshen, *Zhong guo you yi yan jiu* (Shijie shuju, 1946).
9. *Zhong guo cong shu zong lu*, vol. 2, pp. 951–952.
10. *Zhong guo you yi yan jiu*, p. 81.
11. Qu You, *Xuan he pai pu*, in *Shuo fu xu*, juan 38 (Wanwei shantang edition).
12. Gu Yingxiang, *Pai pu*, in *Xin shang bian fu xu bian*, 10 juan (National Central Library, Taiwan).
13. Zhang Qiaosou, *Ying pu*, *Shuo fu xu*, juan 39.
14. See Wang Zhongmin, *Zhong guo shan ben shu ti yao* (Shanghai guji chubanshe, Shanghai, 1983), p. 302.
15. Jin Xingyuan, *Xuan he pu ya pai hui ji* (Hongwenzhai edition, 1888), Fu Sinian Library, Taiwan.
16. *Shuo fu xu*, juan 39, part 7.
17. *Shuo fu xu*, juan 39, part 8.
18. *Shuo fu xu*, juan 39, part 10.
19. It is noted in *Zhong guo cong shu zong lu* that the work is in *Shuo fu xu*, juan 39, but it is not in the School of Oriental and African Studies Library edition. This work may be found in Wang Shihan, *Ye xi yuan qi*, pp. 26b–30a.
20. *Shuo fu xu*, juan 39, part 9.
21. Wu Weiye, *Mei cun jia cang gao*, 26/3b–4b, Sibucongkan edition (Shangwu yinshuguan, Shanghai, 1929).
22. Wang Zhuo, Zhang Chao, eds, *Tan ji cong shu*, Xiajutang edition, SOAS Library, *yuji*, second part, pp. 21–22a.
23. *Zhao dai cong shu*, *bieji*, part 47.

24. Shouan jushi, *Ma diao pu*, manuscript, National Central Library, Taipei.
25. *Zhao dai cong shu, bieji*, part 15.
26. Lanling xiaoxiaosheng, *Jin ping mei ci hua* (Taiping shuju, Hong Kong, 1982).
27. Zhuoyuanting zhuren, *Zhao shi bei* (Shanghai gudian wenxue chubanshe, Shanghai, 1956).
28. Xizhou sheng, *Xing shi yin yan zhuan* (Shanghai guji chubanshe, Shanghai, 1981).
29. Biliange, *Wu se shi* (Chunfeng wenyi chubanshe, Shenyang, 1985).
30. Wuse shi zhuren, *Ba dong tian* (Shumu wenxian chubanshe, Beijing, 1985).
31. Cao Xueqin, Gao E, *Hong lou meng* (Renmin wenxue chubanshe, Beijing, 1985).
32. Suiyuan xiashi, *Lin lan xiang* (Chunfeng wenyi chubanshe, Shenyang, 1985).
33. Li Lüyuan, *Qi lu deng* (Zhongzhou shuhuashe, Henan, 1980).
34. Zhong kui ping gui zhuan', in Lu Gong, Tan Tian, eds, *Gu ben ping hua xiao shuo ji* (Renmin wenxue chubanshe, Beijing, 1984).
35. Xiaoyaozi, *Hou Hong lou meng* (Chunfeng wenyi chubanshe, Shenyang, 1985).
36. Qin Zichen, *Qin xu Hong lou meng* (Chunfeng wenyi chubanshe, Shenyang, 1985).
37. Guichuzi, *Hong lou meng bu* (Tianyi chubanshe, Taipei, 1975).
38. Li Ruzhen, *Jing hua yuan* (Zhonghua shuju, Hong Kong, 1974).
39. Chen Sen, *Pin hua bao jian* (Tianyi chubanshe, Taipei, 1974).
40. Shining Zhuqiushi, *Hong gui chun meng* (Shijie shuju, Taipei, 1969).
41. Yu Da, *Qing lou meng*, in *Wan qing xiao shuo da xi* (Guangya chuban youxian gongsi, Taipei, 1984).
42. Han Bangqing, *Hai shang hua lie zhuan* (Renmin wenxue chubanshe, Beijing, 1982).
43. Jingmeng chixian, *Xiu xiang hai shang fan hua meng chu ji* (Shangwu yinshuguan, Shanghai, 1923).
44. Huang Xiaopei, *Er shi zai fan hua meng*, in *Wan qing xiao shuo da xi* (Guangya chuban youxian gongsi, Taipei, 1984).
45. Zhang Chunfan, *Jiu wei gui*, in *Wan qing xiao shuo da xi* (Guangya chuban youxian gongsi, Taipei, 1984).
46. Menghua guanzhu, *Jiu wei hu*, in *Wan qing xiao shuo da xi* (Guangya chuban youxian gongsi, Taipei, 1984).
47. Wu Jianren, *Jin shi nian zhi guai xian zhuang*, in *Wan qing xiao shuo da xi* (Guangya chuban youxian gongsi, Taipei, 1984).
48. See *Muzhu xian hua*, in *Zhao dai cong shu, bie ji, juan* 43, pp. 7a, 8b.
49. *Zhao shi bei*, p. 78.
50. *Gu ben ping hua xiao shuo ji*, p. 646.
51. *Xiu xiang hai shang fan hua meng*, p. 94.
52. *Xiu xiang hai shang fan hua meng*, p. 170.
53. See *Di liu cai zi xi xiang zhai ju tou pu* in *Di liu cai zi shu shi jie* (Wenyuantang edition, in the British Library); Xu Zhen, *Mu dan ting tou pu*, in *Zhao dai cong shu, bie ji*.
54. See Herbert Franke, 'A Note on Parody in Chinese Traditional Literature', *Oriens Extremus*, vol. 18, 1971, pp. 237–251; 'Literary Parody in Traditional Chinese Literature: Descriptive Pseudo-Biographies', *Oriens Extremus*, vol. 21, 1974, pp. 23–31.
55. Jin Xingyuan, *Xuan he pu ya pai hui ji, xiajuan*, pp. 34a, b.
56. *Xuan he pu ya pai hui ji, xia juan*, pp. 1–24a.
57. Tan Renfeng, *Shi sou pai pu* (Gansu renmin chubanshe, Lanzhou, 1983).

Discussion

In the subsequent discussion, a question was raised about whether games of cards and dominoes were seen as political allegories. Dr Lo described how the 32-piece domino and card games in the Ming were divided into sections: *hua pai* or 'Chinese' and *yi pai* or 'barbarian'. The Qing emperors were not amused by these divisions and cards were divided instead into *wen* and *wu pai* or 'civil' and 'military' sections. Political attitudes to games are evident from legal sources and local gazetteers which contain information on the prohibition of certain games at certain times.

Other connections and origins of games included the early 32-piece domino game which was based on the *Yi jing*, a connection retained when it developed into a 64-piece game which was more acceptable to players. A late Qing game deliberately based on the *Yi jing* was invented by Yu Pingbo's grandfather, Yu Yue. Each card had three lines from the *Book of Changes* and a player won by managing to gather a set and form a number of hexagrams.

Earlier games were frequently based on gambling – for money, chestnuts or wine. Silver or metal tallies (from the Yuan) were used as forfeits: the loser had to take one, do as it said and play the clown. It is interesting to note that during the Tang and Song there were many physical sports such as polo and football, whilst for the Ming and Qing there is little information on physical sports – perhaps the Chinese had become tired and effete.

In Ming and Qing novels, dominoes were usually played by women whilst some variations of the card games with four suits were usually played by men.

Craig Clunas

Books and things: Ming literary culture and material culture

Books *are* things, of course, artefacts in their own right. They enjoy a particularly prominent place in the total material culture of those historical civilizations which have developed the technology of multiple text reproduction. Of these, China was the first. The sociologist Chandra Mukerji has argued that, in the case of early modern Europe, it was the development of multiple image production through the medium of printmaking which stimulated a distinctively materialist culture in the West.[1] The role of books, and in particular of illustrated books, in the burgeoning urban civilization of late Ming China (defined here as the century or so from the commencement of the Jiajing period in 1522 to the fall of the dynasty in 1644) has been often noted, though there still remains much to be found out about the life cycle of the book as artefact: how books were paid for, published, sold, bought, distributed, displayed, discarded, resold and even read. Clearly books formed part of the cocoon of material possessions which were one of the defining marks of élite status. In the considerable 'literature of reassurance', that body of interrelated texts written between about 1580 and 1640 which seeks to define socially acceptable dispositions of dwellings, clothing, utensils and amusements, books, as potent public markers of high culture, have a prominent place. It is hard to escape the conclusion that at least some of this literature is aimed at giving the *nouveau riche* the trappings to which they aspired, in an age when the flood of silver from the mines of the Americas into the Chinese economy was dissolving ancient social barriers. How else is one to explain the passage in Gao Lian's *Shan zhai zhi* ('Record of my Mountain Studio'), (probably written about 1600) where he lists the books one should possess and have on view; *Yi jing, Li sao, Bai jia Tang shi, Cao tang shi yu, Hua jian ji, Li dai ci fu xun, Shi dian dao yin*.[2] What kind of 'scholar' needed to be told he should have a copy of the *Li sao*, or that rubbings of the calligraphy of Huang Tingjian and the monk Huaisu were desirable possessions? Any answer would involve consideration of the problem of social status and social stratification in late Ming China, and would lead away from the main theme of this paper, which seeks to demonstrate at least some of the inter-penetrations and threads of connection between what have until recently been studied as two entirely different entities. The world of books, of bibliography and of the history of literature, and the world of connoisseurship and art history have, over a length period, developed two entirely different discourses, each with its own set of emphases and elisions. What we learn from the *Shan zhai zhi*, a book about things in which books are granted the same status as furniture, pictures and flowers, is that there are insights to be gained from trying to look at a period of Chinese culture in a less fragmented way.

In attempting to persuade colleagues whose primary raw material for the study of China's past lies in books that it is worth seriously considering the evidence of material culture, help can be found in the fact of the overwhelming illiteracy of the population in late traditional times. The exact literacy rate remains a subject of contention,[3] but it is certainly clear that there was by no means an exact fit between an ability to read (and hence to participate in the 'high' cultural tradition) and possession of the necessary wealth to enjoy luxury goods. The example springs to mind of Ximen Qing, louche anti-hero of *Jin ping mei*, with his 'study' full of books, antiques, paintings by famous hands and other scholarly accoutrements, who nevertheless relies on his son-in-law for access to the written word. Of his numerous wives, only Pan Jinlian herself can read, and this unusual accomplishment is the subject of some comment in the novel.[4]

This fact alone raises the possibility that through the study of objects, with their often richly allusive decorative schemes, it might be possible to approach some of those areas of culture which had meaning in the lives of those otherwise excluded from the literary tradition. In particular, the study of objects known from their function to be associated with women allows us, if not to study in depth the cultural life of this generally silenced majority, at least to apprehend something of those areas of the prevailing patriarchal ideology which were manifested in their daily lives. A concrete example is provided by a distinctively shaped and decorated group of lacquer boxes, executed in a variety of lacquer techniques, at least nine examples of which have appeared in publications.[5] They all date from between about 1550 and 1620. They are distinguished by their shape, a rectangular one which is typically about 70cm long, 20cm wide and 10cm high. On all except one of them (no. 3) the decoration 'reads' vertically, so that it can only be viewed when one of the short sides of the box is held towards you. All nine of the boxes carry the same subject matter, either as the only subject or as one of three panels. This is the scene where Li Yuan, the future founder of the Tang dynasty, wins Dou Yi's daughter as his bride by triumphing in an archery competition, hitting the eyes of two peacocks painted on a screen. We might begin legitimately to infer that these boxes thus had something to do with rituals surrounding betrothal and marriage. This inference becomes a near certainty when we consider two other themes which appear with the archery competition on six out of the nine boxes. These show the Emperor Yao seeking the horoscope of his prospective son-in-law and successor, Shun, from Shun's harsh old father Gu Sou, 'The Blind Elder', and those paragons of mutual respect between husband and wife, Liang Hong and Meng Guang, treating one another with the propriety due to a guest, as the wife greets her husband after a journey 'raising the tray level with her eyebrows', *ju an qi mei*.

We do not know the exact use to which these boxes were put, though Wang Shixiang has suggested that they may have been designed to contain the written horoscopes exchanged between the bride and groom's families. What we can infer is that these subjects carried social meaning, and thus had a use beyond the function of preventing the horoscopes from getting wet. They had what the American archaeologist Lewis Binford would describe as a 'socio-technic', as well as a 'technomic' function.[6] There are no boxes of these elongated rectangular proportions which do not have at least the archery scene on them. The archery scene does not appear on objects other than these elongated boxes. The boxes do not exist in any material other than the various lacquering techniques. They and their decorative scheme are only seen during the 70 years or so from 1550 to 1620. (This is worth stressing, as too much writing on Chinese material culture still treats all subject matter as simultaneously valid, after the manner of books like Williams, *Outlines of Chinese Symbolism and Art Motifs*.)

There is in fact a close fit between form and decoration here which allows us to be confident that we are dealing with a collocation of associations which to any participant in late Ming culture, literate or not (and this must include women in this instance) meant 'wedding'. It is perhaps significant that these boxes, unlike most other forms of Ming lacquer, do not appear to have been transmitted to Japan in any quantity at the time of their manufacture. They were just too specific to the cultural context for which they were made.

What then are the sources of these nuptial allusions? They lie deep within the 'high' culture of pre-modern China, in the orthodox dynastic histories. The story of Gu Sou appears in *Shi ji*, in the section *Wu di zhuan*. That of Liang Hong, and the locus of the phrase *ju an qi mei* is in Liang's *Hou Han shu* biography, while *Jiu Tang shu* provides the story of the archery contest. This is hardly surprising. Numerous writers in recent years have drawn attention to the remarkable success of the élite culture of China in exercising hegemony over cultural registers at a much more popular level. The visual culture of the mass drew a great deal of its raw material (however much it may subsequently have been transformed) from the most prestigious types of text, such as the standard dynastic histories. There is no need here to posit a thorough familiarity with the original dynastic history forms of these stories, in order to explain their presence as carriers of meaning on these boxes. The easy passage of ideas downwards through Ming society can be explained in several other ways, by invoking a number of cultural mediators.

Perhaps the most important of these cultural mediators was the drama, as broadly interpreted to include puppet theatre and other performance arts such as *pingtan*, etc. The late Barbara Ward was surely right to maintain that, for the overwhelming majority of China's population from the Ming period to the present day, attendance at periodic dramatic performances was one of the key means by which they learned about history and mythology.[7] The heroic exploits of *Three Kingdoms* generals, the story of Monkey, and the romantic entanglements of Yingying were all familiar to millions who never owned or opened a book. All three of the stories mentioned above have enjoyed a history of slipping in and out of the dramatic repertoire, only a small fraction of which has, in any case, come down to us in the form of printed texts. A version of the Liang Hong and Meng Guang story appears in the 1616 compilation by Zang Mouxun, *Yuan qu xuan*.[8] This is of course the very top end of the market as far as play texts are concerned, and we cannot know how much has been lost of a less literary nature. Illustrating the easy transition between a submerged vernacular performance tradition and a more formalised written one is the history of the two other subjects, both of which appear in the Peking opera repertoire of the late nineteenth and early twentieth centuries. The story of the archery contest was put down in a written version by the noted Peking opera writer Luo Yinggong (1880–1924) who in doing so was not quarrying raw material out of the *Jiu Tang shu*, but simply giving literary form to a story which 'every child knew'.[9]

Other examples of parallels between the subject matter of objects and that of the drama can be given quite easily. Another close fit between a form of lacquer box and a specific corpus of allusion is provided by a group of boxes inlaid in mother of pearl with the story of the 'Eighteen Scholars of Tang'.[10] These boxes were all probably used for the gifts of food which were such an important part of ritual intercourse in Ming society. The box containing a present was not retained by its recipient, but was returned to the giver, often containing a return gift. The emphasis is thus on reciprocal relations between equals, on the mutual esteem alluded to by this famous grouping of colleagues. Once again the decoration forms a central element in the total function of the object, tying the individual gift into socially sanctioned paradigms of behaviour.

The original account of this seventh-century think-tank again lies in *Jiu Tang shu*. It enjoyed favour as a painting subject through the Song, Yuan and Ming dynasties, and by the sixteenth century was a theatrical subject in its own right. An anonymous play in the *zaju* style called *Shi ba xue shi deng Ying zhou* ('The Eighteen Scholars Mount to Fairyland') is recorded in the Jiajing period bibliography *Bao wen tang shu mu*, the contents of which have been described by twentieth-century critics as 'clumsy in language, common in thought and stereotyped in plot.[11] These are the potboilers, not the enduring masterpieces, of Ming drama, and have been studied by Tanaka Issei, among others.[12] It is excerpts from plays like these, arranged by categories such as 'Birthday Congratulations', 'Birth of a Son' or 'Feasting' which fill the 1602 anthology *Yue fu hong shan*.[13] They are not major monuments of Chinese literature, but their social significance as disseminators of ideas about the past cannot be overestimated.

Plays, then, acted as transmitters of cultural values beyond the narrow scope of the fully literate minority. Objects did the same thing, though to a lesser extent, their circulation being limited by economic factors. I have left till last the question of illustrated books, although obviously these played a crucial role in providing the models which were adapted by the decorators of lacquers and porcelain. Turning back to Li Yuan and his feat of archery, we find the scene portrayed in a popular encyclopaedia of the Chongzhen period (1628–1643) named *Wu dou yun* ('Five Clumps of Cloud'), compiled by Zhang Tongchu.[14] This is one of a group of such books, clearly compiled to provide quick and easy access to key elements of the great tradition. They sometimes take the form of collections of *duilian*, couplets suitable for committing to memory. In *Da bei dui zong* of 1600 we find 'The Tang Emperor travels to the moon palace', 'The Four Luminaries take refuge on Mt Shang', 'Su Wu herding sheep', while *Gu wen zheng zong* of 1593 has subjects like 'Yuanming enjoying chrysanthemums', 'Du Fu's spring outing' and 'Dongpo as Grand Secretary'.[15] These are all very well known stories indeed, and an exclusion from an understanding of at least their basic import would surely have disqualified anyone from even a middling position in the Ming cultural spectrum.

No written text was more basic than that of the *San zi jing*, whose jingling rhymes were every schoolboy's introduction to literary culture. The second historical figure to be mentioned in this is a now obscure Five Dynasties figure named Dou Yudiao (or Dou Yanshan):

> Dou Yanshan
> Had the right scheme
> Taught his five sons
> All made their name[16]

The five sons, all of whom rose to high office, were known as the 'Five Cassia trees of Yanshan', after a line in a poem addressed to their father by the poet Feng Dao (881–954AD)[17]. It is this very poem, part of which is teasingly obscured by the old man's head, which appears written on a screen on a piece of mid-sixteenth-century enamelled porcelain in the Victoria and Albert Museum.[18] A bowl of similar date and comparable technique exists in the Topkapi Saray Museum, Istanbul.[19] Once again the subject was an extremely familiar one. Four separate acts from a play on this theme entitled *Cui pan ji* survive in the *Yue fu hong shan* collection of extracts. The text as a whole is lost, but extracts from it are preserved in four other Ming drama anthologies. This is a class of drama, the ephemerality of which is matched only by its very great popularity in its heyday.[20]

Here we are on less firm ground than we are with the 'wedding' boxes or even with the 'eighteen scholars' food boxes, in ascertaining how the iconography of these objects was read by their intended recipients. The V & A jar is probably for wine, and the Istanbul bowl for food or wine. Obviously the imagery operates in the general area of wishes for success (the first *Yue fu hong shan* extract appears under the category 'Educating Sons'), and for a brood of high-achieving offspring, but the exact nuances must continue to escape us. What cannot, however, be avoided is a recognition of the intimate inter-penetration of the world of literary culture with the artefacts of daily life at a certain level of society.

Most of the themes discussed above have their ultimate roots in the writing of history, the genre of narrative which, it has been argued, exercised dominance over vast areas of the Chinese literary culture, fulfilling the role which epic played in the development of the literatures of the Mediterranean. Rather than a simple dichotomy between 'true' history and 'untrue' fiction, Andrew Plaks has argued for the recognition of a historical-fictional continuum in Chinese culture, with the history end enjoying 'quasi-religious pre-eminence'.[21] A historical event such as Li Yuan's triumph can thus be situated at several points on the continuum, from the rigorous orthodoxy of the standard history to the freedom of treatment it enjoys in romantic drama, and even beyond the page or stage into the world of goods, far beyond the control of editors or cultural centralizers. Despite its impeccable origins as an anecdote, it finds no place in *Sui Tang yan yi*, the 'scholar' novel about the rise of the Tang compiled by Chu Renhuo in the 1670s.[22] It may well have been the subject's very hackneyed familiarity which led him to avoid it. Here it is the objects, actual pieces of the Ming dynasty which have come down to us, which add breadth to our understanding by demonstrating the simultaneous existence of more than one set of approaches to the same body of historical narrative. At a period when, for various reasons, figure painting was in decline and arbiters of taste generally held figurative decoration in low esteem,[23] its continued hold on porcelain and lacquer decoration is striking. Study of this decoration seems likely to advance our understanding of that broad stratum of Ming society which was well enough off to afford luxury goods like inlaid lacquer and enamelled porcelain, but was not self-consciously defining 'elegant' style through prescriptive texts. Rather than a simple model of a 'scholar élite' in opposition to a mass 'popular culture', a considerably richer and more complex picture may emerge of the culturally vital, socially insecure world of late Ming China.

Selected names, titles and phrases mentioned in the text

Gao Lian 高濂
Shan zhai zhi 山齋志
Yi jing 易經
Li sao 離騷
Bai jia Tang shi 百家唐詩
Cao tang shi yu 草堂詩餘
Hua jian ji 花間集
Li dai ci fu xun 歷代詞府洵
Shi dian dao yin 釋典導引
Li Yuan 李淵
Dou Yi 竇毅
Gu Sou 瞽瞍
Liang Hong 梁鴻
Meng Guang 孟光
ju an qi mei 舉案齊眉
Wang Shixiang 王世襄
Zang Mouxun 臧懋循
Yuan qu xuan 元曲選
Luo Yinggong 羅癭公
Shi ba xue shi deng Yingzhou 十八學士登瀛洲
Bao wen tang shu mu 寶文堂書目
Yue fu hong shan 樂府紅珊
Wu dou yun 五朵雲
Zhang Tongchu 張侗初
Gu wen zheng zong 古文正宗
San zi jing 三字經
Dou Yudiao (Yanshan) 竇禹鈞
Feng Dao 馮道
Cui pan ji 翠蟹記
Sui Tang yan yi 隋唐演義
Chu Renhuo 褚人穫

References

1. Chandra Mukerji, *From Graven Images. Patterns of Modern Materialism* (New York, 1983), chapter 2.
2. Gao Lian, *Shan zhai zhi*, Shui bian lin xia congshu, undated Ming edition, Suzhou Municipal Library, p. 2b.
3. W L Idema, *Chinese Vernacular Fiction, the Formative Period* (Leiden, 1974), pp. 99–102 proposes a three-tier model of literacy, involving 5 per cent of the population.
4. *Fleur en fiole d'or (Jin pinq mei cihua)*, translated by André Lévy, 2 vols (Paris, 1985), II, Chapter 78, p. 797. The description of Ximen Qing's 'study' is I, Chapter 34, pp. 692–3.
5. These are:
   (a) Black lacquer inlaid with pewter and silver, dated 1580, Linden-Museum, Stuttgart OA 20.852 L. Published: *Laques chinois du Linden-Museum de Stuttgart* (Musée Guimet, Paris, 1986), no. 34.
   (b) Black lacquer inlaid with brass, Mr Robert H. Ellsworth. Published: James C Y Watt, *The Sumptuous Basket: Chinese Lacquer with Basketry Panels* (China House Gallery, New York, 1985), no. 16.
   (c) Lacquer with painted decoration, Honolulu Academy of Arts, gift of Mrs Philip E Spalding. Published: Watt, *Sumptuous Basket*, no. 25.
   (d) Black lacquer inlaid with brass, Yamato bunkakan. Published: *Yamato bunkakan shozōhin. Zuhan mokuroku – 3 Shikkō* (Nara, 1982), no. 157.
   (e) Carved red lacquer, Royal Ontario Museum, Toronto.
   (f) Carved red lacquer, Palace Museum, Peking. Published: *Gu gong bowuyuan cang diao qi* (Peking, 1984), no. 144.
   (g) Carved polychrome lacquer, Palace Museum, Peking. Published: *Gu gong bowuyuan cang diao qi*, no. 146.
   (h) Carved red and black lacquer, Victoria and Albert Museum, 983–1883. Published: Edward F. Strange, *Catalogue of Chinese Lacquer*, Victoria and Albert Museum (London, 1925), no. 50.
   (i) Painted lacquer, dated 1600, Victoria and Albert Museum W.66–1925. Published: Sir Harry Garner, *Chinese Lacquer*, London, 1979, p. 252.
6. Lewis Binford, 'Archaelogy as Anthropology', *American Antiquity*, 28.2 (1962), pp. 217–226.
7. Barbara E Ward, 'Readers and Audiences: an Exploration of the Spread of Traditional Chinese Culture', in *Text and Context*, edited by R K Jain (Philadelphia, 1977), pp. 181–203.
8. Zhao Jingshen and Shao Zengqi, *Yuan Ming bei zaju zongmu kaolüe*, Zhongguo gudai xiqu lilun congshu (Zhengzhou, 1985), p. 481.
9. Tao Junqi, *Jing ju jumu chu tan*, zeng ding ben (Peking, 1980), p. 2 ('Great Shun ploughs the fields.) and p. 119 ('The Peacock Screen').
10. Craig Clunas, 'Human Figures in the Decoration of Ming Lacquer', Oriental Art. NS 22.2 (1986), 177–188 (pp. 182–185).
11. Zhao Jingshen and Shao Zengqi, p. 584.
12. Tanaka Issei, (The Social and Historical Context of Ming – Ch'ing Local Drama', in *Popular Culture in Late Imperial China*, edited by David Johnson, Andrew J Nathan and Evelyn S Rawski, (Berkeley/New York/London, 1985), 143–160.
13. P D Hanan, 'The Nature and Contents of the *Yüeh-Fu Hung-Shan*', *Bulletin of the School of Oriental & African Studies*, 26 (1963), pp. 346–361.
14. Fu Xihua, *Zhongguo gudian wenxue banhua xuanji*, 2 vols, (Shanghai, 1980), II, 648.
15. Fu Xihua, *Zhongguo gudian wenxue banhua xuanji*, I, 75–77 & 250–252.
16. *San zi jing*, lines 13–16.
17. *Quan Tang shi*, Zhonghua shuju ed., 12 vols (Peking, 1960), 11, *juan* 737, 8,405–8,406.
18. C.67–1954.
19. Regina Krahl, *Chinese Ceramics in the Topkapi Saray Museum*, 3 vols, (London, 1986), II, no. 1,631 (TSK 15/3055).
20. Fu Xihua, *Mingdai chuanqi quan mu*, (Peking, 1958), p. 486.
21. Andrew H Plaks, 'Towards a Critical Theory of Chinese Narrative' in Andrew H Plaks ed., *Chinese Narrative. Critical and Theoretical Essays*, 309–352 (p. 312).
22. Robert G Hegel, 'Sui T'ang Yen-i and the Aesthetics of the Seventeenth Century Suchou Elite' in Plaks ed., *Chinese Narrative*, 124–159 (pp. 154–157).
23. Clunas, 'Human Figures', p. 180.

Discussion

In the subsequent discussion, Dr Clunas explained that he regarded Qing manuals on elegant living as distinct from those of the Ming. They seemed to be a form of literature of nostalgia, a continuation of the Ming by other means, whilst the Ming manuals were of the moment, not written out of nostalgia or for consolation but to make money. The genre gradually died out by the mid-Qing when this sort of manual ceased to exist. Indeed, there is an undercurrent in early Qing writing suggesting that the obsession with the details of elegant living was actually one of the causes of the fall of the Ming and that the genre was decadent. Literature of the Kangxi period, even when about enjoying yourself, was sterner stuff.

The question of the development of commodity items is problematic, as artefacts do not come complete with a history; their context can, however, be derived from literature and drama. For example, in the *Jin ping mei*, embroidered handkerchiefs often appear as a woman to woman gift. The identification of the real scholar through his possessions, which was clearly a live issue at the time, is unlikely to be sorted out now as we are probably less aware of possible ironies. The description of Ximen Qing's study and the disposition of his paintings there is quite bland in the text, but according to Wen Zhenheng, it was vulgar and crass, and, as the grandson of Wen Zhengming, he should have been aware of this. No doubt some contemporary readers understood the appalling solecism, whilst some missed it, for artefacts do not have only one meaning, but shifting meanings for different people, and they also have a cultural biography. An object that has come down to use from the Ming has *lived* in the meanwhile; it is not brought to life, like the frog prince, by the twentieth-century museum curator. It would be interesting to know what a mid-Ming lacquer marriage horoscope box did in the Daoguang period. Was it a curiosity in 1820 or was it put away in a drawer? One of the ways of approaching this complicated graph of time and space is to look at how certain objects were employed at certain times by certain interest groups. However, if the hypothesis about manuals of taste defining the *nouveau riche* is correct, then the authors were shooting themselves in the foot by making the *nouveau riche* more difficult to define; the pace-setters have to keep one step ahead. The point of a fashion mechanism (using Jean Baudrillard's definition of the term), which is what may be seen in the mid-Ming, is that some people should fail to keep up with it. If everyone knows what the fashion is and immediately adopts it then it is no longer the fashion, for there have to be leaders and there have to be failures to generate the continuous changes in fashion which in turn generate the continuous production of new cultural products.

The Chair made a call for more intelligent popularisation of Chinese culture. Of the few examples that we have in translation, the *Dream of the Red Chamber* should be as well known as Proust for it is not that much further away, and the *Jin ping mei* should be as well-known as Tom Jones. Many translations are somewhat inaccessible as they are effectively dedicated to sinologists and are hard for 'lay' persons to 'place' in their intellectual scheme. The approach through artefacts and the approach through games are both scholarly and popular, and good popularisation should be encouraged.

Lo Huimin

The Morrison Papers

Libraries and archives are the life-line of scholars like myself. Although I have been less concerned with the Morrison papers in recent years, I will talk very briefly about Morrison the man and his papers and why they are important, and trust that my preoccupation does not bore. Morrison's papers, more than many similar collections, owe their value to the man responsible for them. I have recently edited Morrison's letters (of which the first two volumes have been published by Cambridge University Press and recently translated, very badly, by the Chinese Academy of Social Sciences into Chinese, a translation which I am afraid I find incomprehensible in many places) and consider that they may be viewed in contrast to items such as Lu Xun's diary or Gladstone's diary. In these latter cases, if you didn't known that they were by Lu Xun or by Gladstone, they would be quite meaningless, but Morrison's diary and papers have a quality and value more akin to, for example, Pitt's diary or the Greville memoirs which cast light on the early years of Queen Victoria's reign. Such papers are of interest even if you do not know much about the writers, though their value is certainly enhanced by knowledge of who the writers were and what they did. For that reason it is important to talk briefly about Morrison the man.

During his lifetime he was endlessly mistaken for Robert Morrison and they were assumed to be the same man, though in fact G E Morrison was not born until 28 years after Robert Morrison had died in 1862 (Morrison himself died in 1920). Morrison was a first generation Australian of Anglo-Scottish descent; his father was drawn to Victoria in the early 1850s, at about the same time as the early Chinese gold-miners. Morrison's father, founder of Geelong College, distinguished himself in the field of education, both in Scotland and Australia, and Geelong, together with his uncle's school, Scotch College, was one of the most distinguished Australian private (or in British usage 'public') schools. After graduating from Geelong, Morrison went on to Melbourne University to read medicine, but with the excuse of having failed one subject in his intermediate examination, he left to fulfil the wanderlust which he had already demonstrated at the early age of 16, by walking one summer (in average temperatures of 115 degrees) the 150 or so miles from Melbourne to Adelaide and back. Between the ages of 17 and 21 he undertook four or five more arduous trips in the Pacific Islands and he practically traversed the whole of Australia. Amongst the most famous of his expeditions was his solo canoe trip at the age of 19 along 150 miles of the Murray, one of Australia's longest and, at the time, least explored rivers. He travelled in Northern

Queensland and his report, published in a newspaper, provoked a government enquiry into the slave trade (then called the Kanaka trade) in the area. By far his most famous trip was that from the north of Australia to the south, when he covered 2,000 miles in 123 days, again with the temperatures in the 100s. Some barely believed Morrison's claim at the time although *The Times*, unaware of its close future connection with Morrison, described it as 'one of the most remarkable pedestrian achievements'. Still at the age of 19, he was the leader of an Australian expedition to then little-explored New Guinea, where he was ambushed by what were referred to as 'natives' and had splinters of poisoned spears lodged in two places in his body (one between the eyes). They remained there for five and a half months until they were extracted in Edinburgh by the leading surgeon of the day, in an operation which made medical history when the account was published.

While in Edinburgh, he continued and completed his five-year medical course in two years, though he was never to practise medicine, merely using his profession as a means to travel, to North and Central America, Spain, North Africa and finally, the Pacific Islands, Japan and China. He always travelled in conditions of absolute deprivation; for example, in 1894 with only £18 in his pocket, he set off from Shanghai to travel to Rangoon, a journey of some 3,000 miles, mostly completed on foot. Though he always wrote very detailed accounts of all his journeys, the account of this trip was published in book form as *An Australian in China*. It remains an interesting and perceptive account of the interior of China during the first Sino-Japanese War. The moment of publication was fortuitous for owing to the rapidly changing conditions in East Asia, *The Times* then decided that it needed a special correspondent there. Until then, *The Times* had relied on occasional contributors, among them Curzon, the future Viceroy of India whom Morrison was to get to known well.

When *An Australian in China* was published in London, Morrison lived not far from SOAS in the slums behind Mornington Crescent. Despite having been to China, very much wanting a job, and very much wanting to be a journalist, Morrison turned down *The Times*'s first offer to become the Peking correspondent as he wanted to go to Indo-China instead. It was six months later, at the age of 33, that he arrived in Peking in 1897 as *The Times* correspondent. His subsequent career is well known: not long after his arrival, the 'battle of the concessions' was in full swing; Morrison's reporting was an immediate success, and he was praised in his premature 'obituary' in *The Times* for recording 'day-to-day events with the accuracy of an historian and the prescience of a statesman'. Despite his writing under the anonymous by-line of *The Times* correspondent in Peking, his reports were pored over and were effective in the decision-making of the great powers of Europe, American and Japan. He played a very important part in the Boxer uprising when he was wounded and nearly died, and his account of both the uprising and siege has been compared to Gibbon. Later, through the part he played in it, the Russo-Japanese War became known to his contemporaries as 'Morrison's War' and in 1906 when the Liberal government came to power in Great Britain, it was through Morrison that efforts were finally made to end the century-old opium traffic. The British Minister, Sir John Jordan, appointed to serve in Peking for the next six years, was in fact Morrison's nominee. These events and his involvement in Chinese politics are detailed in his documents and diaries.

Before he became the first Political Adviser to a Chinese government, (to the first President of the Chinese Republic), he had already become one of the 'sights' of Peking, a 'must' for every visitor, whether Chinese or foreign. Several foreigners complained that on arrival at Peking Railway Station (which had been moved from outside the 'Chinese City' to outside the 'Water Gate'), rickshaw pullers, without asking for the address, would take them straight to Morrison's house, assuming that every visitor had come to see Morrison. Morrison then lived in Wangfujing dajie, known for long after as 'Morrison Street'.

As Political Adviser, he was responsible for the exposure of Japan's 'Twenty-one demands'; he was strongly against Yuan Shikai's monarchist movement; he was an intimate recorder and witness of Zhang Xun's imperial restoration of 1917; he played a leading role with the help of the British and American ministers in persuading the Chinese to join the War on the side of the Allies in 1917; and finally, he took part as adviser to the Chinese delegation to the 1919 Peace Conference where he was responsible for correcting all the drafts of the Chinese submissions to the conference. He died in 1920 in Sidmouth. This was Morrison.

During his quarter of a century of China, half of his time was spent travelling to various parts of China, and he criticised the Chinese for not knowing their own country. When Liang Qichao attended the Paris Peace Conference as an unofficial delegate and later asked Morrison, through Ding Wenjiang, to correct his account in *Ou Yu xin ying*, Morrison remarked that Liang Qichao did not know the history of his own country. Morrison was intolerant of sloppiness as he was himself a very meticulous man.

In his diary, correspondence and other papers, at least 5,000 people are mentioned, people he'd met, or corresponded with, and these 5,000 range from emperors and presidents to his house boys. Once a year, Morrison threw his house open for his famous party for the children of Peking, to which four or five hundred childen were invited. The wealth of detail in the papers makes them, as his wife said when they were presented to the Mitchell Library in Sydney, one of the most important sources in the study of Far Eastern history in this very significant 25 years from the first Sino-Japanese War to the eve of the founding of the Chinese Communist Party.

Morrison had visited the Mitchell Library and was most impressed with its collection which concentrated on early Australian history and the Pacific Islands. Perhaps because of this specialisation, Morrison's papers were accepted but not given much attention, except by Cyril Pearl, Morrison's distinguished biographer (whose biography first appeared in 1967). C P Fitzgerald had looked at the papers but decided that his life was too short to make an impact on them, though he gave me tremendous encouragement to work on them. The papers consist of 323 volumes, large bundles and boxes. This is a greatly reduced amount from that which was originally presented for, before they were catalogued in 1974, occasional readers removed items, causing incalculable losses. Even between my first visit in 1965 and their eventual cataloguing, many items which I had seen and noted had sadly disappeared. Apart from the 323 volumes, bundles and boxes, there are other categories of material: 15 big boxes of photographs, a large collection of maps and many visiting cards which help us to identify his visitors, both Chinese and foreign as well as a large collection of newspaper cuttings with his own notes commenting on their accuracy. The most important and richest items in the collection, apart from his correspondence, are the diaries. Morrison kept a diary from a young age, never abandoning the habit, and all the accounts of his trips are, in fact, in diary form. Between 1899 and three days before his death, his diary is virtually complete, with hardly a day's interruption. For the period, I cannot think of any comparable document, in English or Chinese, which offers such continuity, richness and diversity. I often find it difficult to imagine how he found the time to write 3,000 or 4,000 words a day, despite a continuous stream of visitors from early morning until late at night, with several people sitting down to lunch and dinner. Though there are only 323 boxes remaining in the collection, I've consulted some 50 government and private archives in 11 countries and have so far met nothing to compare with the Morrison papers. Their importance lies not only in the period they cover (and there are many items covering earlier periods and other places such as Australia, Indo-China and New Zealand) but also in his wide contacts reflected in the huge name-list and his tremendously serious approach, which is also reflected in the Morrison Library.

Morrison had previously collected books on China but he began collecting seriously when he arrived in China in 1897. When he had been very poor in China and Japan in 1893, he sold his medical instruments and his coat (in winter) but never sold his books. He originally bought books to help him in his work but ultimately he became a collector of every book and journal, or even subject, related to China that he could find, in every language except Chinese and Japanese. The majority are first editions, as the two-volume catalogue of the Morrison library in the Toyo Bunko (*Catalogue of the Asian Library of G E Morrison*, 1924), reveals. It is hard to imagine how he managed to purchase such expensive books, since before 1900 he only earned £600 a year, and subsequently £1,000, rising finally to £1,200. This had to cover everything from his travel expenses to his telegrams to *The Times*, yet many of the books cost as much as £100 each. It is certainly not true that he supplemented his income (as a Chinese journal suggested in the 1950s) by acting as a spy.

It would be presumptuous to suggest that librarians use the catalogue of the Morrison library to check the quality of their own collections on China. Despite his concentration on non-Chinese and Japanese materials, the library contains the most complete collection of Chinese bibles, including dialect versions, and dictionaries.

A valuable collection of material not included in the published catalogue is that of off-prints. These include off-prints from all relevant journals both publicly and privately published, up to 1917. The 9,000 off-prints still remain to be catalogued, despite being an infinitely superior collection to that in, for example, Columbia.

When he donated his library to the Toyo Bunkō, Morrison made three conditions: that the books would be kept together under the name of the Morrison

Library; that the volumes would be available to all readers; and that the library would undertake to continue the serial runs. This was, unfortunately, not done by the Toyo Bunkō. Nor did they retain the name of the library, using the excuse that they have incorporated many other books into the Morrison collection (which is true), though the real reason is that Morrison was very much critical of Japan's actions since the first Sino-Japanese War and, in a period of rising nationalism, the name of Morrison was not acceptable to many Japanese. The library must be seen as an important aspect of the life of Morrison; a remarkable collection for a journalist, remarkable indeed for any man.

Morrison has recently had a rather bad press since the publication of Lord Dacre's *Hermit of Peking*, where his treatment of Morrison is less than fair. I hope that my forthcoming book on the manuscript of Jing Shan's diary will reveal the unfairness of the view. Other speakers in the colloquium have cited Backhouse's purchases for the Bodleian as marking the moment when the collection of Chinese books in this country became a serious matter, but I am afraid that this is inaccurate. Backhouse was a dealer, an antique dealer who knew enough to impress purchasers but he was not a serious scholar like Morrison.

Discussion

In the subsequent discussion, the following points were raised: there are a number of Chinese books in Cambridge University Library acquired in 1908 through a Luzac auction of Backhouse's books, and Bland's descendants have informed the Library that Backhouse received the books from Morrison in payment and that Morrison, in turn, acquired them from a princely mansion which he occupied after the Boxer rebellion. The Librarian is interested in establishing the location of the princely mansion. However, Dr Lo, expanding on Morrison's help to Backhouse, found the story improbable. Morrison had numerous connections, including Zeng Guofan's grandson (who had also acted as secretary to Li Hongzhang) who furnished him with anecdotes. When Backhouse arrived in China in 1898, Morrison, in turn, helped him. It was through Morrison that Backhouse was employed by Satow and as a teacher of English in the Tong men guan (subsequently known as Bei da san yuan). It seems unlikely that Morrison gave Backhouse many Chinese books since his collection was limited to European language works. Neither did he live in a princely mansion at the time stated. Until 1916, he lived in Wang fu jing (where his landlord helped to copy the Jingshan manuscript now in the British Library), but though the street was known as the 'residence of thirteen princes', Morrison's house was a single courtyard, which cannot have been very splendid. It was the house of Zhu Ziqian, Minister of the Interior under Yuan Shikai and creator of Zhong shan park. Morrison eventually moved because the Dong fang market (precursor of the Dong feng market), which was opposite Morrison's house, had become rather noisy and busy by 1916. He moved to Gong xian lane (next door to the birthday-cake building of the Mei shu guan) where his house was famous as the 'Half acre garden' (Ban mou yuan), one of the most beautiful in Peking. It was later occupied by Sir Harold Acton and subsequently the Chinese Secret Service (Jun tong) took it over in 1945 from the Japanese Secret Service which had seized it during the Japanese occupation. Until four years ago you could still see the torture chamber there used by the Japanese and the KMT.

Dr Lo also expanded on Morrison and Backhouse's connections with Sir Ernest Satow (a benefactor of the British Library). Satow was Minister in Tokyo in 1895, and after the Boxer Uprising, he became Minister in Peking, exchanging jobs with Sir Claude Macdonald. Morrison later bought Satow's country cottage, near the site of the 8th Route Army Museum and Satow retired to Sidmouth in 1906. When Backhouse applied for the Chair at Oxford, Satow was amongst the electors who turned him down.

On the question of Morrison's acquisition of expensive books on a small salary, it was suggested that some might have been gifts. Morrison was, however, generally unwilling to accept gifts (though he did accept £1,000 from Yuan Shikai after writing a condemnation of him). After he had helped the Prince of Kashgar, the Prince sent him a carpet and a donkey for his children, but these were returned, together with a tip for the delivery man.

It may be that Morrison accepted volumes from authors that he knew, and his acquaintance was wide. His collection was not entirely restricted to books on China, for on his death his collection of early editions of Robinson Crusoe was said to be the best in the world. It was later broken up and sold piecemeal by his second son.

Nancy Wang

Research materials in the National Palace Museum

The National Palace Museum in Taipei has long been recognised as one of the finest and largest collections of Chinese art on earth. While each year thousands of tourists from every corner of the world visit, and are amazed by, the various art objects in the Museum, few people are aware that a tremendous number of rare books and historical documents are also preserved in this great institution. If the art masterpieces represent the core, the esssence of Chinese civilisation, the books and documents may well be said to constitute a 'key' that unlocks the door leading to a better understanding of that civilization – the diverse subjects covered in these items will inevitably provide many points of access to a greater comprehension of the social milieu and other cultural aspects of the various ages during which the art objects were produced. Indeed, these treasures have been acknowledged by scholars as indispensable sources of information in sinological studies. This presentation is intended to provide the book world, and those interested in Chinese descriptive bibliography, with an introduction to the nature and scope of the rare books and historical documents currently stored in the National Palace Museum.

Rare books

It is important to note at the outset that our definition for 'rare books' is somewhat different from that which has been generally accepted in the Western world. For the purpose of this paper, rare books are those that were finely printed, beautifully copied and meticulously collated prior to the fall of the Ming dynasty (1644). However, it should be remembered that since both rare and ordinary volumes were produced during every period in Chinese history, their distinction lies not so much in the place and time of their production as in the making and condition of the volumes themselves.

Amongst the rare books in the collection at the Museum, there are volumes dating from the Song, Yuan, Ming and Qing dynasties, traced copies of Song and Yuan volumes, delicately copied Ming and Qing volumes, manuscripts and Japanese and Korean volumes. Some of the Buddhist texts are executed in embroidery or tapestry. Books from two imperial collections of the Qing dynasty constitute an important part of the repository. A brief account follows.

The *Tian lu ling lang* is a collection begun in 1742 at the order of the Qianlong Emperor and stored in the Zhao ren Hall. Unfortunately, the fire of 1797, which started in the Jian jing Palace, destroyed the Hall and the collection within. At the time, the second catalogue of the *Tian lu ling lang* was being compiled. The second *Tian lu ling lang* comprising 664 titles, totally different from those in the first catalogue, was inherited by the Museum; however, only a fifth of the Song editions, half of the Yuan editions and two-thirds of the Ming editions were preserved. Of these books, those dating from the Song and Yuan are probably the most treasured. In so far as quality is concerned, this collection contains many editions that cannot be found anywhere else in the world; notable examples include the *Er ya*, *Zhou li*, *Confucian Analects* and the *Works of Mencius*.

The other collection is the *Wan wei bie cang*. This was originally stored in the Yang xin Hall and comprised 160 titles in 784 volumes. These books were steadily collected in South China after the compilation of the *Si ku quan shu* had been completed. They could not be included in the collectanea as it was already complete so they were put together and given the new title *Si ku wei shou shu* ('Works not collected in the *Si ku quan shu*'). They consist mainly of beautiful hand-copied versions of Song and Yuan works whose value equals that of the original editions.

In addition, the following substantial collections from the Qianlong period are also preserved in the Museum:

THE WEN YUAN GE SET OF THE *SI KU QUAN SHU*

In 1772, the Qianlong emperor issued an edict instructing all the provincial viceroys and governors to collect all known books, whether printed or in manuscript form, throughout the empire and loan them to the Emperor. In 1774, the Qianlong emperor found the project so far advanced that he appointed a committee of scholarly officials to decide what books should be transcribed for preservation in four imperial libraries. The name selected for the collection was taken from *si ku*, the four divisions, into which all literature had long been classified: classics, history, philosophy and belles-lettres. It took fifteen years for the scholars to complete the task and the 3,460 titles were bound in 36,383 volumes encased in 6,752 uniform wooden boxes. The books themselves were luxuriously bound in four different colours of silk: green for classics, red for history, blue for philosophy and brown for belles-lettres. A total of seven sets were made; three were deposited in South China (Wen hui ge, Wen zong ge and Wen lan ge) and one in each of the four imperial libraries (Wen yuan ge, Wen su ge, Wen jin ge and Wen yuan ge). Unfortunately, three were later destroyed by acts of God, but the first and best set is now preserved and exhibited in the Museum, its uniqueness lying in the fact that it had been deposited in the Wen yuan ge in the Qing palace for imperial use.

THE CHI ZAO TANG COPY OF THE *SI KU HUI YAO*

In 1773 at the age of 63, fearing that he might not live to see the completion of the *Si ku quan shu*, the Qianlong emperor ordered that the cream of the collection be selected and two copies of each work produced. Each set included 619 titles in

2,001 boxes. One set was subsequently destroyed in a fire, the other was preserved in the Chi zao tang in the Qing palace and is now in the Museum. This is the sole extant copy of this intellectual masterpiece.

The following collections also contain many rare items, rich in research value.

WU YING DIAN EDITIONS

In 1739, the fourth year of the reign of the Qianlong emperor, a publications office was established in the Wu ying hall to produce the Thirteen classics and the Twenty-four histories. As these books were published from the Wu ying dian, they are referred to as 'dian' editions. There were certain set standards for 'dian' editions and they may be grouped into three categories: manuscript volumes such as the *Veritable Records* and *Imperial Injunctions*; volumes printed from movable type such as the *Gu jin tu shu ji cheng* and *Ju zhen ban cong shu* and volumes printed from carved blocks such as those printed by the printshop Yangzhou Shi ju. The following categories from the Museum's collection are classified as 'dian' books and they comprise those authorised by emperors, those made by imperial order and those presented to the emperors.

GU JIN TU SHI JI CHENG

This is probably the largest and most useful encyclopaedia ever printed in China. Like its forerunners, the work was geared towards providing a comprehensive survey of all that was best in the literature of the past, dealing with virtually every branch of knowledge. The scale of this encyclopaedia is truly stupendous: the table of contents alone occupies no fewer than 20 volumes. The first edition was printed using copper movable type in 1728. Three copies were preserved in the Palace and they are now in the Museum.

BOOKS PRESERVED IN THE GUAN HAI TANG

This was originally the private collection of Yang Shoujing who went to Japan in 1879 with the Chinese ambassador. At the time, Japan was undergoing great social reforms and old books were thought to be useless. Yang Shoujing took advantage of this opportunity to collect together many ancient books and brought them back to China in 1884. When Yang died in 1917, the government purchased his collection. The bulk of the books were given to the Song Po Library, the remainder sent to the Palace Museum. The Museum now holds 1,339 titles in 15,471 volumes.

Other books stored in the Museum include the Chinese Buddhist *Tripitaka*, Tibetan Buddhist texts, Manchu and Mongolian books, volumes from the Shi lu ku and miscellaneous titles. These collections of rare books were augmented by books acquired from many other sources; for example, an excellent rare book collection from the National Library in Peking, entrusted to the Library of Congress during the Second World War, was restored to the Museum and became readily accessible to serious readers. Moreover, because of the excellent preservation and conservation facilities, a large number of books have been donated by local bibliophiles and literati. Numbering 4,372 volumes at the present moment, these donations have a considerable role to play in strengthening the Museum's collection. Amongst the donations, that of Shen Zhongtao is probably the most significant. His Yan yi lou collection, consisting of 90 titles in 1,169 volumes, contains rare items from the Song and Yuan periods, many of which are unique copies or editions. A catalogue of the rare books in the Yan yi lou (in Chinese only) was published in 1986 to commemorate Shen Zhongtao's valuable contribution to cultural preservation.

Historical documents

The historical documents in the Museum's collection are extremely broad in scope. Those discussed here represent only a fraction of the various documents that were brought to Taiwan in the late 1940s. For the most part they are grouped in the following categories.

ARCHIVES OF THE GRAND COUNCIL

Of all the historical documents now preserved in Taiwan, the Archives of the Grand Council are of the greatest importance. From the 1730s until the last months of the Qing dynasty, the Grand Council was the highest organ of central government. Originating in the Qian long Emperor's concern for greater efficiency and security in military affairs, it became a sort of imperial privy council. Its archives contain imperial edicts and memorials to the throne, memorials from the frontiers, communications with foreign governments and documents of top-secret nature. The archive contained the most important government documents and could furnish duplicates for any items that went missing from the archives of the Grand Secretariat.

PALACE MEMORIALS

These differ from the archives of the Grand Council in that they contain less information about state affairs and more about the private life of the emperor. They include such items as state papers presented to the emperor by statesmen and officials, memorials bearing comments in the imperial hand, authorised poems and essays, and the daily records of various departments in the Palace. These provide excellent material for research into the court system and the lives of the emperors themselves.

THE *VERITABLE RECORDS*

These records contain entries on such important matters as accession to the throne, the selection and appointment of empresses and the bestowal of titles of nobility.

Copies of the records were made in Chinese, Manchu and Mongolian. Though generally not regarded as first-hand historical research materials, they are rich in content and entries are detailed, hence their value cannot be ignored.

THE QING ANNALS

The annals are the sections of the orthodox histories which present chronological records of events in the monarch's life. All the Qing annals were copied into special books and both Chinese and Manchu versions were made. The Annals preserved in Taiwan include the reigns of the Emperor Tai zu through to Mu zong (1644–1874), though they are incomplete. Further, for the reigns of certain emperors, only the Manchu versions are available.

IMPERIAL MANDATES

These are proclamations from the emperor to the ministers and people. Although the text of the proclamation is said to be in the emperor's words, it was the product of many scholars' work. As the documents became increasingly ornate literary productions, the texts are neither completely reliable nor of first-rank value as historical resources.

DIARIES OF ACTIVITIES AND REPOSE

Although the Diaries were written by the officials-in-attendance who recorded the words and movements of the emperors at all times, they cannot be regarded as authorised history. They provided the material that was later drawn on in writing the official history. The Museum has an incomplete set of these detailed diaries with more written in Manchu than Chinese.

LETTERS OF CREDENCE

These are documents given to a head of state by another head of state or his representative. The Museum holds copies of such documents from Burma, Korea, Japan, Russia, Thailand and the Vatican.

RECORDS OF THE BOARD ON THE HISTORY OF THE QING DYNASTY

The Board on the History of the Qing dynasty began the work of compiling the Qing history in 1914 and its task was completed in the autumn of 1927 although, owing to the untimely death of its Director, the publication did not materialise. The original draft was later taken to Shenyang for publication as the Manchurian edition of the *Draft History of the Qing Dynasty* which was later reprinted by the puppet-state Manchukuo. In 1960, the *Draft History* was re-issued in a photolithographic version in Hong Kong and a Chinese edition was later published, although the editing and scope of the *Draft History* are considered unsatisfactory.

In 1930, the Nationalist Government ordered the Executive Yuan to prohibit the distribution of the Chinese version of the *Draft History* and officials were sent to Beijing to retrieve all copies that had been printed and circulated. The original draft was then put in the Palace Museum for safe-keeping.

LOCAL HISTORIES

Local histories now housed in the Museum are unusual in terms of both quantity and quality. Of the Chinese local histories now preserved in the world's great museums and libraries, 51.7 per cent are in the Palace Museum, according to a survey conducted by Zhu Shijia, and no other repository has a comparable collection particularly extensive in the Ming, and early Qing (pre-19th century) and in the descriptions of the provinces of North and North-west China. To a very large extent, these records constitute a most important resource for the study of local history and genealogy in China since they deal with social conditions in various periods and places as seen from the bureaucratic point of view.

The more than 3,100 volumes in the collection were acquired from the following three major sources: the collection transported to Taiwan with the exodus of the Nationalist government in 1949; the donation made by the Ministry of Defence in 1983; and the collection returned by the Library of Congress after the Second World War. It is worth noting at this point that more often than not the sole extant copy or edition of a particular title is to be found in this collection of local histories.

Administration and bibliographic control

The purpose of a museum, on one hand, is to take charge of the cultural records created in the past and to preserve them without loss. On the other hand, it bears the obligation of transmitting the cultural heritage to later generations so that they can appreciate and be enlightened by what has been preserved. A museum also assumes the responsibility for opening up new horizons in world scholarship. The rare books and historical documents deposited in the National Palace Museum are the records of the civilisation created by our ancestors. These records, manifesting man's loftiest wisdom and ability, have an extraordinarily long history. In virtually every case, they are rich in historical and cultural value, and represent a most important source of information and inspiration in the pursuit of the essence of China's civilisation. But how are these valuable records organised? Through what channels are they made available to the scholarly community and the general public?

Administratively, the library of the National Palace Museum is part of the larger Department of Books and Documents, to which the treasures described above have been entrusted. It is through the library that the bulk of the rare books and historical documents bearing the intellectual significance of Chinese civilisation are made accessible to scholars, researchers and the public. Though the collection *per se* is excellent, the library is, by the nature of the diverse subject matters involved, a general library rather than a research library for a specific discipline. The library is envisioned as a vital part of an international research centre for the study of Chinese arts and history, as well as being an integral part of an eminent institution. Hence, the library's immediate concern is the systematic development and expansion of its holdings to transform the collection into a research centre for the arts and history of China.

Bibliographic control plays a crucial role in the utilisation of the resources in the library. For the arrangement and classification of rare books, the methods delineated in the *Si ku quan shu* and *Shu mu da wen* are employed, with new categories added as necessary. Further, the Museum's published *Catalogue of Rare Books* and the *Catalogue of Engraved Woodblock Books* (both in Chinese only), also serve as access tools to the vast collection of rare materials in the museum. As for the historic documents, their arrangement depends on the nature of the documents themselves but in the main, they are catalogued in chronological order, with separate indices to personal names and topical headings. To date, the following tools for easy access to the Museum's document collection have been published: the *Catalogue of Qing documents* and *Personal name index to documents in Zhuan bao and zhuan gao*.

As noted elsewhere, the library is open to anyone with an interest in broadening his perspectives of China's cultural legacy. Our open-shelf policy in the use of the library's holdings of contemporary publications, for example, is a clear demonstration of our intention to fit library services to the demands of the users. Nevertheless, certain restrictions do apply to the use of the rare books and historical documents because of their inherent fragility. Where photo-duplicates have already been made of rare items as a result of extensive demand in the past, these are provided to readers; otherwise the process of securing a particular title is somewhat complex, involving a certain amount of paperwork. In either case, the materials can only be consulted in the library.

The library has always occupied an important position in facilitating the Museum's various publication projects in cooperation with publishers in the private sector, producing facsimiles of certain rare titles to meet the demands of scholars and serious readers. Titles that have been published using contemporary printing technology include the Wen yuan ge set of the *Si ku quan shu*, *Wan wei bei cang*, the Secret palace memorials of the Qianlong period, and the *Si ku hui yao*. Moreover, for preservation purposes, the Museum has just launched a gigantic microfilming project which will include all the rare books in the collection.

The library of the National Palace Museum, with its long historical tradition, has assumed a position of prominence amongst libraries in Taiwan. Through the development of its collection in Chinese arts and history, it has made a great contribution to the advancement of sinological scholarship. The quality of the rare book and archive collection is no accident and as the library strives to maintain its reputation for excellence, every effort is being made to take full advantage of the Museum's own wealth of intellectual resources. Since its incorporation into the Department of Books and Documents, it has been decided that because of its vast collection of unpublished source materials from the Qing, the library should develop its collection in the field of Qing history and become a centre for the study of the period. Thus the library, by fully utilising its original collection and by the acquisition of books and other graphic materials, can now more adequately serve the needs of those who are coming in increasing numbers to depend on its facilities for research.

Discussion

In the subsequent discussion, the point was raised that there is a need for finding aids in an archive of the size described, and whilst indexes are fundamentally arranged in chronological order, there were also proper name and subject indexes and the staff fully understood the need to guide visitors – personal assistance is a major aspect of work in the Archive.

In response to a question as to how many copies of archival items like *Shi lu* and *Ben ji* were made in each language, it was explained that, on the basis of the items in the archive, it was assumed that there was only one in Chinese and one in Manchu. The question was based on the scattered folios of *Ben ji* and *Shi lu* now in the British Library, in an attempt to discover whether these were duplicated elsewhere in the Chinese version.

Ji Shuying

The Chinese Union Catalogue of rare books and its criteria of inclusion*

The *Chinese union catalogue of rare books* (CUCRB) began publication in 1986.[1] It will be a major catalogue relating to contemporary Chinese collections of rare books, and will list about 130,000 items of such editions in the collections of institutions throughout the country, including: the National Library; the libraries of provinces, municipalities and autonomous regions; of museums, bureaux of cultural relics, schools of higher education, technical colleges, academic organisations and so on, altogether accounting for 791 sites.[2] The arrangement of bibliographic entries is according to the traditional classics, history, philosophy, belles-lettres scheme, with the addition of a section devoted to collectanea, making five sections altogether. To date, the catalogue of the classics section has been published, and this will be followed by the other four. The catalogue of the classics section is in four volumes, with a total of 5,240 titles classified into eleven categories headed: General, 'Book of Changes', 'Book of History', 'Book of Poetry', 'The Rites, The Music', 'Spring and Autumn Annals', 'Classic of Filial Piety', 'The Four Books', 'Commentaries on the Classics', and 'Lesser Learning'. Thus, the classification scheme of this catalogue broadly corresponds to that of the *Si ku quan shu* ('Complete Library of the Four Branches of Books'). Since the items recorded are early editions, and considering their typical contents, it is quite convenient to make use of this classification in practice. Of course, some appropriate adjustments and revisions to section and class headings have been made.

The items recorded in the catalogue are entirely from public collections. Private collections are not incorporated. There may, moreover, be a small number of fine editions whose records have not been forwarded by certain libraries. However, the total number of items involved is very small. For these reasons we can say that this is a comprehensive catalogue of rare books in contemporary China. In the past, the National Library of China – that is, Beijing Library – and other famous regional libraries have published separate catalogues of rare books. Although these listed a large number of such books, they remained separate and limited in scope. In 1975 the President of the State Council, Zhou Enlai, directed that, 'we must thoroughly, speedily gather together catalogues of the entire country's rare books'. By 1978 the

*Translated from the Chinese by John Cayley.

plans and stages of production for compiling the CUCRB had been worked out. In 1980 work on compilation began. In 1983 the final text was produced and handed over for publication to the Shanghai Guji publishing house.

For each entry in the catalogue, apart from title, number of volumes (*juan*), author, annotator, and edition, each work is also given a serial number. At the end of each section of the catalogue an appendix lists these numbers. If one needs to know which institutions hold a particular work, it is possible, using the serial and collection numbers, to find this information at a glance, a great convenience which will save researchers much labour in inquiries.

China has a long history and the number of books and manuscripts which have come down to us through the ages is vast, covering a wide range of subjects. Already, during the Han dynasty (26BC–7BC), for the convenience of collection management and to make it easier to find materials, Liu Xiang and his son, Liu Xin, had begun work towards regularising the cataloguing of books and manuscripts, and so established the foundations of bibliographic science. Before the invention of printing, the transmission of books depended upon manuscript copying. After printing was discovered, woodblock editions proliferated, and one work might often be hand-copied and block-printed repeatedly. The level of erudition of both copyist and block-maker varied, with some of those handling the text being careful and respectful and others lax and cursory. This meant that as a text passed through several editions and was produced by one process or another, differences appeared in textual content and gave rise to the question of which was the best edition. The vast numbers of early editions which now survive must be sorted through systematically, each item according to the circumstances of its textual history and the nature of its contents. All those with special characteristics must be singled out for preservation, so that they may survive long into the future. The books selected in this way are precisely those which have traditionally been known as rare books.

What kind of items are to be considered as rare books? In the past there has not been a commonly accepted standard. The opinions of most scholars and of others engaged in dealing with early works, have been divided. Some advocate strictness; some believe that as time progresses, standards must relax accordingly. In the field of bibliographic science the term 'fine edition' (*shanben*) has consistently referred to editions which have been properly assessed critically and which contain few textual errors; which are rare, old woodcut editions; or which are hand-copied editions (*chaoben*), critical editions (*jiaoben*) or, original manuscripts (*shougaoben*) of well-known scholars and collectors. As for the items recorded in the CUCRB, broadly speaking – in accordance with the above-mentioned criteria – any early edition can be included of which relatively few copies have come down to us with one or two of the following characteristics: it has historical/cultural significance; it is material for scholarship; it contains representative artistic work. Considering the actual qualities of early works within the scope of these criteria, we find, generally speaking, that these categories are still quite broad. We shall now, in the following explanations, address ourselves to the question of how the union catalogue has considered and understood these criteria.

The question of dates

In the past, when dealing with the dates of rare books, there were those who considered only the block-printed editions (*keben*) and manuscript books from the Ming dynasty (1368–1644) or earlier to be fine editions, while in recent years, some scholars have held that Qing editions (1644–1911) can be called 'fine'. Early works share with other cultural objects an intrinsic historical value. Where they differ from other cultural objects is in recording texts. The records in books allow transmission of human historical development, cultural diffusion, and progress in scholarship and thought. They have a huge influence on the life and culture of posterity. From the point of view of 'historical/cultural significance', a book's date is the primary criterion for considering it to be a fine edition. However, it is not an absolute criterion.

There are some items whose status can be determined purely on the basis of date. For instance, the manuscripts and printed items discovered in Dunhuang and dating from before the Tang dynasty (618–906) and up to the period of the Five Dynasties (907–960) must be treated as especially valuable, without regard for their contents, down to each scrap of paper and every single character. The same goes for printed books and manuscripts of the Song and Yuan dynasties. No matter what value they have for reference, these items are, physically, over 600, and sometimes 700 or 800 years old. Looked at simply in the context of the history of printing, they are particularly worthy of preservation. Similar considerations lead us to broaden dates for hand-copied editions.

Early editions are like other cultural objects in that the more recent they are, the greater the numbers which have been preserved. The manuscripts and printed books of the Ming and Qing dynasties account for by far the largest number of early editions which have come down to us. Thus, many more factors must be considered in selecting such books as fine editions. The question of date must be set against other factors in order to deal with each case as thoroughly as possible. We can put it like this: Ming editions are not invariably fine editions; and there are a number of Qing editions which may be selected for inclusion as fine editions. How a decision is made must be discussed with reference to the actual qualities of the item.

One reason why Ming editions are not invariably fine editions is that the dynasty lasted from the fourteenth to the seventeenth centuries and in the course of almost three centuries there was an unprecedented number of publications. There are enormous differences of quality among the books which have come down to us. The first is a difference of contents. When a new edition of an ancient work was prepared during the Ming, there were some who were not rigorous in their approach. They did not undertake a careful collation or correct erroneous characters, and at times they went so far as to tamper wilfully with the work of an ancient author, revising the text and departing from the original. Such new editions (*chuanke*) are of little value, despite their great age. Moreover, simply because the craft of woodblock printing had become highly developed, almost any book could be printed and transmitted in this way. There are certain books which we now believe to have no value for research.

Apart from differences in the contents of Ming editions, differences in block printing techniques are also quite significant. There are some comparatively late Ming editions (that is, those dating from in and around the seventeenth century) which need not be singled out as fine editions since their contents are as unremarkable as their printing and since, in any case, many copies have survived.

On the other hand amongst books printed in the Qing dynasty, there are many works by contemporary scholars of high standards and materials overflowing with research value, which merit our serious attention. Where block printing technique is concerned, there are some Qing editions which have been very finely printed using good quality ink and paper. There are also some remarkable editions with the text cut in a handwritten style, then printed and bound so as to look like manuscripts. During the Qing dynasty there were specialists in the collation of artistic block prints to a high standard. Not many copies of such books have been preserved and they are also noteworthy. Since Qing editions are fairly recent, a large number of items have survived, and so it is even more difficult to choose those which particularly deserve preservation. The criterion of date must be considered together with other criteria, such as the book's contents, its research value and its quality as material for scholarship. The circumstances of transmission must also be looked into – whether many copies have survived or not. The woodblock printing of early works had come to the end of its development in the late nineteenth century. If a Qing edition possesses special characteristics, we should not allow considerations of date to prevent its being singled out as a fine edition.

The question of contents

A book's contents are weighed up in terms of its practical and research value. As time progresses, the sphere of learning is extended and our treatment of early works develops accordingly. For example, in the Qing dynasty and earlier, the 'Five Classics' and 'Four Books' were required reading and so given precedence. However, according to our present way of seeing things, history and philosophy have a much wider range of application. Another example can be taken from printed editions of the late sixteenth and early seventeenth centuries. At that time, many books which were fairly common contained plays or novels, and some had, in turn, additional woodblock illustrations. Such editions of plays and novels were later to acquire greater value as research material than other books, because they were despised by scholars in feudal society despite their high artistic quality. Few of these works have survived.

There are many other books representing a wealth of research material which, when they are being assessed for inclusion as fine editions, can call for a relaxation of criteria. Examples are found amongst some scholars' manuscripts, for example authors' handwritten manuscripts and hand-copied manuscript books with annotations by the author. Amongst these are unique materials. Further instances include collections of poetry and prose by Ming and Qing authors. The contents of these collections are very rich, and famous as literary collections. However, they are not simply literary works. There are a certain number of scholarly/scientific works included amongst the literary texts, forming equivalents of modern collections of scholarly essays. There are other types of materials, such as contemporary biographies, which are also often seen in these 'literary' collections. For these reasons, we must always give as much, if not more, attention to such collections of poetry and prose as we do to contemporary editions of other books. Then there are local histories, records of officials, and genealogies from the various provinces and regions, all of which are of a high research value. The criterion of date can also be relaxed in the case of these books.

Printing technology

During the history of the development of Chinese block printing there have been frequent innovations in printing technology. Early woodblock printed books were not only impressed with carved text, they sometimes had woodblock illustrations of a high standard, demonstrating that the origin of block-print image making is also very early. In the mid-eleventh century, movable type was invented. In the mid-fourteenth century multiple block printing appeared, that is, on each page of a book, characters in two colours could be impressed. By the seventeenth century the techniques of multiple block printing were even better known. On a single page characters in two or more colours – up to four or five – could be printed and multicolour woodblock illustration had also appeared. Books which have special significance relating to these printing technologies naturally merit our serious attention. For example, when choosing between a block-printed edition and one printed in movable type, the movable type edition must be seen as more important, since movable type editions are more rare. Movable type editions, multiple block editions, books with woodblock illustrations or multiple block colour illustrations – all were printed in small numbers, and even fewer have survived. In the past, book collectors thought of Ming movable type editions as being especially precious, second in value only to Song editions.

In addition there are certain books which exemplify some particular aspect of printing technology, and which can be selected as fine editions entirely on the basis of this characteristic. For instance, at the end of the 1950s, two books dating from 1844 were discovered which were printed with clay movable types. Block-printed books from the same period would not necessarily be treated as fine editions, but the special character of books printed from a font of clay types definitely qualifies them as such. Apart from this, there are some books of outstanding artistic quality when looked at in the context of the development of printing techniques or the art of block cutting. Towards the end of the Ming dynasty (mid-seventeenth century), for example, multiple block colour printing – with separate colours printed from separate blocks – was invented. Blocks were cut for each of the different colours of a painting to make a set which was then printed, building up a coloured image which reproduced the original painting. Amongst the works of this time produced in colour there is *Meng xuan bian gu jian pu*, *Shi zhu zhai hua pu*, *Shi zhu zhai jian pu*, etc. This technique of printing from multiple carved blocks has been handed down to the present day. It has been continued and developed in the woodblock watercolour printing of the famous studios in Beijing and Shanghai, the Rongbaozhai and Duoyunxuan. Books like these, having special significance for printing technology, should be regarded as fine editions and treated with proper care.

Critical notes and colophons

In the process of the transmission of an early work, critical comments and notes are often written into a book, or it may be checked against other editions, or introductory remarks and explanations may be added, usually known as 'colophons' (*ba*). Such books also merit serious attention. Two sets of circumstances pertain to such books. On the one hand the book may, itself, satisfy the criteria for a fine edition. Then, when famous scholars or collectors add their critical notes and colophons, it becomes even more attractive. On the other hand, the book may be more or less run of the mill, becoming a fine edition by virtue of the critical notes and colophons which well-known scholars and collectors have added in manuscript. Such circumstances must be very carefully gone into, since not all books with critical notes and colophons should be treated as fine editions. The notes and colophons must be examined in order to discover whether they should or should not be regarded as important. The quality and authorship of these additions must be assessed. To clarify points of this kind a wealth of professional knowledge and considerable power of discrimination are required. Critical notes and colophons can enhance the usefulness of a book, since the contents of the added material may have intrinsic research or reference value.

Early Chinese works have a long history and have been produced in many different places. Because of this a single title is often made into blocks or copied by many people at many different times and places, giving rise to a proliferation of editions. In normal circumstances, textual criticism is carried out by collating texts based on good quality early editions. This work can be used to help to correct errors in the text or supply missing characters. At the same time, the characteristics of other editions can be recorded. Colophons are generally of some substance, introducing the origins and development of the edition, explaining the significance of the text, etc. We can learn a great deal from the colophons of our forbears, and so these critical notes and colophons must also receive our serious consideration.

The form of the book

The quality of a book is also looked at from the point of view of its external appearance. There are four main aspects of this: first, printing technique (quality of the block cutting and impression); second, the quality or otherwise of the paper and ink; third, whether or not the blocks used in printing were newly cut or refurbished from an earlier impression; and fourth, the quality of the binding.

Before it can be block printed, the text of an early work must first be written out and then carved according to the traces of the handwritten characters. Because of this, great care must be taken in the first process to ensure that the text is well written; and in the second production process to ensure that the block cutters have a good technique. Only a book printed from blocks which are cut in this way can manifest strength and vigour in the style of the original writing, and so be counted as first-rate.

The paper and ink used in book production are also important in determining quality. The physical extent of China is vast and there are many different regionally produced papers. Paper made during the same period can be of varying quality because it comes from different regions, and, when books are produced with different papers, corresponding differences arise. There are some sets of books from the same edition in which the paper used during printing differs. Examples are the *Quan Tang shi* ('Complete Tang Poems') printed during the Kangxi period (1662–1723), and the large-scale *Gu jin tu shu ji cheng* ('Synthesis of Books and Illustrations of Ancient and Modern Times') printed in bronze movable type during the Yongzheng reign period. Editions of these books used both *kaihua* paper and *taishilian* paper in different printings.[3] There are many books of the Ming and Qing dynasties which have impressions made on different paper.

Early Chinese works are first carved on to wooden blocks and then printed. Because of this, there arises the distinction between early impressions and later impressions. Printing from newly cut blocks produces crisp, clear impressions of the characters, but after many impressions, the strokes of the characters can become ragged and coarse looking. If the blocks are stored for a long time, it is hard to avoid damage to some of the characters. Sometimes the blocks are refurbished and successive printings are made; however, the quality will not be up to that of the earlier impressions. Thus, in selecting books we must take care of these points. There are some early impressions which are fine editions, while later impressions, from the same set of blocks, are not necessarily so.

Binding is another factor which has to be carefully considered. Bindings and books are a bit like clothing and people. Just as fashions have always changed with the times, so books have always been bound in different ways. Nowadays when speaking of early Chinese editions, the thread-bound book is often mentioned. However the thread-bound book is far from being the earliest form of Chinese binding. From actual surviving objects, we can see that books during the Tang dynasty (618–906) and before were in the form of scrolls. In the Song dynasty (960–1279) the book bindings developed into booklets (*ce*), bound for the most part in the butterfly form. During the Yuan dynasty (1260–1368), the butterfly binding continued to be used, and after the beginning of the Ming dynasty (1368–1644), this was changed to a wrapped-back binding, outwardly very similar to modern book binding. An example of wrapped-back binding is that of the *Yong le da dian* ('Ming Encyclopedia of Yongle, 1403–1424'). Thread-bound books first appeared after the middle of the Ming dynasty, and are still being made right down to the present day. If early editions which have come down to us still retain their original bindings, when they are restored their original form must be preserved. The form of binding must not be altered. The same applies to books of the Ming and Qing dynasties.

External influences

Apart from qualities intrinsic to books themselves, there are external influences which are important elements of any assessment. For instance, during the reign of Qianlong (1773–1786), Gaozong Hongli commanded the compilation of the *Si ku quan shu* ('Complete Library in Four Branches of Literature'), ordering officials of the various provinces to collect books in local libraries. In actual fact this amounted to a vast censorship operation on all books then available. In the course of compiling the *Si ku quan shu*, after receiving the books forwarded from the provinces, the great seal of the Hanlin Academy was, as a rule, impressed on the upper part of the recto of the first leaf each book. Then, after they had been thoroughly examined by the editors, some of the books were selected for inclusion, edited into the *Si ku quan shu*, and provided with brief explanations known as *tiyao*. Amongst the books selected, there were some which had first to be cut or amended before they could be copied into the manuscript of the *Si ku*. The books which were used in this way are collectively known as the *Si ku di ben* ('base texts'). There were also books which were excluded from the *Si ku*. Some of these were included in the *cunmu* ('extant items') and also had *tiyao* written for them. Afterwards all the *tiyao* were collected and went to make up the *Si ku quan shu zong mu ti yao* ('Imperial Catalogue of the Complete Library in Four Branches of Literature'). From the base text of the *Si ku* which has come down to us, it is possible to see the extent of cutting and revision in the case of certain books. From the nature of the material cut or revised, it is possible to understand the motivation of the revisions, and this makes the base text an excellent source for historical research. At one and the same time, the compilation of the *Si ku quan shu* led to many books being listed as 'indexed' (*jinshu*) and destroyed after examination. If we come across a book which has somehow managed to survive despite the 'index', it must be especially highly regarded.

Conclusions

Not all surviving works are fine editions. Only those books which have special qualities deserving of preservation or are relatively 'rare' can be counted as fine editions. By 'rare' we mean that either a particular book or a particular edition is uncommon. The books recorded in the CUCRB have been selected on the basis of the above principles. Generally speaking, in the case of pre-seventeenth-century printed books and manuscripts we are more generous in applying criteria apart from date. In the case of printed books and manuscripts of the Qing dynasty (seventeenth century and later), the particular characteristics of the book have to be rigorously examined, although all those with special qualities should be given generous consideration.

Translator's notes

1. 'Rare book' is here used to translate the term *guji shanben*, especially as it occurs in the title of the union catalogue. The important point to note is that the Chinese term embraces both printed books

and manuscripts satisfying the criteria of rarity and value described in this paper. The use of the word 'book' in the translation is often used in accordance with this Chinese usage. The two elements of *guji shanben* sometimes appear separately in the text where they are most often translated as 'early work' and 'fine edition' respectively.
2. This figure refers to the number of separate items or copies recorded in the catalogue. Mrs Ji informs me that the number of titles recorded is approximately 60,000.
3. *Kaihua* paper, made from paper mulberry, is a fine, strong, high-quality paper which was used for imperial editions. *Taishilian* is a bamboo based paper of lesser quality. The copy of the *Gu jin tu shu ji cheng* in the collection of the British Library is printed on *taishilian* paper.

Discussion

In the subsequent discussion, Mrs Ji revealed that the *shan ben* catalogue was to be published in a limited edition of 2,000. On the question of how to decide whether an item is unique, Mrs Ji said that all existing catalogues, both ancient and modern, were consulted to see whether the item was listed anywhere, but that it was also sometimes a question of experience.

Jean-Pierre Drège

The Dunhuang and Central Asian manuscripts and the history of books

The discovery of the Dunhuang manuscripts at the beginning of the twentieth century was a revelation for researchers in the fields of economics, religion and literature in medieval China, opening up quite unheard-of possibilities. Historians have placed stress on the quantity of new textual and documentary material, to some extent banishing into oblivion another aspect of the manuscripts, their place in the history of the book in China, which has been little explored by scholars.

In the paragraph above, I take the point of view of one who resorts to manuscripts, not that of the historian of science and it is in that context that we may raise a certain number of questions and make some observations.

Many of the fields of investigation enriched after the journeys made by Sir Aurel Stein and Paul Pelliot were already well-developed, but the study of the manuscripts themselves as archaeological objects and not as texts has developed only after the initiative of Fujieda Akira.[1] R H Clapperton, an historian of paper, showed interest in the Dunhuang manuscripts but the science of paper history only started to develop some 20 years ago.[2]

It was also true that until recently, the history of the bound manuscript and the history of paper in the medieval era remained largely dependent on historical sources. A more recent development, the analysis of manuscripts, should cast a new light on these sources. Traced only through texts, the history of books and paper is punctuated with areas of shadow. This is due to the scarcity of texts and to the brevity of references scattered throughout general works. To mention only the period from the fifth to the tenth century, the period when the Dunhuang manuscripts were copied, apart from a few remarks about the uses of paper and the various types of paper used in the administration of the Empire, texts about the manufacture of paper can only be found in Jia Sixie's *Qi min yao shu* (sixth century) or in anecdotes related to the copying of Buddhist sutras in collections of edifying stories. The account in the *Qi min yao shu* deals with the techniques of treatment and conservation of works. Except for Zhang Yanyuan's *Li dai ming hua ji* (ninth century), the mounting of scrolls is mentioned nowhere. As for the evolution of the morphology of the manuscripts themselves, we have not found any mention of it before the Song dynasty where references appear in books such as Ouyang Xiu's *Gui tian lu* (1007–1072) or the anonymous *Xuan he shu pu* (*c.* 1120). These are only brief references, the meaning of which is sometimes rather obscure.

It is for these reasons that the Chinese manuscripts discovered in Central Asia, especially at Dunhuang, are so precious to us, for thanks to this concrete evidence, it is possible to cast a new light on the meagre data from historical sources. As regards the history of books and more particularly the evolution of the format of books, the Dunhuang manuscripts provide all the forms, from handwritten scrolls to the form which would ultimately become the printed book:[3]

1. The 'whirlwind book', *xuan feng zhuang*, sometimes called the 'dragon scales' book.
2. The 'concertina' book.
3. The pothi, in the Indian manner.
4. The 'butterfly book', *hu die zhuang*.
5. Loose leaves.

In addition, there are the combined forms:

1. The 'butterfly' books with 'pothi' style holes.
2. The 'concertina' books with 'pothi' style holes.
3. Books combining the 'butterfly' and 'concertina' styles.

A close study of those various forms allows us to clarify the very few textual references in historical sources and to generate a greater understanding of the influences these formats had upon one another during a period of co-existence, that is to say the eighth century, before many faded away, leaving room only to a few which were better fitted to the expansion of the printed book.

As for the history of paper, we can obtain a certain number of details through morphological study, of the type of moulds used for making sheets of paper or of dying, for instance. As for the mould, we can see that the transition from the primitive, fixed mould to the movable one, composed of a screen, with laid-lines and chain-lines, the traces of which are visible on the sheets, took place before the end of the third century; we can actually still see such traces on the Loulan manuscripts which date from that period, whereas none of the paper fragments supposedly dated back to the Han dynasty apparently show any sign of laid-lines or chain-lines.

Chemical analysis recently pursued in Great Britain, China and France has also cast a new light on our knowledge of the history of paper.[4] We must acknowledge our gratitude to Mr Pan Jixing who has applied his analysis to clarifying early texts on paper history. It is imperative to investigate thoroughly and expand such a form of analysis: far too few manuscripts have been examined in this way. Manuscripts from other places in Central Asia, which do not belong to the same period as that of the Dunhuang manuscripts have hardly been studied. A wider range would allow better comparisons to be drawn. Moreover, to work on too narrow a sampling may lead to interpretations which are poles apart. As yet, in such a type of analysis, the fibre content has been of primary interest, whereas the loading and sizing elements, the pigments and the dyes as well as the inks, have been less thoroughly studied.[5] If the Dunhuang and Central Asian manuscripts have been and will remain a field of investigation for the book and paper historians, those who use the manuscripts and are therefore interested in the history of the manuscripts themselves have undoubtedly to expect something new from the application of techniques of scientific analysis to paper. I will mention only two significant examples which concern the problem of the dating of manuscripts and their authenticity.

First, the dating of undated manuscripts poses a certain number of questions which have not yet been solved. Only a very small proportion of the Dunhuang manuscripts bear a date; for the others, dating is assessed according to the text on the manuscript and its content, but also quite often according to an opinion about the style of the writing. These two criteria are usually not satisfactory for perfect dating. Thanks to the morphological analysis of paper, we can come to more reliable indications, by comparing the manuscripts to those already dated. Nevertheless, quite a large number of manuscripts do not fit into the field of typology already established for the dated manuscripts. This is why a different kind of analysis, such as the one currently being pursued by the paper experts, might provide other dating elements. That would be very useful not only for the Dunhuang manuscripts but also for the other manuscripts of Central Asia, whose origin and methods of production are more diversified. The most striking example is undoubtedly that of 'the ancient Sogdian letters'. These letters were discovered by Sir Aurel Stein in 1907 in a watch-tower located near Dunhuang. First, Aurel Stein, with the support of the paper expert Julius Wiesner, determined that they dated back to the second century AD just after the alleged invention of paper by Cai Lun. In 1948 W B Henning, when translating these letters, established they dated back to the beginning of the fourth century. More recently, in 1971, relying on a brief description of the paper, Mr Fujieda Akira suggested we should date them to the beginning of the sixth century. Recently the controversy has been raised again, with some scholars such as J Harmatta (1979), Huang Zhenhua (1982), and Lin Meicun (1985) suggesting the end of the second century, others like Wang Jiqing (1986) or N Sims-Williams and F Grenet (1985–86) being more inclined toward the early fourth century. A very close comparison of the paper of these letters with Dunhuang and Loulan manuscript paper shows that the most likely hypothesis is probably the one dating them back to the early fourth century. Indeed, the paper bears more similarity to the paper of the Loulan manuscripts (end of the third or beginning of the fourth century) than to the most ancient of the Dunhuang manuscripts which date back no earlier than the fifth century. Contrary to Fujieda's findings, the paper is entirely different from that of the Northern manuscripts dating back to the first half of the sixth century. As far as the second century dating is concerned, no comparison is possible and J Wiesner's opinion is based only on the previous statement by A Stein who, in turn, relied on questionable archeological data. In such a case, it would be very useful to resort not only to a morphological analysis, but to a chemical analysis by comparing the elements which constitute the paper of these letters with those of the Dunhuang manuscripts dated back to the fifth and the sixth century, or those of the Loulan manuscripts dated back to the beginning of the fourth century. Let us hope that such an analysis will be achieved and settle the controversy.

The user of the manuscripts may also expect to find a solution to a second problem he is faced with: the authenticity of manuscripts in some collections. Everybody knows that not long after the discovery of the Dunhuang manuscripts, deliberately produced forgeries spread all over the Far East, filling some private collections and various libraries. Once again, opinions are at odds. Collections such as those of the National Museum in Kyoto, Otani University and the National Central Library in Taibei[7] were regarded as genuine up to the moment when they were discredited by Mr Fujieda. It is, of course, sometimes difficult to judge and a morphological study is not sufficient to make a decision. Some manuscripts in these collections are so different from genuine manuscripts from the Pelliot and Stein collections that it is inconceivable to take them as such. This is why one may suppose that a chemical analysis might disclose new elements allowing us to establish a greater difference between the real manuscripts and the forgeries. A preliminary stage of this type of analysis is being pursued at the moment, for Mr Collins and Mr Milner who have already worked on the Stein manuscripts, are studying some fragments known as forgeries which were produced in the Khotan area by Islam Akhun. We know that not long before 1900, this forger proposed quite a number of manuscripts written in an 'unknown' language, which Dr Hoernle went on studying unsuccessfully until Stein discovered the forgery. Let us hope that new analysis will lead to a better differentiation.

In conclusion, if the Dunhuang and Central Asian manuscripts have enriched our knowledge of the history of books and paper and will continue to do so, the analytical techniques of paper specialists might enable us to answer the basic questions concerning the actual history of the manuscripts themselves.

Notes

1. A Fujieda, 'The Tunhuang manuscripts: a general description', *Zinbun*, 9, 1966, pp. 16–27.
2. R H Clapperton, *Paper, an historical account of its making by hand from the earliest times down to the present day* (Oxford, 1934), pp. 23–26.
3. J-P Drège, 'Du rouleau manuscrit au livre imprimé', in *Le Texte et son inscription*, (CNRS, Paris to be published).
4. J-P Drège, 'L'analyse fibreuse des papiers et la datation des manuscrits de Dunhuang', *Journal Asiatique*, 274, 1986, pp. 403–415.
5. J-P Drège, 'Dun huang xie ben de wu zhi xing fen xi; *Han xue yan jiu*, 4, 2, 1986, pp. 109–114.
6. F Grenet, N Sims-Williams, 'The historical context of the ancient Sogdian letters', *Transition periods in Iranian history* (Paris, 1987), pp. 70–83.
7. J-P Drège, 'Étude formelle des manuscrits de Dunhuang conservés à Taipei: datation et authenticité', *Bulletin de l'Ecole Française d'Extreme-Orient*, 74, 1985, pp. 477–484.

Discussion

In the discussion, the relationship between the simple ninth and tenth century thread-bound booklets found at Dunhuang and the later *xianzhuang* or thread-bound format was raised and M Drège was of the opinion that there was no particular connection between the two. Questioned about changes in paper-making techniques such as moulding which might facilitate dating (as it does with Western paper), he thought that techniques of paper-making changed very little after the Song and that it was difficult to study the paper of printed books for the post-Song period. The Dunhuang finds were easier, providing a great mass of manuscripts from one source, even if some were actually copied in Chang'an or elsewhere.

M Drège thought that there were examples of *xuanfeng zhuang* (whirlwind or dragon-scale binding) in the Paris and London collections but these had been broken up and now consisted of separate sheets. They were all rhyme books, like the Beijing example. It was clear that the discovery of the *xuanfeng zhuang* in the Palace Museum, Beijing, had completely altered the traditional view of what *xuanfeng zhuang* was, and that the description by Li Zhizhong and others superseded that of Professor Kawase Kasuma, for example.

Pan Jixing

The origin of papermaking in the light of scientific research on recent archaeological discoveries

Papermaking, the compass, gunpowder and printing are the four great inventions of ancient China. The invention of papermaking brought about a revolution in writing materials, and played a great role in the development of human culture. According to the historian Fan Yie (397–445 AD), paper was invented by the eunuch Cai Lun (a.61–121) of the Eastern Han dynasty (25–220 AD) in the year 105. But other scholars of the eighth to twelfth centuries thought that paper must have existed before the Eastern Han, and that Cai Lun's contribution was to make an improved paper from plant fibre.

Which raw materials were used for papermaking before Cai Lun, and who was the inventor of paper? There has been controversy for a long time about these problems in China and abroad. In the past, few writers studied the technique of papermaking in early times, and the questions raised above were not solved until after the 1940s. Before then, most people believed that paper was invented by Cai Lun, since there was not sufficient evidence to disprove the traditional account. It is fortunate that modern archaeological excavations carried out during this century in China have provided many valuable practical materials to help solve the problems related to the origin of papermaking. Let me enumerate the newest archaeological discoveries and the results of examination of the excavated paper. The well-known archaeologist, the late Dr Huang Wenbi first found a small sheet of pale yellow paper at the side of a beacon of the second century BC at Lopnor in Xinjiang in 1933. It was made of hemp fibre no later than 49 BC and thus was made at least 154 years earlier than the year 105AD. This important discovery proved that before Cai Lun there actually had been paper made of hemp fibre. But the sheet of paper was destroyed by fire during a war of 1937.

However, in 1957, other pieces of paper were recovered in an old tomb at the Baqiao building site near the city of Xi'an in Shaanxi province. These were made no later than 140–87BC. It had previously been thought that the earliest paper was made of silk fibre, and that vegetable fibre paper was invented by Cai Lun. But after we had done a microscopic analysis of this early paper in 1964 and 1980, we found that it was not made of silk, but hemp fibre. Through further research we recognised it as the earliest paper made of plant fibre. We felt greatly honoured to have the opportunity to provide material evidence to prove that paper was actually invented by craftsmen 2,000 years ago in the Western Han dynasty (206BC–25AD). Since then, excavations of ancient paper have been given much attention by archaeologists. Specimens of early paper made before Christ have appeared gradually in various places and wonderful discoveries have been made one by one.

In 1973 a professional archaeological team in North-western Gansu province found two pieces of hemp paper made in 52 and 6BC respectively at a military post, Jinguan, at a point of the bank of the River Erjina, near the western end of the Great Wall. Five years later in December 1978 archaeologists found a collection of miscellaneous items in a ceramic pot in an architectural ruin of the second to first centuries BC in Zhongyan village, Fufeng county, Shaanxi province. When they examined the contents of the ceramic pot in detail they discovered two pieces of paper. After analysis in 1980 we recognized these as hemp paper, dating from the Emperor Xuan's reign (73–49BC).

The most recent discovery was made in 1979. A professional archaeological team in Gansu province found a lot of wooden tablets and other things, including eight pieces of hemp paper at a beacon ruin of the Western Han at Majuanwan, a north-western suburb of the famous Dunhuang county on the Silk Route. They date from the first century BC to the very beginning of the Christian era. We made a microscopic analysis of the fragments in 1980 which proved they were all made from hemp fibres. In short, plant fibre paper made of hemp datable before Christ has been excavated five times in various places in China in 1933, 1957, 1973, 1978 and 1979. This paper was all dated by experts in published reports. Four of these samples of excavated paper have several times undergone microscopic analysis by us and other scholars in laboratories. According to our analysis, all paper dated before Christ was made of hemp (*Cannabis sativa L*) and ramie (*Boehmenia nivea Gaud*). Not one piece was made of silk fibre. The mean length of the paper fibre is 1–2.2 mm, and mean width is 19–21μ (one μ is equal to 0.001 mm). The mean length of raw hemp and ramie is 12–25 and 120–180 mm respectively. This means that the hemp fibre was not raw but treated. With the exception of the earliest example (the Baqiao paper), all the fibres were broken up by beating to various degrees. The excavated ancient paper has a density of 0.28–0.33 g/cm^3 which is within the range for common hand-made paper. All ancient paper consisted mainly of individual and dispersed fibres interwoven in different directions by beating and pounding.

Apart from Baqiao paper, which is pale yellow, Jinguan paper, Zhongyan paper and Majuanwan paper-V all have a brightness of more than 40 per cent. After treatment with a reagent of zinc chloride and iodine solution (ZnICl) the paper fibres appeared a wine-red colour. This indicates that the raw material for papermaking was digested with a basic solution. In ancient times the ash of white goosefoot vine, (*Chenopodium album*) was often used to prepare the basic solution, because it contains potassium carbonate (K_2CO_3) which is the salt of a weak acid (carbonic acid H_2CO_3) and a strong alkali (potassium hydroxide, KOH), so the solution should show an alkaline character. On the surface of the Zhongyan paper and Majuanwan paper we are able to see faint screen marks of the type of the so-called 'wove mould'. From the preceding observations and technological data we reached the following conclusions:

1. Paper was invented in the Western Han dynasty, in the second to the first century BC. Its inventor, therefore, was not Cai Lun, but craftsmen whose names are unknown.

2. Paper dated before Christ was all made of hemp or ramie fibres, just like that made in the later periods. We have not found paper made of silk fibres from this period.

3. We have been able to determine the raw materials, character and outward forms of early paper. With the help of imitative experiments done in the field we have also gained a clear idea of the technical processes and apparatus for making early paper.

Now let me describe the process of papermaking in the Western Han period on the basis of our imitative experiments. First, the raw materials (rags, used fish-nets, waste hemp, rope stubs, etc.) were put in water and then cut into smaller pieces with an iron axe. After washing carefully in the river, and pounding either with the feet or a wooden bar, the raw materials were treated with a basic solution. Craftsmen burnt some kind of plant (white goosefoot vine is the best one), then mixed the vegetable ash with water. This was filtered to obtain the solution used for digesting the fibres. The solution was poured into an iron pot over which there was an iron grating connected to a wooden bucket. The raw material was put into the bucket, some basic solution poured on, and then the bucket was closed. The raw material was digested for more than 20 hours. After digesting, it was taken out of the bucket and washed in the river, then put into a stone mortar to be pounded into paper pulp. Two kinds of mortar were used. The pulp was then washed again and put into a stone or wooden vat, mixed with clear water, and stirred continuously. An experienced papermaker would put the paper mould into the vat to make a sheet of paper, then take it out of the vat and place it outside. After drying he took the paper from its mould, and stacked up many sheets which were trimmed on all four sides. In this way many sheets of paper could be made to the same size.

From the description above, the problems concerning the origin of papermaking have been resolved through scientific research on early samples. It is unnecessary to maintain the traditional theory, since 'practice is the sole criterion to examine truth'. We believe that there will be new discoveries of ancient paper in the future. The new point of view has been supported by leading Chinese and foreign scholars and here we want to express our thanks to them. However, has the contribution and role of Cai Lun been entirely negated? Our answer is no. Cai Lun should still be credited with his own contribution. First, he summed up his predecessors' technical experience in making hemp paper and organised the production of high quality paper for writing. He therefore improved and popularised the technique.

第二章 两汉时期的造纸技术

图2—11 汉代造纸工艺流程图

Fig. 3 Technological flow diagram of the making of hemp paper in the Han dynasty (221BC–220AD).

Secondly, he led craftsmen to produce bark paper from paper-mulberry (*Broussonetia papyrifera* Vent) fibre, thus extending the sources of raw materials for papermaking. Bark paper was actually the product of a technical innovation. In short, he was a technical innovator serving as a link between past and future.

Papermaking, like other ancient techniques, could not have been invented accidentally by a single person, but must have gone through a historical evolution. Our experience of making paper has taught us that an individual could not perfect the processes of papermaking, which is a collaborative labour. According to historical records, the Chinese brush was invented by Meng Tian, a senior general of the Qin dynasty (third century BC) but archaeological findings have proved that people started to use writing brushes in the Shang dynasty in the sixteenth to twelfth centuries BC or earlier. This is another area in which historical records have been disproved by facts. There is no basis for further perpetuating the theory that Cai Lun invented paper.

[This paper was distributed but not read at the conference as Professor Pan was unable to join the colloquium as planned]

Peter Lawson

Conservation of Chinese materials in the British Library

In order to introduce our current methods of work, and, in particular, the after-care aspect of conservation, I will first describe briefly some of the earlier approaches to early Chinese material after it arrived in the British Museum. The most significant collection, that of the Stein manuscripts, was first stored in blue board boxes and some of the scrolls and fragments were mounted on a chemically unstable paper, mainly of European origin. This mounting method was short-sighted in that it precluded the possibility of future paper analyses. It would be impossible, for instance, to look for evidence of starch sizing, for any original sizing would lose its identity when the scroll was re-lined with starch paste prior to mounting. The boxes were also liable to slowly destroy the manuscripts as they contained a tray resting on an inner ledge which tended to fall down on the manuscripts below.

Our policy in the library today is very different. We have abandoned the boxes for more secure storage, to which I will return, and in treatment of the manuscripts, where we use two distinct methods, our fundamental philosophy is that of minimal intervention, in other words we interfere with a manuscript as little as possible.

The first of the two methods we use today, with manuscripts of a restricted size that require no further treatments (perhaps to reverse earlier mountings) is simply to stitch them into a polyester film (produced by ICI and trade-named Melinex), using an industrial sewing machine so that the manuscript is encapsulated in a very stable plastic. If in future we need to do anything further to the manuscript or need to take a paper sample for analysis, it is a simple matter just to cut it out. Though the method is easily reversed, as the cost of the material and labour involved is probably about £40 a folio, we cannot undertake removal without a very good reason.

The second method of treatment, used in cases of damage and in longer scrolls that are, because of their length, unsuited to encapsulation, is more lengthy. We first begin with the case history of the scroll, a description of all its characteristics, a fibre sample and a record of proposed actions. Taking the fibre sample is particularly important; though we ourselves are not specialists in fibre analysis, we can often recognise common fibres such as paper mulberry, and we hope in time to build up a bank of fibre slides to go with the manuscripts themselves. It is a simple matter to take a few fibres and make a slide prior to mounting or conserving. Scrolls that are too long to be put into Melinex have to be mounted.

Damage often has to be repaired and making up missing areas is necessary to prevent tearing or further damage if the scroll is to be unrolled and used. Horizontal tears can result from scroll ties weakening the centre of the document. The springiness of a lined document can cause a small central tear to expand progressively along the whole length of a document if it is carelessly handled. There are complicating factors in mounting Dunhuang scrolls, for some have text or inscriptions on both sides. In such cases we must leave the back either wholly or partially visible.

Prior to mounting, dust and dirt must first be brushed off for if this is still present when the paper is damped, it will be carried by the water into the paper and it is extremely difficult to remove the ensuing stains without recourse to strong chemicals. In conservation, careful preparation is everything and it is, for instance, just as important to spend time preparing a stable paste as it is to search out stable paper for repair. The paste we use is made from wheat starch with nothing added at all except water. It is mixed, cooked and kept under water in a refrigerator at some 2 degrees centigrade, (and not allowed to freeze). When required, a lump is taken from the water, placed on a horse-hair sieve, worked through several sieves with progressively finer meshes and eventually a very small amount is pushed through a silk sieve to produce a thin paste with a small particle size. The paste is also spread very thinly for thickly spread paste (in the European manner) is another contributing factor to scroll cracking. After preparing the paste, it is equally important to prepare the paper which is going to be used for mending or infilling. After much searching and experimentation, we have found that the only way to get a compatible tone of paper with the original is to dye it ourselves. Much time has been spent on the search for a dye that is chemically stable and reasonably light-fast and it seems virtually impossible to achieve the two: light-fast dyes often contain sulphonic acid whilst non-light-fast dyes are very chemically stable (or, in other words, acid-free). We now use a dye that is the most stable of the light-fast dyes.

If possible, we try never to line a scroll completely, for this interferes with possible future analysis of paper (for starch-sizing, for example). Partial lining also alleviates the problem of cracking. In European materials, the problem of cracking is just as acute, as heavier backing materials and much heavier paste were generally used, though the format is different: European rolls do not measure up to 30 feet or longer like many of the Chinese rolls from Dunhuang. If a scroll is fully lined, the outside circumference of the paper has further to travel round the scroll than the original on the inside, and this almost invariably causes the whole to crack across the scroll.

In the case of small cracks or tears which can be repaired without relining, these are mended with small pieces of compatible paper pasted over the tear, not made invisible but blended with the original. The dyed repair paper is cut into shape to infill by means of a water cut: a line is drawn with water outlining the desired shape and the paper is pulled apart along the water line, pulling out the long fibres. The point is to attach the drawn-out fibres to the original paper, rather than cover parts of the original with solid blocks of repair paper. The water-cut paper is then applied to the scroll and the scroll has to be carefully damped, using a deer hair brush to get a small amount of water into the paper so the edges can be fixed and the paper can contract and be pulled tight when it is fixed to the drawing board. The paste used to join the fibres is very thin, of the consistency of milk. When the scroll has been infilled and is damp, all the paper fibres tend to pull against each other, contracting and moving at different rates, so in order to fix the scroll onto a drying board, 'concertina strips' (of folded paper) are used, which allow movement on the drying board without the danger of tearing when the scroll contracts. In this way, the scroll is 'hung' on the board for at least three months as it needs to expand and contract with the varying humidity in order to settle down finally and mature as one sheet of paper.

When the scroll has been removed from the drying board, the 'concertina strips' are cut off and all repairs have to be trimmed square. If the trimming is even a fraction of a millimetre out, it takes little to imagine what would happen at the end of a 25 foot long scroll.

For convenience of consultation the finished scroll must be able to be unrolled and to stay unrolled; it is no use mounting a scroll that will roll up like a spring. The finished scroll is placed in a silk bag or a silk bag lined with cotton. The cotton is treated with a fungicide and an insecticide for, although neither of these problems afflict the library at the moment, it is always possible that something might go wrong with the air-conditioning in future.

Today, the Stein manuscripts are stored in wooden cabinets. Wood is preferred because it provides a better seal and insulation so that the cabinets are virtually airtight. They also have glass doors so that documents can be instantly checked for security purposes – these would be very hard to fit on steel cabinets. The only drawback to the system at present is that those scrolls that have not been treated need to be wrapped in paper or silk to alleviate the possibility of abrasion as they are moved in and out of their individual pigeon-holes.

Note

A more detailed paper on a similar subject: 'The preservation of pre-tenth century paper' will be delivered by Peter Lawson at the 12th International Congress of the International Institute for the Conservation of Historic and Artistic Works, Kyoto, 19–23 September 1988, and the paper will subsequently be published.

Discussion

In reply to a question on the possible deterioration over time of the plastic used in mounting, it was pointed out that the ICI polyester film is as inert as possible and is far more stable than most paper. It has been used for 20 years now and no deterioration has been noticed. It is also very widely used, the only difference in British Library practice being that is is sewn rather than welded. It is difficult to weld without expensive ultrasonic equipment and for British Library purposes sewing seems remarkably efficient.

Obviously Library policy is to encourage readers to use substitute microforms rather than original Dunhuang manuscripts and use of the originals is restricted.

In response to a question on the restoration of Chinese thread-bound books, it was necessary to explain that during the eighteenth and nineteenth centuries, and indeed until recently, it had been the practice to use European binding formats. Many of these early European bindings are now in need of repair and current practice is to re-sew in the Chinese style wherever possible, using the original holes and making a Chinese-style *tao* case. In some cases, the European-style binding involved too much trimming of the paper and it is no longer possible to re-sew the *ce*, but in the *Tu shu ji cheng*, for example, the original stab holes have been preserved and the encyclopaedic work is gradually being restored to Chinese *ce* and *tao*. In some of the early fiction volumes, the binding is so tight that even microfilming is impossible; the volumes have to be unbound for microfilming and then either rebound, European-style, or have each page separately remounted, an expensive task. The cost of such operations is considerable: the 5,000 volumes of the *Tu shu ji cheng* could represent 20,000 hours of work. If this is divided by weeks, with 40 working hours per week, plus materials at £15 a week, the final cost is not inconsiderable. Unfortunately, many decisions are now fundamentally decided by cost.

A question was raised as to whether books should be allowed to 'breathe' and whether they could do so in an airtight, glass-fronted case. This depends upon location. In a dirty, dusty city, with atmosphere bearing damaging hydrogen sulphide, it is better to exclude air. In the use of Melinex, there has been a constant debate over the virtues of total encapsulation versus ventilation. The wooden, glass-fronted cabinets were purpose designed and one of the features was that their careful finish emphasised the specialness and rarity of the Dunhuang material. Much time was spent on the design and also the finish, for as wood has a very poor pH, the protective varnish is of considerable importance.

Automation and co-operation

John Cayley

Automation and Chinese studies

'... where there are machines, there are bound to be machine worries; where there are machine worries, there are bound to be machine hearts. With a machine heart in your breast, you've spoiled what was pure and simple; and without the pure and simple, the life of the spirit knows no rest. Where the life of the spirit knows no rest, the Way will cease to buoy you up. It's not that I don't know about your machine – I would be ashamed to use it!'[1]

These are the words of what Angus Graham terms one of the 'primitivist' writers of the Daoist classic *Zhuang zi*. They were set down sometime in the third or second century BC.[2] Interestingly, they were not directed against a computer or even an abacus. It is a reactionary horticulturist who speaks these words, one who draws an absolute limit of technological corruption at a level above buckets and ropes, but *below* that of the humble well, sweep or shadoof, the 'machine' he berates in this passage. On the one hand, we have here some measure of our technological progress, and, on the other, an indication of how little change there has been in some attitudes towards it.

More seriously, however, machines do introduce 'machine worries', which is to say that, when applied to the solution of a particular problem, machines inevitably change the nature of the original problem and/or create new, related problems which may not have been foreseen. As an obvious example, we might consider the way that library automation has affected both the nature of catalogues and the nature of the cataloguing process. We move away from a conception of 'catalogue' as a book or card file – a severely limited number of fixed arrangements of physical records (which may or may not be published as such) – and towards the ideal of a flexibly indexed machine-readable file of records accessible 'on-line', eventually without any need of traditional publication because other institutions are able to share the file on a network. On the way we have to design and agree on a complex cataloguing format which is both more rigorous and less flexible than traditional manual systems. Somewhat more 'machine-worryingly' we also find ourselves splitting existing catalogues, thus significantly limiting the convenience of any automated catalogue, and raising the difficult question of 'retrospectively converting' our remaining manual catalogues. Daoist primitivists and Western traditionalists begin at this point to nod sagely, wag their fingers and murmur, 'We told you so'. Only time (inevitably more of it than we have budgeted for) will prove the levellers wrong.

The application of computers to Chinese studies has also generated its special 'machine worries'. It has and will continue to modify our understanding of the nature of both the computing and the research problems involved. It has and will continue to generate new problems for both partners in this still fairly novel cooperation. This paper goes so far as to suggest that insufficient attention has been paid to the way in which automation developments influence the problems being faced. Today, the relationship between computers as (potential) tools and Chinese research applications seems to have reached a crucial stage. At such a point it may be useful to attempt a brief analytical overview and analysis of past and present developments.

It is necessary first to make a couple of more or less isolated introductory points. At this colloquium, we are chiefly, though not exclusively, concerned with computer applications in the Humanities and Social Sciences. This needs to be said at the outset because one of automation's most egregious faults is, as we shall see, to encourage us to exchange non-technical problems for technical ones and as we do so our interests seem to veer misleadingly towards those of science and technology. It is also important – again given the nature of this colloquium – to make an initial point concerning the relationship between the automation problems of the librarian and those of the academic. In this context, we take them to be of the same nature though perhaps of a different order. The main use of computers in the Humanities is to build textbases or databases. A library's catalogue *cum* bibliographic database is simply the academic's most fundamental research tool. In theory, one of the more important effects of automation should arise from the increased potential for making the databases created and maintained by school and library mutually available with much greater flexibility, reinforcing their proper relationship against the false tendency to see them as having separate or even competing interests. Finally, as is probably clear by implication, we are mainly concerned with automation developments which face up to the problems of incorporating coded data in Chinese script. More will be said about the alternative, romanised or translated applications, later.

A promise implicit in the original title of this paper was to provide a survey of what is presently happening in Chinese automation in the UK. A partial survey will be built into the paper with, however, an intention to make the projects covered serve to illustrate the paper's main purpose, which is (once again) to try and indicate how attempts to develop useful automated applications to research in Chinese studies are influenced and altered by the field's special 'machine worries'.

Computing structures

At this point, it may be useful to remind ourselves of certain concepts and distinctions from the world of computing, while passing comment on how they effect aspects of Chinese automation development.

The distinction of levels in the provision of computing resources is now fairly familiar. Nearly everyone has heard something of the differences between micro, super-micro, mini and main-frame computers. The phenomenal and continuing decrease in hardware costs always accompanied by increase in processing power, has shifted the whole of this structure upwards a notch or two, so that, for example, personal microcomputers now have the capabilities of erstwhile minis. A related recent trend has produced an increase in the distribution of computing power to small separate systems or networks of such systems.

There have been important implications for Chinese automation in these developments. The vast increase in the power/cost ratio of small systems has been especially important because it has allowed the proliferation during the past three to four years of microcomputer systems with built-in character handling facilities. In the West this has meant that the provision of such special capabilities has 'found its own level'. Whereas previously it had been necesssary to make use of mini or main-frame power to handle an adequate Chinese character set, it is now quite easy to pack such facilities into a microcomputer which is still able to function either as a general stand-alone system or as a terminal attached to a mainframe. In the West there will be no real need to develop mainframe or even mini computer operating systems which can handle Chinese, the job can be left to the micro/terminal, while the larger machines deal with the heftier information management tasks.

In mainland China, where expensive computer resources are at a premium, there is still a place for the large system with Chinese character operating software. This is despite the historical dominance of computing by the West which has meant that Eastern computer scientists have been trained in a roman-script environment. However, because of scarce resources the computing which is spreading most quickly in today's China is microcomputing: precisely the stand-alone microcomputer systems with Chinese character handling just mentioned. The most common configuration is an IBM XT or AT Personal Computer (or clone), running under a Chinese operating system known as CCDOS, developed by the Number Six Research Institute of the Ministry of the Electronics Industry. Such a set-up is usually combined with a 'sinified' word-processor and/or database and thus allows organisations of many types in China to implement small but useful separate applications, including limited local bibliographic databases. The logical next step, the networking of such systems both with each other and with more powerful central systems managing *shared* databases and applications, is still at an early stage of development on the mainland.

The proliferation of such small systems in the People's Republic means that mainland China is in a position to all but skip over the stage – which we are steadily moving out of in the West – of the centralised, mainframe-dominated provision of computer resources. In a way which was not possible here, the Chinese will be able to get on with applications on dispersed equipment and, as more resources become available, build larger systems 'from the bottom up', as it were, seeking to integrate existing micro-based applications with new mini and mainframe systems, designed to manage and share the dispersed data.[3]

Appropriate hardware resources can be provided at any of the levels (micro, mini, etc.) outlined above, while at each level systems can be analysed along another dimension beginning with the design and capabilities of the hardware itself, and progressing through 'firmware' and 'software' proper. Basically, the 'softer' parts of a system have more specific functions, but are easier to change. The 'harder' parts of the system have more general functions, but are more difficult, if not impossible, to alter. Computers are driven by a number of more or less fundamental programs. The more fundamental programs are more likely to be associated with the 'harder' parts of the system. One of the *most* fundamental programs running a computer is its so-called 'operating system'. This is the program which, amongst other things, handles the input, output and display of the whole system's 'atoms' of (human readable) information, typically roman characters. An operating system works very closely with specific hardware and is often resident as what is known as firmware (in neat accord with the hard-soft metaphor).

Now, the only reason for bringing these potted technicalities into a paper like this is to try to emphasise the point that the development of a system for handling Chinese characters – which has normally been thought of as a legitimate aspect of 'automation and Chinese studies' – really amounts to developing part of an operating system. It is very clearly part of *making* a system and certainly not part of *using* it. A computer system only becomes a tool when it is running an 'application program'. The user of an application need know nothing about how the system works. All he or she has to be able to do is make it answer to the original research or information management problem.

The application of computers to Chinese studies has previously concerned itself overmuch with problems which were, more properly, system problems. Now that working Chinese systems and terminals are achieving slightly more generality and currency we must more carefully distinguish between the development of a system and its use. In our role as researchers and information providers (not computer technicians) we must resist, where possible, the temptation to become involved in anything approaching systems development. When hardware and software packages which handle Chinese script at the various computing resource levels exist to be 'bought off the shelf', as it were, this is not an unreasonable requirement and should lead to better general management of resources.

Ironically but inevitably, this paper itself commits the heresy it attempts to analyse and expose. In a way which parallels the development of Chinese automation and its application, it dwells too long on system designs which should now be taken for granted, rather than reporting on the – at present – fairly restricted uses which are being made of these new tools for the benefit of Chinese studies.

The special worries of Chinese automation

THE NATURE OF THE SCRIPT

Delegates to this colloquium will be more or less familiar with the special problems of Chinese automation. However, it may be useful to briefly rehearse some aspects of these problems in order to highlight certain shifting concentrations of concern.

The first problem of the script is, of course, the sheer quantity of Chinese characters, the number of separate graphic elements pointing to morphemes in the Chinese language (syllables in the spoken language, corresponding to distinct meaningful units but not always or even often to free words) which have to become 'atoms' of input and output for any truly sinified computer system. In total there are over 50,000 separate graphic forms. For serious bibliographic work, over 20,000 characters are required and there may still be occasions where an even more uncommon character must be used. In practice a slightly smaller set of characters will serve for the bulk bibliographic work. The Research Libraries Group East Asian Character Code (REACC), based on the Taiwanese-developed Chinese Character Code for Information Interchange (CCCII) includes 14,063 characters (plus 174 kana and 1,996 hangul characters), and in using the Research Libraries Information Network, Chinese-Japanese-Korean system (RLIN/CJK), at the British Library for the past year and a half, we have only once or twice been short of a character for some particular record.[4]

The size of the Chinese character set has generated four worrying questions for Chinese automation:

1. Given a particular state of hardware and software development, could a computer's operating system handle a character set of the necessary size efficiently?

2. How were the characters to be input and output?

3. How should the internal code of the characters be structured and how would this relate to the codes for existing alphabetic character sets?

4. How would the standardisation of character codes be dealt with?

The early days of Chinese automation were largely occupied with the first two questions. For obvious reasons, language specialists and other sinologists became involved in attempts at various solutions to this problem. They became, in fact, more deeply involved than their counterparts in Western language studies had been in earlier corresponding developments for roman-script languages. Computer scientists could not assume for Chinese, as they had (wrongly many would argue) for Western languages that, for example, designing and using a character set was a simple matter of common sense and expediency, with typewriters providing an obvious model for an input device.

Earlier difficulties were increased because the simple answer to the first of our worries above was, until quite recently, 'no'. Before the advent of powerful microcomputers able to handle character input and display locally – at the level of the stand-alone system or intelligent terminal – an efficient way to deal with the Chinese character set did not exist. It is really only in the past three to four years that microcomputer terminals have become available with sufficient power to build in character processing software. Earlier solutions often depended upon directly using the power of a main-frame or mini-computer for character generation, which is impracticable in the long term.

None the less, work on the development of systems for processing characters went ahead with the consequence that Chinese automation has passed through the same sort of period of immaturity which characterised much Humanities and Social Science computing more generally. Its history has been shorter and more intense, and the symptoms of immaturity have, if anything, been more marked. In a context of under-funding, with Humanities computing a sort of Cinderella in terms of resource allocation and Chinese automation even further down the pecking order, specialists and researchers at a quite high level were tempted to involve themselves with development work. The unavoidable consequence, during what is here called the period of 'immaturity', is that machine worries over-determine or even suspend work on problems which the machine is ultimately intended to solve or serve.

The good news is that, as implied in the above, the first problem of script handling can now be answered positively and the second is also no longer a difficulty which should concern the specialist seeking to make use of Chinese automation. Good quality character displays can be catered for by a variety of output devices such as 24-pin dot-matrix printers, laser printers or high resolution video displays. Schemes for character input abound and while there are many disputes over the merits of those which are currently available, many of these are perfectly servicable. The user has a choice of many ready-to-go working systems and there is no longer any excuse for reinventing the wheel in feigned isolation. No review or analysis of input systems will be attempted here. In the short history of Chinese automation they have already attracted much too much of our attention and effort. Refinements will be made to existing systems, but the basic problem had best be considered solved.[5]

In sharp contrast, no one interested in the further development of Chinese automation can ignore our other two worrying character set questions: those which concern coding standards. Again, the problems are technical but here they require the continuing involvement of specialists and librarians mainly because of the far-reaching consequences for information exchange. In an ideal world one computer system, and one over-arching encoding system would handle the characters of all the world's scripts. Unfortunately, because the number of Chinese characters is at least an order of magnitude larger than any other character set in the world, and because the original computer character sets were developed in the West for the relatively simple roman alphabet, there are problems for computer processing of coded CJK data which will take some time to resolve. Moreover, the contradiction between CJK character codes and the rest of the world's is compounded by the fact that a number of *different* CJK coding standards have now emerged.

On the one hand we have the three-byte codes: the Taiwanese CCCII and the RLIN REACC code which was developed from it. The latter is now published and maintained by the Library of Congress as EACC (East Asian Character Code). It is being used by OCLC's CJK system and is likely soon to become an American national standard. On the other hand, we have the two-byte standard GB 2312-80, 'basic set' from the People's Republic. The latter, presently handling only 6763 simplified characters will be supplemented by further sets of traditional forms and more rare simplified forms.[6] The PRC set is registered with ISO, and will cluster together with the similarly registered Japanese and Korean standards which are also two-byte. The huge code space of the REACC code has room to incorporate the published mainland 'basic set', which would make translation in and out of this limited set relatively easy, but this does not answer the fundamental incompatibility of the two coding systems, which, when they are both fully elaborated would demand hefty translation tables for exchange purposes.[7]

As a brief aside, it is also perhaps worth pointing out that, at present, even though processing and memory costs continue to drop, there are other consequences of adopting a particular coding scheme besides exchange difficulties. Records with characters coded in three-bytes obviously take up more room than those using two-byte codes (even if there are occasional extra bytes to shift from one set to another). Large numbers of three-byte records would be significantly more expensive to process and store, and this has demonstrably influenced the attitudes of some mainland institutions to certain systems.[8]

Despite the fact that there are now, in the People's Republic of China, systems which use the REACC code, interested institutions seem to be firmly set on supporting the extended two-byte national standards in the long term. This has obvious implications for any automation planning in Chinese studies and the situation needs careful monitoring.

WESTERN ORIENTATION; RESOURCES

In the early low-power days of computing the problem of representing natural language data from the Humanities was low priority. Over-sanguine and imaginative users quickly discovered short-comings in the input, output and processing of even roman script data, let alone non-roman alphabets. Few were considering taking a quantum leap upwards to engage problems with the huge morphographic character set of Chinese. The Western, science and technology-led, orientation of computing is still a determinant of what is possible in natural language processing, but the nature of certain concomitant contradictions has changed. At first, there was the simple clash between the computer's capability and the requirements of a large character set. Now, in the West we have machines powerful and cheap enough to cope with the quantitative aspects of this problem but we remain hamstrung by what might be called the 'parochialism' of our systems. We are coming to the point when, faced with non-roman character sets, some of us will be less able to cope than colleagues in the East who are either developing applications from scratch or who are committed to adapting bought-in systems for Chinese. Here we are speaking mainly of developments in China with an eye to how they have been spurred on by occasional cooperative efforts with the Japanese and access to some of their advanced hardware and systems. Despite lack of resources, Chinese institutions in the People's Republic – two recent important examples are the National Library and the library of Beijing University – are now planning to implement automation projects which are intended not only to handle Chinese characters but to provide computing environments which are fully 'sinified'.[9] The problems of other non-roman scripts, since they are of a lesser order, can, given will and resources, be handled within the new framework.

Contrast this with the way some Western systems, despite benefiting from far more resources in terms of investment, computing power and experience, can be straight-jacketed within the roman-script world for historical reasons. An example is the British Library's own Blaise system. Where it would be desirable, at the very least, to make it possible for this major British bibliographic system to handle a wide range of non-roman alphabets, in practice, even this will take a great deal of development as the present Blaise is geared up to become Blaise System II. On present projections, the likelihood of its being able to incorporate coded data for Chinese is slight. The major bibliographic databases of our American colleagues have, as we can see from other papers, fared better in tackling these problems, but the ironic contradiction mentioned here will still prevent significant opportunities for exchange unless Western systems generally face up to the non-roman world.

Funding considerations have already been touched upon occasionally in this paper. Frustratingly, with a sort of wicked irony, resources for Chinese automation development in mainland China and the West are scarce in complementary ways. In the West, Chinese automation – like Chinese studies – is a relatively limited, low-priority facet of something much bigger. In mainland China advanced, widespread automation development cannot yet achieve the momentum of its Western counterpart. Chinese budgets cannot cope with the expense of advanced hardware on an appropriate scale and much of the requisite technological infrastructure is still lacking. Taiwan and Japan provide an alternative source of impetus for developments in Chinese automation, but we are all bound to wait and see in which direction China is moving, however slowly.

Applications, East and West

The database is by far the most important type of computer application for research and information provision in the Humanities and Social Sciences. If we consider a textbase to be a special type of database, and see statistical functions as now more or less integrated with the modern computerised data management system, then the vast majority of significant research applications can be seen as databases of one sort or another. The word processor, along with its natural successor and partner, the desk-top or in-house publishing program, is an equally common but much more general tool. Helpful as it is, a word processor and/or publishing aid does not make the direct contribution to research which a well-designed data- or textbase does. Another important area of computer application with great potential is computer aided instruction (CAI, embracing computer aided language learning, CALL). However, maintaining the traditional teaching – research distinction for our present purposes, we will leave aside discussion of the latter sort of application.

In discussing (so late in the proceedings) applications which have earlier in this paper been singled out as the proper but previously neglected focus for automation and Chinese studies, we should pause to consider those which contain data which is of Chinese interest, but not coded as Chinese characters. In fact, databases can be divided into those whose contents can be either translated into another language or romanised without losing significant information and those whose contents must be in the original language (or, more accurately, the original script). Typically, databases serving the social sciences may contain translated and romanised data, where the aim is to analyse and collect statistics about distributions of entities which are accepted within the field and across linguistic cultures.

Partly because they are databases of the 'translatable' variety and partly because of present limitations on character handling systems available in this country, two existing Chinese studies databases in this country contain translated data. The University of Newcastle East Asia Centre's Database of Chinese Provincial Leadership now contains over 9,500 records relating to tours of duty for provincial officials from 1949 to the present day (a considerable expansion since the publication of the directory of the database as it was at the beginning of 1986), and now includes biographical information relating to these individuals. Data for Central officials will be added during the next couple of years. At the University of Leeds, Department of Chinese, an index with translated abstracts for two major mainland Chinese short story periodicals, *Xiao shuo yue bao* and *Xiao shuo xuan kan*, has been set up and entries covering 1983–85 have been entered. Simple content analysis of the stories, veering towards the sociological, can be carried out using this database by searching for translated key terms built into a thesaurus. For these purposes there is not an absolute requirement to have the original form of the text encoded. However, in this latter application we begin to feel the desire for data which more directly represent the raw material, for accuracy's sake and future flexibility. Interestingly both Newcastle and Leeds have purchased character-handling microcomputers and software which, at the very least, they will use to generate separate character indices – of names, titles, positions etc. – for their databases, with the potential to later integrate these parallel indices with the main system.

For social science databases, translated data may suffice, but for literary and linguistic research an accurate representation of the original material is an absolute requirement. At the University of Cambridge Centre for Literary and Linguistic Computing, one of the earliest-developed and simplest devices for computer input of Chinese characters, their IdeoMatic Encoder, linked to mainframe based character generation software has been used to build up a small – and presently static – Chinese textbase. It also provides character data for an important palaeontological dictionary project. At the School of Oriental and African Studies, an office under the supervision of Dr Paul Thompson of the Department of the Far East is involved in a number of projects mainly concerned with developing systems to process Chinese (including participation in the cooperative Alvey speech recognition project) and programs for computer assisted language learning. Presently the projects under Dr Thompson's supervision are taken up more with development and not so much with research, but his ultimate and personal aim is to see the creation and manipulation of major textbases – linguistic and literary corpora of modern Chinese and pre-Qin texts. When a totally 'transparent' and user-friendly Chinese language system is able to interrogate such textbases for research purposes, the automation of at least one branch of Chinese studies will have come of age. It will also be making possible for a Chinese textbase the sort of statistical work and concordancing which is totally impractical without computers.

At the outset of this paper we stated that the library and its catalogues are simply the researcher's mot fundamental tools. Similarly a library's machine-readable bibliographic databases may be considered as primary research databases. In this country, there exists at least one database of romanised Chinese bibliographic records, the China Library Group's *Union List of Current Chinese Serials*, which is maintained at the British Library as part of a Blaise-Locas file for the Oriental Collections. The database provides a very useful service, but one which would be far more useful and easier to use if its records contained characters. In general, a bibliographic database needs to be more like a literary or linguistic application than the sort of 'translatable' social sciences applications we've mentioned above. The data in bibliographic records should be full and accurate, for the most obvious of reasons and also for the sake of the potential future exchange of such records.

In the UK, the best model available to us of an appropriate and more or less 'mature' application of Chinese script handling computing to Chinese studies has been the RLIN CJK system on loan to the British Library. The similar, rival OCLC system is also represented at the colloquium and discussion of these database is intentionally abbreviated here as they will be described in detail in other papers and can be demonstrated to anyone interested. There will be many opportunities to discuss the merits and demerits of these important systems which have heralded the end of East Asian bibliography's isolation from library automation. But I do hope that this paper will encourage delegates to look more carefully at the two databases themselves – how they are managed, which libraries contribute to them, what opportunities for cooperative projects exist – not just at the merits of the front-end system: in other words, not at how it does it, but at what, in the end, it does.

Conclusions

In conclusion we must chant the refrain for a last time. The automation of Chinese studies has been preoccupied with technical, system developments. We have only recently reached the point where fully 'sinified' systems will be able to engage and enhance genuine research applications. Now that this point has been reached, however, we can begin to look forward to the great unprecedented benefits which have already accrued to colleagues in other disciplines, those for which automation has proved slightly less troublesome.

Finally, it may be useful just to highlight a couple of likely and/or desirable trends in Chinese automation. Firstly, as automation gathers pace on the mainland, and because of the necessity to exchange information, computer projects in Chinese studies – including those in the West – will turn away from translated or romanised data, towards the incorporation of full and accurate character data. Secondly, the coding and machine readable bibliographic standards being developed now in the People's Republic will gradually become dominant in

Chinese automation, with standards originating elsewhere either coming into line or providing facilities for code conversion.

The well sweep which our primitivist gardener from the *Zhuangzi* railed against at the outset of this paper, appears in a somewhat better light elsewhere in the book:

> Have you seen a well sweep? Pull it, and down it comes; let go, and up it swings. It allows itself to be pulled around by men; it doesn't try to pull them. So it can go up and down and never get blamed by anybody.[10]

While it seems much more threatening at times, the computer truly is just such a neutral, blameless tool as the well sweep, unworthy of the awe and reverence sometimes accorded it. There is the point, however, that well sweeps — and metaphorically computers — only leave men free to push them around for their own benefit if they have been well-made, well-balanced, provided with leak-proof buckets and, most importantly, set up close to a good supply of water.

Notes

1. Burton Watson, trans., *The complete works of Chuang tzu*, (Columbia University Press, New York, 1968), p. 134.
2. A C Graham *Chuang-tzu: the Seven Inner Chapters and other writings from the book Chuang-tzu* (George Allen & Unwin, London, 1981). See especially pp. 185–87. Graham's translation of the same passage differs from Watson's in a number of ways, particularly in using 'tricks' for 'machines'. I have preferred to use Watson's version in this somewhat light-hearted context for obvious reasons.
3. These trends — in the use of Chinese script handling micros and in the use of micros to be later integrated with minicomputers or mainframes — were much in evidence during visits I made in May and June 1987, under the British Library's asupices, to certain institutions in Beijing involved in problems of setting up databases holding data in Chinese script. In the computing section of the Library of the Academia Sinica and at the Institute for Scientific and Technical Information, China (ISTIC), Beijing, IBM PC's are being used to input records which will later be downloaded for management on larger systems. The use of micros allows these institutions to get down to work on the databases at hand, solving bigger problems — including those of finance — at a later stage. A brief report of this visit will be printed in the forthcoming (1988) issue of the Bulletin of the European Association of Sinological Librarians.
4. For a description of the original REACC coding scheme see Karen Smith-Yoshimura and Alan M Tucker, 'The RLIN East Asian Character Code and the RLIN CJK Thesaurus', *Proceedings of the second Asian-Pacific conference on library science*, 20–24 May 1985, Seoul: The Cultural and Social Centre for the Asian and Pacific Region and the Central National Library, Republic of Korea. The administration of this code has now been taken over by the Library of Congress and copies of what is now called EACC or *USMARC character set for Chinese, Japanese and Korean*, November 1986, Supt. of Docs. no. LC 30.2:C37, ISBN 0 8444 0548 5 may be obtained from the Library's Cataloguing Distribution Service. A description of the Research Library Group's Chinese–Japanese–Korean enhancement to their bibliographic database, the Research Libraries Information Network, can be found in Dr John Haeger's paper elsewhere in this volume. The Chinese Section of the British Library had a CJK terminal cluster on loan for a year and a half from April 1986, and we hope to be able to assess the new equipment being produced by RLG in 1988.
5. A useful bibliography is that of Christina Lackschewitz and Richard Suchenwirth, *A bibliography on computer applications in Chinese language and script processing*, (Goettingen University, Hamburg, Ostasiatisches Seminar, 1983) although there is much more recent material. One of the most useful *practical* surveys I have seen of existing input systems — especially those available in the West — can be found in Damon Koach, *Processing Chinese characters with MINISIS: Consultant's report to the IDRC* (Arlington, Virginia, August 1984). MINISIS is a mini-based database system, initially set up for third-world users by the IDRC (International Development Research Council). This consultant's report was to advise on the suitability of various Chinese systems as 'front-ends' for this database.

6. *The People's Republic of China National Standard Code of Chinese Graphic Character Set for Information Interchange: Primary Set GB 2312-80* (Technical Standards Press, Beijing, 1981). The Chinese Standardisation Research Institute for Electronic Technology announced the development (since 1985) of new standards to the relevant ISO committee in early 1987. These are as yet unpublished but are said to include two supplementary sets of simplified characters (7,237 and 7,039 characters respectively). Two further sets of complex characters are also said to be under development. These are supposed to be related to the primary and one of the supplementary sets. We shall all await the publication of these standards with interest.
7. Since this paper was written and presented, a conference having some bearing on the question of East Asian scripts automation has taken place, namely the 'First International Conference on the Scholarly Information Network – East Asian Applications and International Co-operation', 8–11 December 1987, Tokyo, National Centre for Science Information Systems (NACSIS). Representatives of the major western and Japanese databases with CJK capabilities (including RLG, OCLC and UTLAS) attended to discuss the question of national and international standard character codes, and how to administer them better for the purpose of exchange. However, the attitude of the Chinese standards-making bodies themselves – whose interests may have been somewhat under-represented in this context – is crucial in the long term. National standards, and particularly the Chinese national standard, will continue to develop nationally, and any internationally oriented administrative body must take this into account.
8. Increased overheads in terms of storage was given as an argument against using three-byte codes by computer personnel (including Mr Zhou Shengheng) at the National Library when I visited in June 1987. This was despite the fact that for the automated circulation system currently being implemented, the National Library has bought in a CLSI system which uses the equipment and coding standard originally developed for RLG (the three-byte REACC code!). The Library's computer personnel were quick to point out that the circulation system would be limited in scope and would not influence future developments for either automated catalogues or the National Bibliography. *See* below, and also the paper by Zhou Shengheng, pp. 198–204.
9. *See* Zhou Shengheng's paper, pp. 198–204, and my report mentioned in note 3, above.
10. Burton Watson, *op. cit.*, p. 160.

Zhou Shengheng

Chinese bibliographic data processing

As of the end of 1986, the National Library of China (NLC) had a total collection of 13 million volumes, of which, 45% were in Chinese. As the general repository for China's national collection, the NLC has collected 26,000 volumes of books and nearly 8,000 periodical titles published in China yearly. In order to develop and utilise Chinese bibliographic data resources and conduct bibliographic information interchange, the automation of Chinese bibliographic data processing has become an important task in recent years.

To perform the internationally acknowledged functions required of a National Library, the automation objective of NLC is to establish, step by step, a national centre for bibliographic data in Chinese and foreign languages. With regard to automatic processing for Chinese bibliographic information, the specific tasks at present are as follows:

1. to create an integrated on-line computer system for cataloguing, retrieval, acquisition and serials control in Chinese, in order to automate library operations.

2. To create and maintain bibliographic and authority databases in Chinese, to implement standardisation of Chinese bibliographic data.

3. To prepare and publish the Chinese National Bibliography, produce and distribute China MARC tapes and floppy discs, centralised catalogue cards and other catalogue products in Chinese to realise resource-sharing of Chinese bibliographic data.

In order to fulfil the tasks mentioned above, we studied basic theory for bibliographic data and Chinese character information processing, drew up a series of national standards and undertook the following fundamental projects:

Standardisation of bibliographic data

By the end of 1979, the National Technical Committee for Document Standardisation was set up in China. The following major national standards were issued after many years of effort.

1. General Bibliographical Description (GB 3792.1–83).

2. Bibliographical Description for Monographs (GB 3792.2–85).

3. Bibliographical Description for Serials (GB 3792.3−85).

4. Bibliographical Description for Non-book Materials (GB 3792.4−85).

5. Bibliographical Description for Archives (GB 3792.5−85).

6. Descriptive Rules for Periodical Entries in Information Retrieval Systems (GB 3793−83).

7. Transliteration Rules for the Chinese Phonetic Alphabet in Titles for Books and Periodicals in Chinese (GB 3259−82).

8. Codes for Document Types and Document media (GB 3469−83).

In addition, a 'Bibliographical Description for Maps', 'Bibliographical Description for Old Books', and a 'Bibliographical Description for Music' have been worked out, and will soon be published. All these national standards were based on *International Standard Bibliographic Descriptions* (ISBDs), combined with traditional Chinese bibliographic characteristics. They not only conform to the requirements of international bibliographic exchange but also meet the needs of bibliographic data processing in China. Furthermore, China has acceded to the ISBN and ISSN numbering system, which has been effective since 1987. These national standards are now in common use in the libraries and other documentation institutions of China, thus creating favourable conditions for bibliographic data exchange.

Authority control

As is well known, subject authority and name authority are critical questions in the standardisation of bibliographic data. In an attempt to attain the aim of unified headings, ensuring integrity and consistency of Chinese bibliographic data and raising the efficiency of bibliographic data retrieval, the following authority lists have been established or are in course of preparation:

CHINESE THESAURUS

This was begun in 1957 as a component part of the 'Chinese characters information processing' project. Sponsored by the Institute of Scientific and Technical Information of China (ISTIC) and the National Library of China, a strong professional force was organised throughout the country to participate in its compilation. The group comprised 1,378 scientific personnel from 505 institutions. The thesaurus was published in three volumes of ten separate fascicles, embodying 108,568 descriptions in all, arranged by two major categories of humanities and social sciences and natural sciences, each with an appendix and three indexes. This is the first comprehensive thesaurus China has ever compiled for use by libraries and information institutes, directed specially at making the automatic retrieval of documents possible. The centralised catalogue cards produced by the National Library of China have had subject headings since 1985. The Chinese thesaurus is presently being widely used by libraries and information institutes, and is being made available in machine-readable form.

CHINESE LIBRARY CLASSIFICATION FOR BOOKS

This is a major comprehensive set of classification rules compiled after the founding of the People's Republic of China. Its compilation took four years of cooperative efforts by 36 institutions headed by the National Library of China and ISTIC. The first edition appeared in 1975. In 1980 it was revised into four different versions with the same basic structure in order to suit the classification needs of libraries and information institutes of different sizes and purposes. Since its publication the Chinese Library Classification Rule for Books has been adopted by 9,070 libraries and information institutes and has become a commonly used classification scheme dealing with books and other materials as well as the retrieval of documents through classification.

In order to perfect a retrieval language system in China and meet different needs for document indexing, we are now compiling a 'Chinese Classification-Thesaurus List' in which classification numbers are cross-referred to descriptors and vice versa. This list is expected to be completed in 1988.

CHINESE NAME AUTHORITY

Name heading control is very necessary to achieve a high cataloguing standard and more effective record retrieval. The National Library of China is now compiling a 'Chinese Name Authority List' which contains Chinese ancient and modern authors, transliterated names for foreign authors, cooperative and conference names, uniform titles, series titles, translated titles, etc. It will be completed by 1995.

CHINESE CHARACTER SET

In the processing of Chinese bibliographic data, Chinese character processing is a particularly complicated problem. In the last few years, with the progress of Chinese character information processing techniques, many computerised Chinese character information systems have been developed. PC-based systems have become particularly widespread in China. The National Library of China, as the Chinese bibliographic centre, must handle a great number of publications with simplified Chinese characters as well as ancient books and publications from Hong Kong and Taiwan which contain Chinese characters in a complex form (including variant characters). The total number of Chinese characters required for this purpose is roughly 20,000. Obviously, the 6,763 Chinese characters issued in national standard (GB 2312–80) will not be enough for practical use. In order to satisfy the need in this field, many Chinese character experts in our country have made great efforts in correcting the form, meaning, pronunciation and sequence of Chinese characters. Standards for supplementary sets and their interchange codes have been drawn up and will soon be issued.

In the national standards, each Chinese graphic character is represented by 7-bit or 8-bit doublets. The sets G0,G2, G4 contain Chinese characters in simplified form, and their mapping sets G1, G3, G5 contain Chinese characters in complex form.

The Code of Chinese Graphic Character Set for Information Interchange – Basic Set' (GB 2312–80) contains 7,445 frequently used graphic characters, consisting of 628 non-Chinese graphic characters and 6,763 Chinese characters. The Chinese characters are divided into two levels, 3,755 in level I arranged in the order of Chinese National Phonetic Alphabet, 3,008 in level II arranged by radicals.

The 'Code of Chinese Graphic Character Set for Information Interchange – Second Supplementary Set' and 'Code of Chinese Graphic Character Set for Information Interchange – Fourth Supplementary Set' contain 7,426 rarely used Chinese character codes. Both are arranged by radicals in their encoding matrixes. The codings of Chinese characters in the Basic Set, Second Supplementary Set and Fourth Supplementary Set are:

CHARACTER SET	CODING RANGE (HEXD.)				GRAPHIC CHARACTERS	USAGE
	First byte		Second byte			
	7-bit code	8-bit code	7-bit code	8-bit code		
BASIC SET	21–7E	A1–FE	21–7E	A1–FE	7,445 (682 non-Chinese characters)	frequent
SECOND SUPPLEMENTARY SET	21–7E	A1–FE	21–7E	21–7E	7,237	rare
FOURTH SUPPLEMENTARY SET	21–7E	21–7E	21–7E	A1–FE	7,049	rare

In addition, we will draw up the standard for control codes to be used in Chinese character processing systems.

CHINESE CHARACTER ATTRIBUTE DICTIONARY

In the processing of Chinese bibliographic data, it is very important to study various attributes, basic features and regularity of use of Chinese characters. In the last few years, the National Library of China has integrated the research results of Chinese character attributes, completed the compilation of the Chinese Character

Attribute Dictionary and developed the corresponding support software system for Chinese character processing.

About 50 attribute values pertaining to form, pronunciation, sequence and so on, of each of the graphic characters in the officially issued Basic Set, are without exception listed in this dictionary. The major functions of its support software system are:

1. To provide corresponding codes developed in other countries and regions for Chinese character codes and non-Chinese character codes defined in the officially issued Basic Set. It will facilitate the machine-readable information interchange between the PRC and other countries or regions as a result of mutual character code conversion, for example, between the National Standard code and Japanese JIS 6226 and HITACHI code, the CCCII Chinese character code and the 'Universal standard code of Chinese characters' of Taiwan, and between the ASCII and EBCDIC codes for non-Chinese characters.

2. To provide sequencing data to allow the sorting of Chinese characters by the authorised Chinese Phonetic Alphabet, character components and radicals, stroke number and stroke form, and the four-corner system, in order to meet the sorting requirements for file creation, display and printing of Chinese characters in a computer system.

3. To provide conversion tables for Chinese characters and their Chinese Phonetic Alphabet and Wade-Giles Phonetic Alphabet equivalents, to meet the romanised requirements for computer application systems at home and abroad.

4. To provide linking information between the normalised form and variant form (including complex form) of Chinese characters, to meet the requirements for information retrieval and standardisation of Chinese characters.

5. To provide attribute information for Chinese characters pertaining to pronunciation, tone, radicals, stroke number, stroke sequence and stroke form, to facilitate statistical analysis and research into Chinese characters using computers.

To summarise, this system offers us good facilities for data sorting and the code conversion of Chinese bibliographic data. It has important practical uses. In its present state it has had dozens of users and achieved good results. We are now compiling the Chinese character attributes of the National Standard Second Supplementary Set and Fourth Supplementary Set in order to expand the capability of the Chinese Character Attribute Dictionary.

CHINA MARC FORMAT

To promote bibliographic data exchange in China, the 'Format for Bibliographic Information Interchange on Magnetic Tape' (GB 2901–82) was issued in 1982. But owing to a lack of practical experience in machine-readable data processing, this standard is not satisfactory, and there are some problems and obstacles in its implementation. In the past few years, the National Library of China has made a serious study of relevant foreign standards and experience, analysed the characteristics of Chinese bibliographic data, and a 'China MARC Format' was drafted in 1986. Opinions on this draft are now being solicited from the library world, and it will be published after further revision.

This format is designed to facilitate bibliographic data exchange between the National Library of China and other national bibliographic agencies. The National Library of China will distribute China MARC tapes at home in this format before the national standard for China MARC Format is officially issued.

At present, this format is only suitable for monographs and serials. It will expand gradually to cover maps, music and other materials. The draft of the China MARC Format has the following features:

1. It observes the design principle of the UNIMARC format, and is based on the UNIMARC format and relevant international standards. Consequently, this format should be completely suitable for international bibliographic data exchange.

2. It adequately combines characteristics of Chinese bibliographic information and Chinese character processing, and conforms to officially issued national standards for bibliographic data processing. Appropriate fields, sub-fields and content designators have, however, been added in order to meet the needs of bibliographic data processing in China.

3. It takes account of international standards for the processing of bibliographic records with multiple character sets switched by escape sequences. Therefore, it will be able to meet requirements for the processing of bibliographic data with either single or multiple byte character sets.

A batch processing system for Chinese bibliographic data has also been developed. In order to create a Chinese bibliographic database, we are now preparing data and inputting it into the computer according to the new bibliographic data standards and the new record format. Next year we are going to issue China MARC tapes and floppy discs, and also compile the *Chinese National Bibliography* on computer. We are currently making good progress in the selection and import of computer systems. Within a few years, an integrated on-line processing system for Chinese bibliographic information will appear and at that time our goal will have been attained.

We are well aware that Chinese bibliographic data processing is a far from easy problem to solve. More problems remain to be dealt with and there is still much to be done. For this reason, we are looking forward to exchanging views and experience with experts and professional personnel from other countries.

Discussion

In the subsequent discussion, questions concerning the draft MARC format, Chinese ISSNs and ISBNs and the National Bibliography were raised. The Chinese draft MARC format is only being circulated for comment within China. ISSNs, allocated by the National Library of China, are by now pretty well universal and ISBNs should appear on all Chinese books in 1987.

The National Bibliography is intended to cover comprehensively works published in China, Hong Kong and Taiwan (if, in the case of the last, publications can be obtained). It is intended to include material in national minority languages (which will have to be manually input), although some categories (including children's books and picture books) are deliberately excluded. Chinese material is included on the basis of copyright deposit and it is thought that the coverage is 80–90% complete.

There are over 400 different inputting systems in China, although the preferred method is *pinyin* transliteration, closely followed by radical and stroke order methods. The compilation of the thesaurus (which has been going on since 1957) has been carried out by libraries and subsidiary research groups under the direction of a State Commission.

John W Haeger

RLIN–CJK: a review of the first four years

Eight years ago, the Research Libraries Group (RLG) and the Library of Congress executed a Memorandum of Understanding which laid the corner-stone for automated bibliographic control of East Asian materials in North America. RLG and LC recognised their common interest in automated processing of East Asian materials, and committed themselves to the development and use of a capacity for entry, retrieval, storage, maintenance, display, and transmission of bibliographic data in East Asian scripts. With the support of the American Council of Learned Societies and the Association of Research Libraries, RLG received grants from the Andrew W Mellon Foundation, the Ford Foundation, and the National Endowment for the Humanities to develop the so-called 'CJK enhancements' to the Research Libraries Information Network (RLIN).

In the spring of 1983, the first RLG–CJK terminals were delivered to LC and to RLG member institutions. On 12 September 1983, the first bibliographic records to contain East Asian vernacular data were created in RLIN. Almost four years later, 22 institutions, collectively representing approximately 70% of the East Asian holdings in North America, use RLIN for most or all of their CJK vernacular processing. Seventy-two CJK terminals have been installed in the United States, Canada, and (on an experimental basis) here in the United Kingdom. On 2 March 1987, the number of CJK records in the RLIN data base passed the quarter-million mark, growing at a rate of about 8,000 per month. 40% of these records represent unique titles, and about half of these were created by LC. Marsha Wagner, Director of Columbia University's C V Starr East Asian Library has written:

RLIN has profoundly changed the way East Asian scholars do their research. Formerly, this was a matter of tedious and labor-intensive searching by hand for authors, titles, and subjects in the card catalogs of individual libraries, sometimes coping with cumbersome arrangements of entries in non-alphabetic scripts. The rapidly growing number of CJK entries in RLIN frees them from this arduous process. In seconds, one can retrieve information about available resources and their library locations using Chinese, Japanese, Korean, and Western languages.

On 1 March 1987, RLG implemented the final module of the on-line CJK system: the RLIN–CJK Thesaurus. The Thesaurus is a resource file of approximately 35,000 records, with each record representing an East Asian character. Each character is identified by an RLIN East Asian Character Code (REACC), which is then mapped to equivalent codes in the national standards that have been established in the PRC, Japan, Korea, and Taiwan. For RLIN–CJK users, the Thesaurus is an on-line, multi-indexed, multi-lingual dictionary; each character record shows such information as radical, stroke-count, and readings in the three East Asian languages, as well as instructions for composing the character on the RLG–CJK keyboard. The CJK Thesaurus also shows all variant forms associated with a particular character. The CJK Thesaurus can be consulted independently or while creating or updating a bibliographic record.

The RLIN–CJK Thesaurus can be considered an 'East Asian character authority file' for CJK bibliographic records. Beginning this year, it is being administered by the Library of Congress. As extensions to East Asian code standards are implemented, LC will add to the Thesaurus file whatever mappings are necessary to ensure that East Asian MARC records can be accurately converted.

It is important to understand that the CJK processing capabilities of the RLIN system are *enhancements*, not a separate system. Records which contain vernacular characters reside in the same database with Roman-only and Cyrillic records. CJK is supported for both cataloguing and acquisitions for all MARC bibliographic formats. All RLIN indexes and search capabilities can be applied against CJK records, and additional indexes have been created to handle vernacular searches. An especially attractive feature of the so-called 'character indexes' which support vernacular searching is the ability to confine a search to one exact form of a particular character (e.g., PRC *jianti*) or expand it to retrieve records containing any variant form (all *yiti*) of the same character. Last year, RLIN's powerful searching capabilities were further enhanced (for all records including CJK) by the implementation of ALSO logic, which permits users to narrow a large initial search result by, *inter alia*, the holdings of a particular library or libraries in a certain geographic area, by publication dates, by language or geographic code, by publisher, and by text entered in Roman or in CJK characters anywhere in a bibliographic record, including notes fields. This means that RLIN now supports, in effect, full-text searching for all bibliographic records, CJK and non-CJK alike.

Given that the design of the CJK enhancements to RLIN began seven years ago; that hardware choices were made six years ago; and that the system has been in production for nearly four years, it is hardly surprising that we have now reached the end of the first generation. It is axiomatic that nearly all computer hardware becomes obsolete in terms of price-performance, capacity, power-consumption, functionality, and even maintainability in double digit months. The CJK cluster, based on a DEC LSI 11/23 mini-computer, with a Motorola MDS4000 monitor, and a General Electric 3000-series printer, is no exception. Accordingly, RLG announced a second-generation product in February 1987: a multi-script workstation that will support RLIN bibliographic functions using Chinese, Japanese, and Korean characters, plus Hebrew, Cyrillic, and other non-Roman scripts as and when they are implemented.

The new workstation will be based on AT-class personal computers configured with:

1. A redesigned CJK keyboard, produced by Transtech International Corporation of Natick, Massachusetts, with a modified Chinese character component input method.

2. An ASCII keyboard for use when CJK input is not required.

3. A Wyse-700 high-resolution monitor.

4. A CJK character-generator read-only memory board developed by JHL Research Inc., of Anaheim, California.

5. RLIN terminal emulation software.

6. A choice of dot-matrix and laser printers.

The new workstation will have numerous advantages. Each unit will be free-standing, which eliminates the constraints associated with the LSI 11/23 'cluster' architecture. Because only boards and keyboards will require specialised service, maintenance costs will drop dramatically, and contracted field maintenance will be eliminated. Video screen display and print resolution will be enhanced by an increase from a 16 × 18 dot-matrix font for CJK characters to 24 × 24.

In addition, each workstation, independent of its use as an RLIN terminal, will have all the functions associated with JHL Research Inc.'s ChinaStar (tm) product, including in-board word processing and CJK interfaces to numerous commercial software products including WordStar, Lotus 1-2-3, and dBase III. The entire configuration, including printer and software, will cost less than US $6,000 per unit, which represents approximately an 80% reduction from the cost of first-generation equipment. Getting so much more for so much less is nice, but scarcely surprising. It mimics, in fact, recent developments with large mainframes, direct-access storage devices, and personal computers themselves.

RLIN's capability for managing East Asian vernacular records, and for maintaining an on-line union data base of such records, provides a technical infrastructure for a number of cooperative projects. Of these, two merit special attention in this forum.

The East Asian microfilming project

This is a US $270,000, two-year effort, begun last September, to preserve the intellectual content of brittle materials important to scholarship and research printed in China during the late nineteenth and early twentieth century, many of which are believed to exist now *only* in North America. Columbia, Yale, Princeton, Chicago, the Hoover Institution, the University of California at Berkeley, and the Library of Congress are filming 3,850 volumes of serials, monographs, and sets in their collections. The intent to film and a catalogue record for the finished microfilm are both recorded in RLIN, eliminating the risk of redundant activity.

The International Union Catalogue of Chinese rare books

Plans are also well-advanced for an *International Union Catalogue* – in RLIN – *of Chinese Rare Books (shan ben)*. A Task Force drawn from RLG libraries has now developed a working definition of *shan ben*; a list of cataloguing issues which need attention (caption titles, uniform titles for early Chinese publications, differentiation of holograph and manuscript copies, detail level for collation and notes, etc.); and arrangements for 'expert' consultation to resolve difficult problems in edition discrimination. The first phase of the project will be limited to rare books in RLG collections, but the Task Force also wishes to establish a plan which will integrate this project with work already completed at the National Central Library in Taibei, and with the PRC's Union Catalogue of Chinese Rare Books. In all probability, records from those projects will be converted to RLIN-MARC and loaded from tape; and RLIN records could be provided in exchange.

Summary

RLIN-CJK was the first system of its kind. When it was designed, even word-processing for East Asian scripts was a costly and clumsy application. Now inexpensive boards are available to make an IBM PC-XT into a fairly sophisticated Chinese word-processor. A number of Japanese and Taiwan-based vendors have affordable products in the marketplace. Other bibliographic networks, including OCLC and UTLAS, have implemented East Asian script capabilities. Although office automation and computerised information management in East Asia still lags far behind analogous development in North America and Western Europe, enormous progress has been made in a very short time. The challenges for RLG are:

1. To recognise that CJK processing is a continuing development process, not a one-time project.

2. To put its best efforts toward establishing and maintaining standard codes and formats for data communication across disparate systems. Such standardisation is essential to the development of a universal science of man and his works, drawn as much from the cultures of East Asia as from the traditions of the West.

Discussion

In the subsequent discussion, questions were raised on local processing facilities, relocation of the database and romanisation. Local processing will be possible in the future and whilst there is no plan to relocate the RLIN database, there are plans to make the RLIN system available, under certain circumstances and in certain locations, for operation on other computers with other databases; others will have the opportunity to operate RLIN. This is because of changes that are about to be made in the operating system environment and telecommunications network.

On the question of the 'problem' of romanisation, from the North American perspective there is no romanisation problem. Since the Library of Congress was unable to persuade the sinological library community to change from Wade-Giles to *pinyin*, there has been no change at all in the attitude of librarians (though this is not necessarily true of the academic community), who prefer to maintain their existing catalogue and existing cataloguing practices. There seems to be no insuperable barrier to the maintenance of more than one romanisation system but as no one except the British Library has asked for it, no resources are invested in this.

Andrew H Wang

The OCLC Library Network of Chinese, Japanese and Korean Characters

Introduction

OCLC (Online Computer Library Center) Incorporated (6565 Frantz Road, Dublin; Ohio 43017-0702, USA) is a non-profit making organisation and operates an international computer and telecommunication network. Through this bibliographic network, libraries acquire and catalogue library materials, arrange inter-library loans, maintain location information on library materials, retrospectively convert card file into machine-readable records in support of library automation, gain access to other databases, and order custom-printed catalogue cards and machine-readable records for local catalogues.

About 7,000 libraries in 20 countries use the OCLC Online System. About 30 new users join OCLC each month. OCLC membership includes all kinds and sizes of libraries.

OCLC pursues the following two goals for its membership:

1. To reduce the rate-of-rise of per-unit costs in libraries.

2. To increase the availability of library resources to library patrons.

The hub of the OCLC Network is the OCLC Online Union Catalogue, a database of over 16 million unique bibliographic records and over 300 million location symbols of libraries that hold these materials. This database grows by about 40,000 unique records weekly, or about two million unique records annually.

The OCLC CJK350 system

AUTOMATION OF CHINESE, JAPANESE, AND KOREAN CHARACTERS

In its first 15 years of operation from 1971 to 1986, the OCLC Online System was able to process information in the roman alphabet and arabic numerals only. Information in non-roman alphabets had to be romanised before it could be processed by the OCLC Online System. Unfortunately, romanised Chinese, Japanese, and Korean (CJK) characters are very difficult, if not impossible, for readers of these languages to understand. As a result, despite its riches in information, the OCLC Online Union Catalogue had been of limited use to scholars and students who needed materials in these Asian languages.

Recognizing the needs of librarians and scholars, as well as other library patrons of the CJK materials, OCLC developed the OCLC CJK350 system, and has made it available to all interested libraries world-wide since January 1987.

CATEGORIES OF USERS

The OCLC CJK350 system is intended to serve two categories of users, namely, dedicated users and casual users. In other words, it is designed to be a cataloguing workstation as well as a public access workstation.

Given adequate training and practice, dedicated users can learn to operate any keyboard and use any input method. However, since they spend many hours on the workstation daily, efficiency is crucial to their productivity. On the other hand, casual users, such as faculty members, students, and higher level library staff, use the system only occasionally. It is not practical for them to set aside days or weeks to learn to operate a keyboard or use an input method that they are not familiar with.

For this reason, the OCLC CJK350 system adopts the standard OCLC English-language keyboard without special CJK keycaps. Consequently, if a user is already familiar with the English-language keyboard, no training on the operation of the keyboard is needed. In addition, the OCLC CJK350 system adopts five input methods for users of various backgrounds (*see* below).

A MULTI-SCRIPT, MULTI-PURPOSE WORKSTATION

Since the OCLC CJK350 system is an enhancement to the OCLC Online System rather than a separate system with a separate database, the only hardware required for the CJK operation is the front-end OCLC CJK350 Workstation. The OCLC CJK350 workstation is a micro-computer-based workstation with 640K memory, supporting the CJK and American Library Association (ALA) character sets. It is capable of processing information in Chinese, Japanese, Korean, Vietnamese, English, French, German, Spanish, and other roman-alphabet languages. Besides, when not in communication with the OCLC Online System, the OCLC CJK350 workstation is a stand-alone micro-computer. Any software package that runs on IBM PC will also run on the OCLC CJK350 workstation.

INPUT METHODS AND CHARACTER SUBSETS

Since there is no one best input method for all users, the OCLC CJK350 system provides the following five input methods for various users.

1. *Cangjie*, the only character-based input method of the five, is rated the best input method by the Institute for Information Industry. This input method, primarily to be used by dedicated users, can be used for generating Chinese characters in both full and simplified forms, Japanese *kanji*, and Korean *hanja*.

2. Wade-Giles, a pronunciation-based input method, can be used for generating

Chinese characters in both full and simplified forms. Since libraries in the United States have adopted the Wade-Giles romanisation scheme for cataloguing materials in the Chinese language for decades, cataloguers as well as library patrons in the United States are used to this scheme.

3. *Pinyin*, another pronunciation-based input method, can be used for generating Chinese characters in both full and simplified forms. OCLC adopts this input method due to the increasing world-wide popularity of this romanisation scheme.

4. Modified Hepburn, a pronunciation-based input method, can be used for generating Japanese *kanji, katakana,* and *hiragana.*

5. McCune-Reischauer, another pronunciation-based input method, can be used for generating Korean *hanja* and *han'gŭl*. Since there was no previous provision for McCune-Reischauer romanisation for *hanja* and/or *han'gŭl*, OCLC's McCune-Reischauer romanisation dictionary is the first, if not the only, such dictionary that has been published.

The following chart summarises the input methods provided, and the characters they generate.

	CHINESE		JAPANESE			KOREAN	
	Full	Simplified	Kanji	Katakana	Hiragana	Hancha	Han'gŭl
Cangjie	●	●	●			●	
Pinyin	●	●					
Wade-Giles	●	●					
Modified Hepburn			●	●	●		
McCune-Reischauer						●	●

Cangjie input method is known for its efficiency, and is ideal for dedicated users. Input methods based on romanisation schemes are friendly to casual users such as scholars and students who do not have the time for learning an unfamiliar input method. Efficiency of an input method in terms of the number of keystrokes is critical to dedicated users, but not to casual users.

REDUCTION OF HOMOPHONES

All phonetic-based input methods will inevitably generate homophones. The OCLC CJK350 system provides two optional qualifiers at the end of the input keystrokes to reduce the number of homophones. Users of Wade-Giles and *pinyin* input methods may add to the end of the input keystrokes a numeral 1, 2, 3, or 4 to signify the tone of the character desired. In addition, all input methods other than *cangjie* may add to the end of the input keystrokes as a second qualifier, the first letter of *cangjie* input method of the character desired.

When homophones occur, the OCLC CJK350 workstation will beep and display up to eight characters at a time in the homophone block of the status line. Each character so displayed is associated with an arabic numeral from 1 up to 8. The user then enters an arabic numeral and depresses the space bar to generate the desired character. When there are more than eight homophones, the last character in the homophone block will be an up-arrow symbol to indicate that there are more homophones. The user can depress the space bar to see the next set of up to eight homophones. The last homophone in the list will be followed by a blank space and an exclamation mark.

SCREEN DISPLAY

The OCLC M300 or M310 Workstation, which does not have the capability of processing Chinese, Japanese, or Korean characters, displays a maximum of 24 lines per screen. Data from the OCLC Online System is transferred to these workstations one screen at a time as requested by the user. However, the OCLC CJK350 Workstation displays only up to 16 lines at a time. Therefore, instead of transferring to the workstation one screen at a time as is the case with the OCLC M300 and M310 Workstations, the OCLC Online System transfers all screens of a record to the OCLC CJK350 Workstation. The OCLC CJK350 Workstation then stores the entire record, and reformats the text for display on the screen. All CJK characters are displayed in a 16 × 16 dot matrix.

RETRIEVAL OF THE CJK RECORDS

OCLC maintains only one database, the OCLC Online Union Catalogue, for both roman and non-roman alphabet records. As a result, the OCLC CJK350 Workstation can retrieve both CJK and non-CJK records in the OCLC Online Union Catalogue. At the present time, OCLC provides seven possible numeric search keys and four possible derived search keys, as listed below, for searching and retrieving roman alphabet records in the OCLC Online Union Catalogue. All of these search keys are also applicable for retrieving CJK records. In the OCLC Online Union Catalogue each field that contains CJK characters links with another field that contains corresponding information in romanised form. In addition, users of the OCLC CJK350 system can also use four additional derived search keys in CJK characters.

I. NUMERIC SEARCH KEYS

1. LCCN: the Library of Congress Card Number.
2. ISBN: the International Standard Book Number.
3. ISSN: the International Standard Serial Number.
4. CODEN: a five-letter code assigned to serials by Chemical Abstract Service.

5. OCLC Control Number: a unique number assigned by the OCLC Online System to each bibliographic record as it enters the OCLC Online Union Catalogue.
6. Government Document Number.
7. Music Publisher Number: plate and publishers' numbers for printed music, and serial numbers and matrix numbers for sound recordings.

2. DERIVED SEARCH KEYS IN ROMAN ALPHABET

1. Title search key (3,2,2,1) consists of the first three letters of the first word in the title, excluding an initial article, followed by a comma, the first one or two letters of the second word in the title, another comma, the first one or two letters of the third word in the title, another comma, and the first letter of the fourth word in the title.
2. Personal name search key (4,3,1) consists of the first four letters of the author's surname, followed by a comma, the first one, two, or three letters of the author's forename, another comma, the author's middle initial which is optional.
3. Corporate name search key (=4,3,1) consists of an equal sign, followed by the first four letters of the first significant word in the name, excluding words on the stop list, a comma, the first one, two, or three letters of the word following the first significant word, another comma, and the first letter of the next word which is optional.
4. Name/Title search key (4,4) consists of the first three or four letters of the first word in the author's surname, corporate name, or uniform title, followed by a comma, and the first three or four letters of the first word in the title excluding initial articles.

3. DERIVED SEARCH KEYS IN CJK CHARACTERS

(1) Title search key (ti:5) begins with a prefix 'ti:', followed by the initial one, two, three, four, or five CJK characters in the title. The more characters there are in the search key, the fewer records it will retrieve.
(2) Personal name search key (pn:4) begins with a prefix 'pn:', followed by the initial one, two, three, or four characters in the personal name, beginning with the surname.
(3) Corporate name search key (cn:4) begins with a prefix 'cn:', followed by the initial one, two, three, or four characters in the corporate name.
(4) Name/Title search key (nt:1,4) begins witha prefix 'nt:', followed by none, or the first character in the name, a comma, and the initial one, two, three, or four characters in the title.

Users can qualify all derived search keys by type of material, year of publication (or range of years of publication), and whether the material is a microform reproduction.

Derived search keys in CJK characters will only retrieve records that contain CJK characters. When variant forms of a character exist, one form of the character in the search key will retrieve records containing all variant forms of that character if these records are retrievable by that search key. When one search key retrieves more than one record, these records are sorted by the romanised alphabet instead of the CJK characters.

SOFTWARE PACKAGES

The OCLC CJK350 system offers the following three software packages:

1. Online Cataloguing Package enables users to enter CJK records into, and retrieve CJK records from the OCLC Online Union Catalogue.

2. Card Production Package enables users to print complete sets of catalogue cards in CJK characters in the user's library. CJK characters are printed in a 24 × 24 dot matrix.

3. Word Processing Package contains features usually found in a general-purpose word processor. However, the OCLC CJK350 Word Processing Package has a multilingual capability and supports the same CJK character set and internal code as used in the OCLC CJK350 Online Cataloguing Package.

CHARACTER SET AND INTERCHANGE CODE

The Research Library Information Network (RLIN) pioneered the CJK project in 1983, and developed the RLIN East Asian Character Code (REACC). In order to make OCLC's CJK records compatible with RLIN's CJK records so that both sets of CJK records can be exchanged with minimum technical difficulty, OCLC adopts REACC and its character set. REACC adopts the three-byte structure of Chinese Character Code for Information Interchange (CCCII) and contains the following interchange codes:

1. Chinese Character Code for Information Interchange (CCCII).

2. Code of Chinese Graphic Character Set for Information Interchange (CCGCSII).

3. Japanese Industrial Standard (JIS).

4. Korean Information Processing System (KIPS).

RLIN-CJK character set consists of 15,850 characters which include 13,650 Chinese characters, 174 Japanese kana, and 2,026 Korean han'gŭl.

BUILDING A CJK DATABASE

OCLC is making efforts to build an international database of the CJK bibliographic and location information. Following are the major sources of this information in the OCLC Online Union Catalogue:

1. Records input and/or enhanced by the users of the OCLC CJK350 system.

2. Records distributed by the Library of Congress.

3. Records from RLIN-CJK users.

4. Records from National Central Library in Taipei and other libraries in the Asia and Pacific region.

Conclusion

The purposes of the OCLC CJK350 system are to reduce libraries' costs of processing materials in CJK languages, to reduce the time required to process these materials, and to increase the availability of bibliographic and location information of materials in CJK languages to librarians, scholars, and students world-wide. The OCLC CJK350 system not only links the scholars and the needed materials, but also provides a bridge for the East to meet the West.

Discussion

The 94% hit-rate mentioned was a system-wide average which naturally varies from library to library and material to material. No statistics are available for CJK but since the CJK database is small, the hit-rate must, at the moment, be lower. At present there are 50 libraries in the United States using OCLC-CJK and none elsewhere, but within six months there should be two on-line users in Taiwan, the National Central Library and Tamkang University Library, and hopefully one in West Berlin in early 1988.

Charles d'Orban

The China Library Group

In June 1966, the Library Committee of the School of Oriental and African Studies asked the Librarian to consider the problems of organising specialist library groups on the model of the Standing Conference on Library Materials on Africa (SCOLMA), which had been active since 1962. The result of these deliberations was the organisation of a Conference on the Acquisition of Library Materials from Asia which was held under the auspices of SOAS on 30 June 1967. In the recommendations put forward in its final session the conference concluded that regular meetings of librarians and scholars should be organised for Japanese, Chinese, South Asian and Southeast Asian collections. These meetings would discuss problems of book acquisition and coordination of policy.[1]

A further conference was held on 1 July 1968 to check on the progress of the regional library groups and the China Library Group submitted a report on its first meeting.[2] However, because of problems of organisation and lack of commitment, the Group had become inactive by 1972. No doubt there was a certain amount of disillusionment following the failure of an ambitious plan to employ a bibliographer who would serve all the member libraries of the group. His role would have been to supply members with information on British and world holdings, thus facilitating coordinated acquisitions. Despite the fact that a grant had been secured from the Council on Library Resources in Washington, it proved to be impossible to find a suitable candidate and so the grant (and with it the entire scheme) lapsed.[3]

Constitution and membership

The Group was reconstituted in its present form in October 1976. According to its constitution, the China Library Group exists to discuss and promote matters of common interest to British libraries with holdings of Chinese books. Its membership consists of representatives of such libraries, but anyone with an interest in the Group's objectives may be invited to attend its meetings. The Group usually meets twice yearly, once in London and once elsewhere in the country. The Group has two officers: the Convenor, who is responsible for the administration of the Group and for chairing its meetings, and the Treasurer, who attends to the finances. The funding available to the Group is very limited, depending mainly on the sale of the two bibliographical works which have been produced under its auspices. When undertaking bibliographical projects, the

Group is forced to seek funding from other bodies and must otherwise rely on the goodwill of individual members in giving up their free time.

The diverse nature of the Group's membership means that to a certain extent the collections complement each other and provide a ready-made guideline for cooperative acquisition. Although most of the participating libraries deal mainly in the humanities and social sciences, one deals with science and another with the history of Chinese science exclusively. Oxford and Cambridge tend to concentrate on pre-modern China, whereas SOAS and Leeds lay emphasis on contemporary China. Some members have strong research collections whereas others are responsible mainly for undergraduate provision. The difference in function between national and university libraries must also be recognised.

Co-operative policies and achievements

These differences in function make it very difficult to organise a cooperative policy for the purchase of monographs, except in the case of large sets and very expensive items (and Group members frequently consult one another on the acquisition of such items). Moreover, many of the Group's members feel that a rigid division of subject interests between participating libraries would not be a good idea. Despite great improvements over the last seven years, the vagaries of book supply from China are such that it is safer for several libraries to seek to acquire an important title and increase the chances that at least one will manage to obtain it; for the moment, Chinese publications remain cheap enough for this to be practical. The same argument applies to periodical subscriptions: several libraries are likely to subscribe to an important title and so if one misses a particular issue, there is a reasonable chance that another will have received it. There is also a certain amount of regional cooperation. SOAS and the British Library Oriental Collections will often consider the needs of London specifically.

Periodicals have proved to be a much more fruitful area for co-operation. The major achievement of the Group in the last few years has been the compilation of the *China Library Group Union List of Current Chinese Serials*. This has proved to be a very helpful tool for researchers, teachers and students as well as librarians and it is hoped that the list will form the basis for the UK contribution to a similar European union list.

The CLG has used the list to eliminate duplication of less important titles and for the identification of titles not yet taken by any UK library. Where possible, members have undertaken to take on subscriptions for these titles according to the particular strengths and interests of their own collections. Thus, the overall coverage of Chinese periodicals in the UK has now been strengthened. A periodicals sub-committee now meets once a year to divide up titles newly available for subscription.

New developments in Chinese bibliographical automation are regularly discussed at Group meetings. Among the topics which have been debated at recent meetings are the problems of collecting Japanese sinological works and the possible impact of the 'Parker report' on teaching, research and library provision.

Despite the real progress that has been made in cooperation between members, perhaps the greatest value of the China Library Group for individual members lies in something less tangible, in the reassuring feeling that 'we are not alone'. Sinological librarians exist in a strange limbo between the librarians who oversee their work and the sinologists whom they serve. Although we often have more in common with the latter group, who face the same deluge of new documentation available from China, it is still easy to feel isolated. China Library Group meetings provide a brief respite which helps to make it easier to bear the burdens we share.

Participants and officers

At present, the following institutions participate in the activities of the China Library Group: British Library Oriental Collections, British Library Science Reference and Information Service, British Library Document Supply Centre, the Department of Oriental Books of the Bodleian Library, the University of Oxford Oriental Institute, the Far Eastern Department of the Cambridge University Library, the Cambridge University Faculty of Oriental Studies, the Needham Research Institute East Asian History of Science Library, the University of Durham School of Oriental Studies Library, the Brotherton Library of the University of Leeds, the East Asia Centre of the University of Newcastle upon Tyne, Edinburgh University Library, the Library of the Polytechnic of Central London and the School of Oriental and African Studies Library (University of London). The current Convenor is Charles d'Orban of SOAS Library and the Treasurer is Anthony Hyder of the Oriental Institute, Oxford.

References

1. *Conference on the Acquisition of Library Materials from Asia, 30 June 1967: report* (London: SOAS, 1967). Further information on the background and activities of the regional library groups may be found in Anne J Benewick, *Asian and African collections in British libraries: problems and prospects* (Stevenage: Peter Peregrinus, 1974).
2. *Conference on the Acquisition of Library Materials from Asia, 1 July 1968: report* (London: SOAS, 1969). Conferences of this sort have continued to take place but are now organised under the auspices of the Standing Conference on National and University Libraries (SCONUL) Advisory Committee on Orientalist Materials (ACOOM). The China Library Group, along with the other regional library groups, continues to submit yearly reports to SCONUL/ACOOM's annual conference. These form a useful account of CLG activities.
3. SCONUL Group of Orientalist Libraries, *Newsletter of library developments 1970*, p. 3, and *Contemporary China Institute annual report 1972* (London: SOAS, 1972) p. 9.

David Helliwell

The European Association of Sinological Librarians

Most of the Chinese collections in Europe are maintained by a single librarian with a slender budget: there are few, if any, which can approach at least a dozen American institutions in the level of either their staffing or funding. Nor is it given to the custodians of European collections of Chinese books to preoccupy themselves with administration while subordinates carry out the essential functions of library management: they are not only concerned with all aspects of book selection, acquisition and cataloguing, but despite the high level of their training and expertise, must at times become personally involved in such matters as stamping, labelling and moving books, or even dusting shelves. Furthermore, the sinological librarians of Europe operate in such complete isolation that in the same country and even in the same city there is scarcely any contact between them: they rarely experience the professional and social intercourse that their colleagues in other branches of librarianship take for granted.

Aware of these matters, John Ma, who was then the librarian of the Sinologisch Instituut, convened a workshop for sinological librarians in Europe in Leiden in 1981. The participants found this event to be so informative, and the company of their colleagues so congenial, that they inaugurated the European Association of Sinological Librarians (EASL) and decided to meet annually. At its meeting in Cambridge in 1982 the Association sought, and was subsequently granted, affiliation with the European Association of Chinese Studies (EACS). In Paris in 1983 it was agreed that we should have a bulletin, and in Tübingen in 1984 the chairman of EASL, currently myself, was elected to the Board of EACS. EASL has subsequently convened in Berlin in 1985, Turin in 1986, and London in 1987.

The framework therefore exists for a considerably better exchange of information among European sinological librarians than has been possible hitherto, and the bulletin is its published expression. In a profession which has become obsessed with theory, members of EASL, perhaps owing to their unusual circumstances within that profession, have stressed from the outset the importance of practice. With this in mind, the production of a union list of Chinese periodicals in European libraries has been a major objective of EASL almost since its inception, and is now on the brink of realisation. A related enterprise, the compilation of a union list of *cong shu* in European libraries, was also considered but judged to be too large an undertaking at this stage. To those who are engaged in sinological research, the importance of both these projects is scarcely in need of elaboration.

As the prospect of automation draws closer each day, EASL has devoted much time at its annual conferences, and many pages in its bulletin, to discussion of the issues involved. As our collections are so small and fragmented, international inter-library loan has also been a subject of common interest.

EASL counts the professional sinological librarians of all European libraries with holdings of Chinese books as its members, and its bulletin is distributed to them free of charge. Attendance at the annual conferences increases each year, and aside from the considerable professional advantages which the participants in those meetings have gained from the discussions, members have also benefitted greatly from their visits to major historic collections.

Final discussions

These were concerned with library co-operation, both national and international. The British pattern of meeting twice a year as the China Library Group was envied by the Scandinavians who had difficulty in persuading their libraries to provide financial support for so many meetings. The reason was partly historic, for when the regional library groups were first established, the hope was expressed that they would, indeed, meet often, preferably twice a year. Though distances were considerable and fares expensive, it was perhaps easier to meet on a national basis. From distant colleagues in Australia came the news of the availability of a list of *cong shu* in the National Library of Australia, a challenge to the long-cherished dream of the China Library Group to produce a union list of *cong shu* in Great Britain. It was suggested that the European Association of Sinological Librarians' activities be reported to LIBER with the possibility of attracting funds to support future projects. For the moment, the support of the Staatsbibliothek in West Berlin was acknowledged both for the EASL Bulletin and the final realisation of the union list of Chinese periodicals on which compilation work would begin in 1988. For many of those who attended the colloquium, their work was not yet over as the 1987 meeting of the European Association for Sinological Librarians was to begin the next day.